GOOD WORKS!

MARKETING AND CORPORATE INITIATIVES THAT BUILD A BETTER WORLD... AND THE BOTTOM LINE

PHILIP KOTLER
DAVID HESSEKIEL
& NANCY R. LEE

WILEY

John Wiley & Sons, Inc.

Published by John Wiley & Sons, Inc., Hoboken, New Jersey
Published simultaneously in Canada

For general information on our other products and services or for technical support, please contact our Customer Care Department within the United States at (800) 762-2974, outside the United States at (317) 572-3993 or fax (317) 572-4002.

Wiley publishes in a variety of print and electronic formats and by print-on-demand. Some material included with standard print versions of this book may not be included in e-books or in print-on-demand. If this book refers to media such as a CD or DVD that is not included in the version you purchased, you may download this material at http://booksupport.wiley.com. For more information about Wiley products, visit www.wiley.com.

Library of Congress Cataloging-in-Publication Data:

Kotler, Philip.
  Good works! marketing and corporate initiatives that build a better world . . . and the bottom line / Philip Kotler, David Hessekiel, Nancy Lee.
     p. cm.
  Includes index.
  ISBN 978-1-118-20668-3 (hardback): ISBN 978-1-118-26578-9 (ebk); ISBN 978-1-118-24096-0 (ebk); ISBN 978-1-118-22860-9 (ebk)
  1. Marketing—Social aspects. 2. Social responsibility of business. 3. Relationship marketing. I. Hessekiel, David, 1960- II. Lee, Nancy, 1945- III. Title.
   HF5415.K6246 2012
   658.8'02—dc23
                                                                        2012004742

Printed in the United States of America.

10 9 8 7 6 5 4 3 2 1

Contents

Acknowledgments

The authors want to acknowledge the following people for sharing their stories and perspectives regarding marketing and corporate social initiatives, and in many cases taking the time and effort to complete surveys, confer with other colleagues and partners involved in these initiatives, research historical files, and proof copy. We thank you.

Allstate: Kate Hollcraft, Emily Pukala
Avon Products: Susan Arnot-Heaney
Best Buy: Kelly Groehler
The Boston Beer Company: Michelle Sullivan
Cause Consulting: Mark Feldman, Risa Sherman
Chipotle Mexican Grill: Chris Arnold
Church & Dwight Co.: Stacey Feldman
Clorox: David Kellis
Coca-Cola: April Jordan
Comic Relief: Anne-Cecile Berthier
Corporate Culture: John Drummond, Dave Thomas
Cone Communications: Craig Bida, Whitney Dailey, Alison DaSilva, Sarah Kerkian
ConAgra Foods: Kori Reed
Do Good, Make Money: Laura Probst
Edelman: Carol Cone, Amy Kalfus, Ann Clark
Energizer: Harriet Blickenstaff (Blick + Staff Communications)
Farmers Insurance: Charles Browning, Roger Daniel, Doris Dunn, Josh Krupp
FedEx: Julia Chicoski, Philip Blackett
Food Network: Katie Ilch, Kirstin Knezevich, Leah Lesko, Irika Slavin
General Mills: Berit Morse, Zack Ruderman

IBM: Stan Litow

Johnson & Johnson: Andrea Higham

Kraft Foods: Stephen Chriss

Levi: Sarah Young, Sarah Anderson

Macmillan Cancer Support: Katya Borowski, Francesca Insole

Macy's: Holly Thomas

March of Dimes: Chad Royal-Pascoe

Marks & Spencer: Richard Gillies

Mars Petcare US: Lisa Campbell, Melissa Martellotti

Miron Construction: Kristen Naimoli

MSLGROUP Americas: Anne Erhard

Monterey Bay Aquarium: Ken Peterson

Nike: Jill Zanger, Tessa Sayers

OneSight: Greg Hare

Park and Company: Park Howell, Holly Lim

Patagonia: Mark Shimahara, Bill Klyn

Pearson Foundation: Mark Nieker

Pepsico: Andrea Canabal, Anamaria Irazabal

PetSmart Charities: Susana Della Maddalena

Pfizer: Ray Kerins, Jennifer Kokell, Peter Zhang

Phillips Wyatt Knowlton: Lisa Wyatt Knowlton

Procter & Gamble: Caroline Bozonet, Nada Dugas, July Ung

Recharge: Doug Bamford

Said Business School, University of Oxford: Linda Scott

Sainsbury's Supermarkets: Jat Sahota

Seattle Children's Hospital: Laura Tufts

Sellen Construction: Todd Lee, Dave Scalzo

Share Our Strength: Theresa Burton, Christy Felling, Catherine Puzo

Starbucks: Ben Packard, Anna Kakos, Beth Baggaley

Subaru of America: Brian Johnson

SUBWAY: Cindy Carrasquilla, Les Winograd

Target: Sarah Bakken, Liz Brennhofer, Laysha Ward

TELUS: Jill Schnarr, Trisha Tambellini

TOMS Shoes: Allie Dominguez

U.S. Fish & Wildlife: Joe Starinchak

UNICEF: Laura De Santis

V/Line: Linda Brennan

Western Union: Talya Bosch

Whole Foods: Ashley Hawkins, Carrie Brownstein

Introduction

A commitment to doing the right thing is no guarantee of winning in the marketplace, but over the past 30 years numerous companies have demonstrated that you can simultaneously build a better world and the bottom line. Experience has also shown that creating successful marketing and corporate social initiatives requires intelligence, commitment, and finesse. Whether you work for a Fortune 500 giant or a start-up, generating financial profits and social dividends is a delicate balancing act. For many businesspeople, it proves to be among the most satisfying chapters of their professional lives.

If you are reading this introduction, there is a good chance you work in a company's department of community relations, corporate communications, public affairs, public relations, environmental stewardship, corporate responsibility, or corporate citizenship. Or you may be a marketing manager or a product manager, have responsibility for some aspect of corporate philanthropy, or run a corporate foundation. It is also quite possible that you work in a public relations, marketing, or public affairs agency and that your clients are looking to you for advice on marketing and corporate social initiatives. You may be the founder of a new business or the CEO of a large, complex enterprise.

If you are like others in any of these roles, it is also quite possible that you feel challenged and pulled by the demands and expectations surrounding the buzz for corporate social responsibility. You may be deciding what social issues and causes to support (and which ones to reject). You may be screening potential cause partners and determining the shape of your financial, organizational, and contractual relationships with them. You may be stretched by the demands of selling your ideas internally, setting appealing yet realistic expectations for outcomes, and building cross-functional support to bring programs to life. Or perhaps you are currently facing questions about what happened with all the money and resources that went into last season's programs.

If any of these challenges sound familiar, we have written this book for you. Dozens of your colleagues in firms around the world such as Allstate, Johnson & Johnson, Levi Strauss & Co., Marks & Spencer, Patagonia, PepsiCo, Starbucks, Subaru, TELUS, and TOMS have taken time to share their stories and their recommendations for how to do the most good for your company as well as for a cause.

Years of experience and months of research have strengthened our belief that *doing well by doing good* is more than just a catchy phrase. Corporations that apply rigor to creating effective marketing and corporate social initiatives can help build a better world and enhance their bottom line.

Even though this book has been written primarily for those working on behalf of for-profit corporations, it can also benefit those in nonprofit organizations and public sector agencies seeking corporate support and partners to realize their missions. It offers a unique opportunity for you to gain insight into a corporation's wants and needs and prepares you to decide which companies to approach and how to approach them. The final chapter, written just for you, presents recommendations that will increase your chances of forging successful cross-sector alliances.

Our aspiration for this book is that it will better prepare corporate managers and staff to choose the most appropriate issues, best partners, and highest potential initiatives. We want it to help you engender internal enthusiasm for your recommendations and inspire you to develop programs worthy of future case studies. And, perhaps most important, we hope it will increase the chances that your final report on what happened will feature incredibly good news for your company and your cause.

1

Good Intentions Aren't Enough: Why Some Marketing and Corporate Social Initiatives Fail and Others Succeed

When we come out of this fog, this notion that companies need to stand for something—they need to be accountable for more than just the money they earn—is going to be profound.[1]

—Jeffrey Immelt, Chairman and CEO, General Electric
At the November 2008 Business for Social Responsibility Conference

In the oft-cited 1970 article *The Social Responsibility of Business Is to Increase Its Profits*, economist Milton Friedman argued that business leaders had "no responsibilities other than to maximize profit for the shareholders."[2] Four decades later, the public statements of corporate leaders such as General Electric CEO Jeffrey Immelt quoted above and surveys of the general population indicate Friedman's argument is far from the majority view. A 2011 global consumer study by Cone Communications found only 6 percent of consumers in 10 countries agreed with the philosophy that the role of business in society is to "Just make money"[3] (see Figure 1.1).

More recently, Harvard's Michael E. Porter and Mark R. Kramer have argued that businesses must adopt a "shared value" mindset that seeks out and capitalizes on business opportunities to create "economic value in a way that also creates value for society by addressing its needs and challenges."[4] They criticize most companies for being "stuck in a 'social responsibility' mind-set in which societal issues are at the periphery, not the core."[5]

One need not be a follower of Friedman, Porter, or Kramer to agree that some activity carried out over the years in the name of social responsibility has

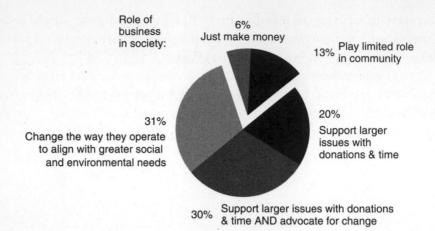

Role of business in society:

6%
Just make money

13% Play limited role in community

31%
Change the way they operate to align with greater social and environmental needs

20%
Support larger issues with donations & time

30% Support larger issues with donations & time AND advocate for change

FIGURE 1.1　The overwhelming majority of consumers surveyed in 10 countries in 2011 for the Cone/Echol Global CR Opportunity Study indicated they believe businesses have societal responsibilities beyond generating profits.

been poorly conceived and ineffective at producing benefits for the companies or causes involved. Conceptualizing, creating, executing, and evaluating marketing and corporate social initiatives is challenging work. This book is intended to be a practical management guide for the executives tasked with allocating scarce resources to strategically craft policies and programs that do good for their companies and their communities.

We will distinguish *six major types of marketing and corporate social initiatives* and provide perspectives from professionals in the field on strengths and weaknesses of each in terms of benefits to the cause and benefits to the company. We've divided these initiatives into two groups: those that are marketing-oriented (cause promotion, cause-related marketing, and corporate social marketing) and those that more broadly express and advance corporate values and objectives (corporate philanthropy, workforce volunteering, and socially responsible business practices). To firmly familiarize you with the breadth of options, Chapter 2 provides an overview of the six types of initiatives and then each is covered in depth in its own chapter. (It should be noted that in practice, many programs are hybrid combinations of several initiative strains.)

Then we will guide you through recommended best practices for choosing among the varied potential social issues that could be addressed by a corporation; selecting an initiative that will do the most good for the social issue as well as the corporation; developing and implementing successful program plans; and evaluating program efforts.

This opening chapter sets the stage by providing a common language for the rest of the book. We highlight trends and statistics that demonstrate that corporations have an increased focus on social responsibility; describe the various perceived factors experts identify as fueling these trends; and conclude with current challenges and criticisms facing those attempting to do the most good.

What Is *Good*?

A quick browse of Fortune 500 websites reveals that the umbrella concept of *good* has many names including: *corporate social responsibility, corporate citizenship, corporate philanthropy, corporate giving, corporate community involvement, community relations, community affairs, community development, corporate responsibility, global citizenship, and corporate societal marketing.*

For purposes of this focused discussion and applications for best practices, we prefer the use of the term *corporate social responsibility* and offer the following definition:

> *Corporate social responsibility* (CSR) is a commitment to improve community well-being through discretionary business practices and contributions of corporate resources.

This definition refers specifically to business activities that are *discretionary* as opposed to practices that are mandated by law or are moral or ethical in nature and perhaps, therefore, expected. We are referring to a voluntary *commitment* a business makes to choose and implement these practices and make these contributions. It will need to be demonstrated in order for a company to be described as socially responsible and will be fulfilled through adoption of new business practices and/or contributions, either monetary or nonmonetary. And when we refer to *community well-being*, we are including human conditions as well as environmental issues and communities from local to global that are defined by geography, demographics, challenges, aspirations, and many other factors.

We use the term *marketing and corporate social initiatives* to describe major efforts under the corporate social responsibility umbrella and offer the following definition:

> *Marketing and corporate social initiatives* are major activities undertaken by a corporation to support social causes, strengthen its business, and fulfill commitments to corporate social responsibility.

Causes most often supported through these initiatives are those that contribute to community *health* (i.e., AIDS prevention, early detection for breast cancer, timely immunizations); *safety* (i.e., designated driver programs, crime prevention, use of car safety restraints); *education* (i.e., literacy, computers for schools, special needs education); *employment* (i.e., job training, hiring practices, plant locations); the *environment* (i.e., recycling, elimination of the use of harmful chemicals, reduced packaging); *community and economic development* (i.e., low-interest housing loans, mentoring entrepreneurs); and *other basic human needs and desires* (i.e., hunger, homelessness, protecting animal rights, exercising voting privileges, anti-discrimination).

Support from corporations may take many forms including cash contributions, grants, promotional sponsorships, technical expertise, in-kind contributions (i.e., donations of products such as computer equipment or services such as printing), paid and earned media support, employee volunteers, and access to distribution channels. Cash contributions may come directly through the corporation or indirectly through foundations they have established.

Corporations may be sponsoring these initiatives on their own (e.g., Procter & Gamble's Tide Loads of Hope sends mobile clothes washing units to disaster zones) or in partnership with others (e.g., Food Network and Share Our Strength collaborate on public service announcements). They may be conceived of and managed by one department within the corporation, or by a team representing multiple business units.

What Are the Trends?

In the past decade, directional signals point to increased corporate giving and investment in cause sponsorship, increased corporate reporting on social responsibility initiatives, the establishment of a corporate social norm to do good, and a migration from giving as an obligation to giving as a strategy.

Increased Giving

In spite of the recession, corporate cash and in-kind giving in the United States rose 10.6 percent in 2010 to $15.29 billion (including $4.7 billion in grants and gifts made by corporate foundations), according to the Giving USA 2011 study.[6] Two-thirds of companies reported increasing their contributions from 2009 to 2010, according to the Committee Encouraging Corporate Philanthropy's annual survey.[7]

Growing at a rate of 6.7 percent, corporate cause sponsorship was the fastest-growing sponsorship segment in 2010, according to analysts at the IEG Sponsorship Report.[8] In 2011, corporate cause sponsorship grew a more modest 3.7% to $1.68 billion according to IEG.[9]

Increased Reporting   Corporate social responsibility reporting is nearly ubiquitous among the largest companies and is growing rapidly around the world.[10] According to KPMG, a professional services firm, their 2011 survey found that 95 percent of the Global Fortune 250 companies reported on corporate responsibility activity.[11] That's more than double the level KPMG found in 2002.[12] "Almost half of the G250 companies report gaining financial value from the[ir] CR initiatives," KPMG reported.[13]

Establishment of a Corporate Social Norm to Do Good

Within those printed and digital reports, there are consistent and similar messages from CEOs, signaling that commitments to corporate social responsibility have entered the mainstream of corporate dialogue as a must do, as indicated in the following examples:

- General Mills: "Our goal is to stand among the most socially responsible consumer food companies in the world. Every day we work to earn the trust of consumers beginning with the safety of our products. Being a responsible corporate citizen is integral to maintaining that trust." —Ken Powell, chairman and CEO[14]
- IBM: "Addressing the issues facing the world now—from clean water, better healthcare, green energy and better schools, to sustainable and vibrant cities, and an empowered workforce and citizenry—does not

pose a choice between business strategy and citizenship strategy. Rather it represents a fusion of the two." —Samuel J. Palmisano, chairman, president, and CEO[15]

- Nike: "It's time for the world to shift. All companies face a direct impact from decreasing natural resources, rising populations and disruption from climate change. And what may be a subtle effect now will only become more intense over the next five to ten years. Never has business had a more crucial call to innovate not just for the health and growth opportunities for our companies, but for the good of the world." —Mark Parker, president and CEO[16]

- Seventh Generation: "We seek to build the most trusted brand on the planet. We seek to reach more consumers, partner with like-minded retailers, and collaborate with responsible suppliers, as we double our business in the next five years. We will anchor our growth by investing in the Seventh Generation Community and our brand and by discovering exciting and innovative ways to meet consumer needs more sustainably." —John B. Replogle, president and CEO[17]

- Starbucks: "Today, perhaps more than ever, people are looking to the business community to help address many of the complex issues facing our world. At Starbucks, we acknowledge that responsibility, and will once again set a new standard of corporate responsibility." —Howard Schultz, president and CEO[18]

A Shift from Obligation to Strategy

In a seminal article in the *Harvard Business Review*, Craig Smith identified *The New Corporate Philanthropy*, describing it as a shift to making long-term commitments to specific social issues and initiatives, providing more than cash contributions, sourcing funds from business units as well as philanthropic budgets, forming strategic alliances, and doing all of this in a way that also advances business goals.

A milestone he identified that contributed to this evolution was a Supreme Court decision in the 1950s that removed legal restrictions and unwritten codes that up to that point had restricted, or at least limited, corporate contributions and involvement in social issues. Subsequently, by the 1960s, most U.S. companies began to feel pressures to demonstrate their social responsibility and established in-house foundations and giving programs.[19]

One of the next milestones Smith cited was the *Exxon Valdez* oil spill in 1989 that brought into serious question the philanthropy of the 1970s and 1980s, a period when corporations tended to support a variety of social issues least associated with their line of business and turn over management of their giving to separate foundations. When Exxon then needed access to environmentalists for expertise and support, management was "without ties to environmental leaders nurtured by the foundation."[20] A final milestone that Smith identified was the emergence and visibility of models in the 1990s such as the one used at AT&T that was "designed as much to reform the company as to reform society."[21]

Hess, Rogovsky, and Dunfee suggest that another force driving this shift is *The New Moral Marketplace Factor*, which is creating an increased importance of perceived corporate morality in choices made by consumers, investors, and employees. They point to several examples of marketplace morality including "investors choosing socially screened investment funds, consumers boycotting Shell Oil because of its decision to sink the Brent Spar oil rig, and employees' desires to work for socially responsible firms."[22]

In the following section, we contrast the more traditional approach to corporate philanthropy with the now strategic approach in terms of our best practice issues of selecting, developing, implementing, and evaluating marketing and corporate social initiatives.

The Traditional Approach: Fulfilling an Obligation

Prior to the 1990s, decisions regarding the selection of social issues to support tended to be made based on themes reflecting emerging pressures for *doing good to look good*. It was most common that corporations would establish, follow, and report on a fixed annual budget for giving, sometimes tied to revenues or pretax earnings. Funds were allocated to as many organizations as possible, reflecting a perception that this would satisfy the most constituent groups and create the most visibility for philanthropic efforts. Commitments were more short-term, allowing the organization to spread the wealth over a variety of organizations and issues through the years. Interestingly (given where we are today), there was more of a tendency to avoid issues that might be associated with core business products, as this might be perceived as self-serving, and to steer clear from major and often controversial social issues such as AIDS, judging that these were best handled by government and nonprofit experts. Decisions regarding issues to support and organizations to sponsor were also more heavily influenced by preferences (and wishes) of senior management and directors of boards than by needs to support strategic business goals and objectives.

When developing and implementing specific initiatives, the rule of thumb might have been described as to *do good as easily as possible*, resulting in a tendency to simply write a check. Most were satisfied being one of many corporate sponsors, as visibility for efforts was not a goal or concern. And because it would require extra effort, few attempts were made to integrate and coordinate giving programs with other corporate strategies and business units such as marketing, human resources, and operations.

And in terms of evaluation, it appears little was done (or asked for) to establish quantifiable outcomes for the business or the social cause, *trusting that good happened.*

The New Approach: Supporting Corporate Objectives, Too

As noted earlier, Smith described that in the early 1990s, many turned to a new model of corporate giving, a strategic approach that ultimately impacted what issues corporations supported, how they designed and implemented their programs, and how they were evaluated.

Decision-making now reflects an increased desire for *doing well and doing good.* We see more corporations picking a few strategic areas of focus, ones that fit with corporate values; selecting initiatives that support business goals; choosing issues related to core products and core markets; supporting issues that provide opportunities to meet marketing objectives such as increased market share, market penetration, or building a desired brand identity; evaluating issues based on their potential for positive support in times of corporate crisis or national policy making; involving more than one department in the selection process, so as to lay a foundation of support for implementation of programs; and taking on issues the community and customers and employees care most about.

Developing and implementing programs in this new model looks more like *doing all we can to do the most good, not just some good.* It is more common for managers to make long-term commitments, to offer in-kind contributions such as corporate expertise, technological support, access to services, and donation of retired equipment. We see more efforts to share distribution channels with cause partners; to volunteer employee time; to integrate the issue into marketing, corporate communications, human resources, community relations, and operations; to form strategic alliances with one or more external partners (private, public, non-profit); and to see funding coming from additional business units such as marketing and human resources.

Evaluation now has increased importance, perceived as critical to answering the question *What good did we do?* Trusting is not good enough. This input is valued, as a part of a strategic framework that then uses this feedback for course correction and credible public reporting. As a result, we see increased pressures for setting campaign goals, measuring outcomes for the corporation, and measuring impact for the cause. Even though there are increased pressures for evaluation of outcomes, program partners are still challenged with determining methodologies and securing resources to make this happen.

The rapidly escalating growth of digital, social, and mobile communications over the past five years has provided companies with new tools for engaging stakeholders in corporate social initiatives. Frequent changes on relatively established major platforms like Facebook, Twitter, and YouTube and the emergence of other specialized and mass online and mobile tools means that knowledge of how to best use them is still in its infancy. To provide insight into some emerging best practices, we've laced this book with *Social Media Spotlights*.

In addition to creating new opportunities, the changing digital landscape has also presented companies with serious challenges. The decentralization of communications tremendously amplifies and accelerates the power of individuals and groups to spread criticism of corporate efforts.

Why Do *Good*?

Most healthcare professionals promise that if we engage in regular physical activity, we'll look better, feel better, do better, and live longer. There are many who say that participation in Marketing and Corporate Social Initiatives has similar potential benefits. It appears that it looks good to potential consumers, investors, financial analysts, business colleagues, in annual reports, in the news, and maybe even in congress and the courtroom. It is reported that it feels good to employees, current customers, stockholders, and board members. There is growing evidence that it does good for the brand and the bottom line as well as the community. And there are some who claim that corporations with a strong reputation for corporate social responsibility actually last longer.

Let's examine the existing evidence that participation in marketing and corporate social initiatives can impact key performance factors, ones that could then support these claims.

Business for Social Responsibility is a leading non-profit global organization providing businesses with information, tools, training, and advisory services related to integrating corporate social responsibility in their business operations and strategies. Their research and experience concludes that companies have experienced a range of bottom-line benefits, including several of the following:[23]

- Increased sales and market share
- Strengthened brand positioning
- Enhanced corporate image and clout
- Increased ability to attract, motivate, and retain employees
- Decreased operating costs
- Increased appeal to investors and financial analysts

Increased Sales and Market Share

Cone Communications has been surveying U.S. consumers and employees on their attitudes concerning companies and causes since 1993. Perhaps spurred by the economic downturn, the 2011 U.S. data revealed some of the highest levels of consumer expectations and preferences Cone had ever recorded.[24]

- Ninety-four percent reported that they were likely to switch brands, about equal in price and quality, to one that supports a social issue—an all-time high. (That figure was 66 percent back in 1993 and 79 percent two months after September 11, 2011.[25])
- Ninety-one percent said they would buy a product associated with a cause if given the opportunity. Sixty-two percent said they had purchased a cause-related product in the past year.
- Eighty-one percent said they would donate to a charity supported by a company they trust, if given the opportunity. Seventy percent reported they had made such a donation in the past year.

In 2011, Cone added citizens in nine other countries to its research and found that "consumers globally believe companies have an explicit responsibility to help change the world."[26] Taken together, 94 percent of 10,000 citizens surveyed in Canada, Brazil, the United Kingdom, Germany, France, Russia, China, India, Japan, and the United States indicated they were likely to switch brands to one associated with a cause.[27]

Such contentions that corporate involvement in social causes can increase brand preference are corroborated by other surveys by public relations and branding firms (e.g., the Edelman goodpurpose study[28] and PRWeek/Barkley Cause Survey[29]), as well as academic researchers.

Bloom, Hoeffler, Keller, and Basurto, for example, contend:

> Consumers these days monitor and pay attention to how brands are marketed, and if they like the way that marketing is done because they have some type of positive feelings about or affinity toward the social cause being supported in the marketing program, then consumers will weigh the brand's marketing approach more heavily and positively compared to how they would weigh a brand's marketing program if it were supporting a non-social cause (e.g., commercial sponsorship in forming preference).[30]

In the chapters to come, you'll find many case examples of programs that increased sales and market share. A pioneering program that has inspired many others over the years is the American Express restoration of the Statue of Liberty campaign, a cause-related marketing initiative in the early 1980s. Instead of just writing a check to help with the cause, American Express tried a new approach: They pledged that they would make a contribution to a fund to restore the Statue of Liberty every time their card was used and would apply an additional contribution for every new card application. The campaign generated $1.7 million in funds for *the lady*, a 27 percent increase in card usage, and a 10 percent jump in new card member applications.[31]

Strengthened Brand Positioning

In their book *Brand Spirit*, Pringle and Thompson make a strong case for the contribution that linking a company or brand to a relevant charity or cause can make to the "spirit of the brand." They contend that consumers are going beyond "the practical issues of functional product performance or rational product benefits and further than the emotional and psychological aspects of brand personality and image. Consumers are moving towards the top of Maslow's Hierarchy of Needs and seeking 'self-realization.'"[32] What they are asking for now and are drawn to now are demonstrations of good. "In an anthropomorphic sense, if consumers know how a brand functions and how it 'thinks' and 'feels,' then the new question that has to be answered is 'what does it believe in?'"[33]

Bloom, Hoeffler, Keller, and Basurto see

> . . . marketing initiatives containing a larger amount of social content having a more positive effect on brand judgments and feelings than initiatives that are similar in size and scope but contain less social content. By 'social content' we mean activities in the marketing initiative that are meant to make tangible improvements to social welfare. Thus a program that would make a donation to an environmental organization every time a purchase was made would be higher in social content than a program that gave a consumer a free toy every time a purchase was made.

Consider, for example, the spirit that participation in corporate social initiatives has given to the Ben & Jerry's brand. Thanks to years of company activity and communication, the words *Ben & Jerry's* conjure up for many consumers an image of a philanthropic company that promotes and supports positive social change through such efforts as the PartnerShops program that waives standard franchise fees for nonprofit organizations in order to offer supportive employment; the *Lick Global Warming* campaign that teaches people how to reduce their carbon dioxide emissions and to advocate for policies that fight global warming; or the sourcing of brownies for their ice cream from Greyston Bakery, a nonprofit that provides employment and support services to former homeless, low-income, and disenfranchised people. For many consumers, the product of the brand's many pro-social activities is a positive feeling toward Ben & Jerry's lineup of ice creams in the grocer's freezer section.

Improved Corporate Image and Clout

Several existing and respected reports cover standards and assessment of performance in the area of Corporate Social Responsibility, including the following:

- *Fortune* publishes an annual list of the "World's Most Admired Companies" and social responsibility is one of the eight attributes executives and securities analysts around the world are asked to rate companies on. Among those topping the 2011 social responsibility rating list were Statoil (Norway), Ferrovial (Spain), Walt Disney (USA), ENI (Italy), and Whole Foods Market (USA).[34]
- *Corporate Responsibility Magazine* publishes a list of "100 Best Corporate Citizens," recognizing companies' corporate social responsibility toward stakeholders including the environment and the community. In 2011, the top five Best Corporate Citizens were Johnson Controls, Campbell Soup Company, IBM, Bristol-Myers Squibb, and Mattel.[35]

In addition to positive press from reports such as these, "Companies that demonstrate they are engaging in practices that satisfy and go beyond regulatory compliance requirements are being given less scrutiny and more free reign by both national and local government entities,"[36] according to *Business for Social Responsibility.*

A strong reputation in the community can be a real asset in times of crisis. Hess, Rogovsky, and Dunfee describe a dramatic example of this in the McDonald's experience during the 1992 South Central Los Angeles riots. "The company's efforts in developing community relations through its Ronald McDonald's houses and its involvement in developing employee opportunities gave the company such a strong reputation, McDonald's executives stated, that rioters refused to harm their outlets. While vandalism caused tremendous damages to businesses in the area, all sixty of McDonald's franchises were spared harm."[37]

Increased Ability to Attract, Motivate, and Retain Employees

Consumer surveys indicate that a company's participation in social initiatives can have a positive impact on prospective and current employees, as well as citizens and executives. According to the 2011 Cone Cause Evolution Study, 69 percent of Americans indicated that a company's commitment to social and environmental issues would influence whether they would want to work there.[38] Employees involved with their company's cause programs were far more likely than those not involved to say they had a strong sense of loyalty to and pride in the company.[39] "Companies who are not fully engaging their employees are clearly leaving equity on the table," according to Cone.[40]

Perceiving an increased desire among students in social entrepreneurship and careers with socially responsible companies, graduate schools of business have been increasing their course offerings related to examining the social, environmental, and ethical impacts of business decisions, according to the Aspen Institute's 2011 *Beyond Grey Pinstripes* survey.[41]

Decreased Operating Costs   Several business functions can cite decreases in operating costs and increased revenue from grants and incentives as a result of implementing marketing and corporate social initiatives, especially altering business practices. One arena easy to point to is the adoption of environmental initiatives to reduce waste, reuse materials, recycle, and conserve water and electricity.

At AT&T, for example, a program that entices customers to sign up for paperless, electronic billing statements by offering to contribute to The Arbor Day Foundation has cut the company's paper, printing, and mailing costs by millions of dollars, saved trees from being harvested to make paper and funded the planting of hundreds of thousands of trees.[42]

Another area for potential reduced costs is in advertising expenditures, especially as a result of increased free publicity.

From its founding in the 1970s, The Body Shop was noted for its stands on issues such as fair trade, protecting the environment, and using animals for cosmetic testing. According to an article in the World Council of Sustainable Development, "The Body Shop was launched on the basis of fairer prices for fairly produced cosmetics. Anita Roddick, its founder, generated so much favorable publicity that the company did not need to advertise: a win-win on the cost-benefit front, leaving aside the do-gooding."[43]

More recently, the social entrepreneurs at TOMS Shoes have ridden a wave of consumer and media fascination with the company's philanthropic business proposition: Buy one pair of shoes and a pair is given to a child in need. An advertising agency executive happened to hear a television report on the company in 2008. That started a chain of events that led ATT to feature the company in a widely aired commercial in 2009, which generated millions of dollars worth of business-building free publicity for TOMS Shoes.[44]

Increased Appeal to Investors and Financial Analysts

Some argue that involvement in marketing and corporate social initiatives can increase stock value.

- In *Firms of Endearment*, Rajendra Sisodia, David Wolfe, and Jagdish Sheth present data indicating that firms that "endear" themselves to all stakeholders wildly outperformed the broader stock market during the 3-, 5-, and 10-year periods ending June 30, 2006.[45] "Great companies sustain their superior performance over time for investors, but equally important in our view, for their employees, customers, suppliers, and society in general," the authors contend.

- In "Corporate Social Responsibility and Shareholder Value: The Environmental Consciousness of Investors," Caroline Flammer of the MIT School of Management studied the relationship from 1980 to 2009 between corporate announcements of positive and negative environmental news and stock movement. "We find that companies that are reported to behave responsibly towards the environment experience a significant stock price increase, whereas firms that behave irresponsibly face a significant stock price decrease."[46]

- According to the Social Investment Forum Foundation's *2010 Report on Socially Responsible Investing Trends in the United States*, "Sustainable and socially responsible investing (SRI) in the United States has continued to grow at a faster pace than the broader universe of conventional investment assets under professional management. At the start of 2010, professionally managed assets following SRI strategies stood at $3.07 trillion, a rise of more than 380 percent from $639 billion in 1995 . . . Over the same period, the broader universe of assets under professional management increased only 260 percent from $7 trillion to $25.2 trillion."[47]

What Are the Major Current Challenges to Doing Good?

Managers and program planners are challenged at each of the fundamental decision points identified throughout this book—decisions related to choosing a social issue; selecting an initiative to support this issue; developing and implementing program plans; and evaluating outcomes. In the next few pages, we identify issues that commonly crop up within organizations. Guidance on grappling with these issues is a key component of the chapters to come.

Choosing a Social Issue

Challenges are perhaps the greatest in this very first step, as experience has shown that some social issues are a better fit than others, and this first decision has the greatest impact on subsequent programs and outcomes. Those making the recommendations will end up juggling competing priorities and publics. They will be faced with tough questions, including:

- How does this support our business goals?
- How big of a social problem is this?
- Isn't the government or someone else handling this?
- What will our stockholders think of our involvement in this issue?
- Is this something our employees can get excited about?
- Won't this encourage others involved in this cause to approach us (bug us) for funds?
- How do we know this isn't the *cause du jour*?
- Will this cause backfire on us and create a scandal?
- Is this something our competitors are involved in and *own* already?

Selecting an Initiative to Address the Issue

Once an issue has been chosen, managers will now be challenged regarding recommendations on what initiative or initiatives among the six identified in Chapter 2 should be selected to support the issue. Again, they will need to be prepared to answer tough questions:

- How can we do this without distracting us from our core business?
- How will this initiative give visibility for this company?
- Do these programs really work? Who pays attention to these?
- What if consumers perceive the amount of the sale that actually goes to the cause is too small?
- Have you calculated the productivity cost for giving our employees time off for volunteering?
- Giving visibility, especially shelf space in our stores for this cause, doesn't *pencil out*. Shouldn't we just write a check or give a grant?

Developing and Implementing Program Plans

Key decisions at this point include whether to partner with others and if so, who; determining key strategies including communications and distribution channels; assigning roles and responsibilities; developing timetables; and determining budget allocations and funding sources. The questions continue, especially around issues of time and money:

- How can we do this when money is needed for increased performance?
- What do we say to stockholders who see this as money that belongs to them?
- Why is our department being asked to fund this?
- Will having partners bog down the decision-making process and therefore take more of our staff time?
- Will we be doing as much good for the cause as we spend?
- Isn't this just brand advertising in disguise?
- What is our exit strategy?
- How do we keep from looking hypocritical?

Evaluation

Ongoing measurement of marketing activities and financial investments for corporations has a track record, with decades of experience in building sophisticated tracking systems and databases that provide analysis on returns on investments and compare current activities to benchmarks and gold standards. By contrast, the track record for measuring return on investments in Corporate Social Initiatives is very young with little historic data and expertise. Marketing professionals and academic experts in the field confirm this challenge.

- Curt Weeden, former CEO of the Association of Corporate Contributions Professionals and formerly the vice president in charge of Johnson & Johnson's corporate philanthropy, put it this way: "Full-scale, highly quantitative evaluations are simply not practical or affordable for 99 percent of the contributions a company elects to make."[48]

- Sinha, Dev, and Salas describe, "Since the benefits related to CSR are not directly measurable, and most firms do not disclose expenses related to such activities, it is difficult to directly assess the return on CSR investment."[49]
- McDonald's, for example, reports that even measuring a major event is challenging: "Most of our current goals and measurements are related to processes, systems development and standard setting . . . We are 70 percent franchised around the world: Currently, we do not have systems to collect and aggregate what some 5,500 independent owner/operators do for their community, people and environment at the local level."[50]
- Gourville and Rangan confirm this difficulty: "Rarely do firms fully assess a cause marketing alliance and its potential impact on both the for-profit and the non-profit entities. Yes, there are several stunning success stories . . . but most for-profit businesses would be hard pressed to document the long-term business impact of their cause marketing campaigns and most non-profits would have trouble pin-pointing the value they bring to the partnership."[51]

Fortunately, many of the case examples in this volume include valuable data on program impact. Businesses and society at large have so much to gain from well-conceived, well-designed, and well-executed corporate social initiatives. Read on for practical knowledge generously shared by dozens of practitioners intended to help future managers escape the pain of avoidable mistakes and craft more successful programs moving forward.

2

Six Social Initiatives for Doing Well by Doing Good

At Starbucks, the values that guide every decision we make can be found in our mission statement: to inspire and nurture the human spirit—one person, one cup and one neighborhood at a time. For 40 years, we have lived these values in the ways we ethically source our coffee beans and work to improve the lives of the people who grow them; in how we participate in the neighborhoods where we do business, operate our stores and care for the environment.[1]

—Howard Schultz
Chairman, President, and Chief Executive Officer
Starbucks

In Chapter 1, we defined *marketing and corporate social initiatives* as major activities undertaken by a corporation to support social causes and to fulfill on commitments to *corporate social responsibility*. We have identified six major initiatives under which most socially responsible-related activities fall—three that are developed and managed primarily by the corporation's marketing function, and three that are developed and managed by other corporate functions including community relations, human resources, foundations, and operations. Brief descriptions of each are presented in this chapter. In subsequent chapters, each initiative will be described in more detail, one at a time, presenting typical programs, potential benefits, potential concerns, keys to success, when to consider the initiative, and steps in developing program plans. In our final chapters, we will summarize these perspectives, presenting 25 best practices for choosing, implementing, and evaluating these initiatives.

The six social initiatives explored in this book are:

Marketing-Driven Initiatives

1. **Cause Promotion:** A corporation provides funds, in-kind contributions, or other corporate resources for promotions to increase awareness and concern about a social cause or to support fundraising, participation, or volunteer recruitment for a cause. The corporation may initiate and manage the promotion on its own (e.g., The Body Shop successfully promoting a ban in the European Union on the use of animals to test cosmetics); it may be a major partner in an effort (e.g., Amgen-Pfizer sponsoring the Arthritis Foundation's fundraising walk); or it may be one of several sponsors (e.g., Keep America Beautiful 2011 major sponsors for the Great American Cleanup included The Dow Chemical Company, Lowe's, Pepsi-Cola, Solo Cup Company, Scotts, Glad, and Nestlé).

2. **Cause-Related Marketing:** A corporation links monetary or in-kind donations to product sales or other consumer actions. Most commonly, this offer is for an announced period of time and for a specific product and for a specified charity. In this scenario, a corporation is most often partnered with a nonprofit organization, creating a mutually beneficial relationship designed to increase product sales and to generate financial support for the charity (e.g., Kraft Foods donates meals to Feeding America when consumers redeem coupons or get involved online with its Huddle to Fight Hunger program). Many think of this as a win-win-win, as it provides consumers with avenues to support charities as well to their favorite charities.

3. **Corporate Social Marketing:** A corporation supports the development and/or implementation of a behavior change campaign intended to improve public health, safety, the environment, or community well-being. It is most distinguished by this behavior change focus, which differentiates it from *cause promotions* that focus on supporting awareness, fundraising, and volunteer recruitment for a cause. A corporation may develop and implement a behavior change campaign on its own (e.g., Allstate encouraging teens to sign a pledge not to text and drive), but more often it involves partners in public sector agencies (e.g., Home Depot and a utility service promoting water conservation tips) and/or nonprofit organizations (e.g., Pampers and the SIDS Foundation encouraging caretakers to put infants on their back to sleep).

Corporate-Driven Initiatives

4. **Corporate Philanthropy**: A corporation makes a direct contribution to a charity or cause, most often in the form of cash grants, donations, and/or in-kind services. This is perhaps the most traditional of all corporate social initiatives and for many decades was approached in a responsive, even ad hoc manner. As mentioned in Chapter 1, more corporations are now experiencing pressures, both internally and externally, to move to a more strategic approach, choosing a focus and tying philanthropic activities to the company's business goals and objectives. And the advent of social media has led some companies to enlist consumers in determining which nonprofits should receive contributions (e.g., the Chase Community Giving program).

5. **Workforce Volunteering**: A corporation supports and encourages employees, retail partners, and/or franchise members to *volunteer* at local community organizations and causes. This activity may be a standalone effort (e.g., employees of a high-tech company tutoring youth in middle schools on computer skills) or this may be in partnership with a nonprofit organization (e.g., AT&T working with the American Red Cross to supply phones for disaster relief efforts) Volunteer activities may be organized by the corporation or employees may choose their own activities and receive support from the company through programs, including providing time off and volunteer database matching programs.

6. **Socially Responsible Business Practices**: A corporation adapts and conducts discretionary business practices and investments that support social causes to improve community well-being and protect the environment. Initiatives may be conceived of and implemented by the organization (e.g., DuPont deciding to slash energy use and greenhouse gas emissions) or they may be in partnership with others (e.g., Whole Foods Market working with the United Kingdom's Department of the Environment, Food, and Rural Affairs to increase purchasing of sustainable fish).

To further illustrate and bring to life these distinctions, three case examples follow: Starbucks, Target, and Johnson & Johnson. In each case, background information on the corporation's focus for social initiatives is briefly described, followed by an example of a social initiative in each of the six areas.

Starbucks

A Strategic Focus on the Environment

In 2008, Starbucks made a bold move when they established a set of ambitious global responsibility goals that would have the greatest impact on the environment, ones related to ethical sourcing, environmental stewardship, and community involvement. They believed then, and still believe now, that their responsible business performance is inextricably linked to their progress against these goals.[2] We think it's working. In 2011, they appeared among those on the Fortune 500 list who had, in 2010, the fastest profit growth (#47[3]), been voted by business leaders as one of the most admired companies (#16[4]), named a Best Corporate Citizen by *CR Magazine* (#1 in industry sector), and considered one of the best companies to work for (#98[5]). And a variety of environmental-related recognitions and awards attest that their efforts are not going unnoticed, including ones from the EPA (for their support for Green Power), the National Recycling Coalition (for their recycling leadership), industry peers (for their support of fair trade farmers), and the U.S. Composting Council (for donating coffee grounds for consumers to use for backyard composting).

FIGURE 2.1   Starbucks logo.

In Table 2.1, note how this commitment is fulfilled with clear environmentally focused efforts in each of our six social initiatives. Read on for more detail (and inspiration) on how they were developed and implemented.

Cause Promotions: Cup Summits

The challenges of recycling are not unique to any one company. The entire food industry, including retail and beverage businesses, needs to work together

TABLE 2.1 Examples of Marketing and Corporate Social Initiatives for Starbucks

	Marketing Social Initiatives				Corporate Social Initiatives		
	Cause Promotions	Cause-Related Marketing	Corporate Social Marketing	Corporate Philanthropy	Workforce Volunteering	Socially Responsible Business Practices
Description	Supporting social causes through promotional sponsorships	Linking monetary or in-kind donations to product sales or other consumer actions	Supporting behavior change campaigns	Making direct contributions to a charity or cause	Supporting employees to volunteer in the community	Adapting and conducting discretionary business practices and investments that support social causes
Example	Encouraging the food industry to serve beverages in either reusable or recyclable containers (Earth Day brand spark and Cup Summits)	Making a contribution to water projects around the world with every purchase of Ethos Water at a Starbucks store	Encouraging and supporting customers to engage in backyard composting	Providing grants for environmental education of youth	Organizing opportunities for employees to participate in community projects that enhance the environment (hosted Global Month of Service in April 2011)	Committed that all new company-owned stores would be built to achieve LEED® certification (U.S. Green Building Council's Leadership in Energy and Environmental Design)

along with suppliers, recyclers, and government entities to make meaningful and sustainable changes needed to reduce waste. Starbucks has an ambitious environmental goal. By 2015, 100 percent of their beverages will be served in cups that are either reusable or recyclable, and they'd like others in the food industry to strive to do the same.[6]

In 2008, Starbucks engaged the Massachusetts Institute of Technology and the Society for Organizational Learning to help explore a systems thinking approach to cup recycling. They applied a problem-solving approach to analyze how the various segments of a structure are interconnected.

This led to the first Cup Summits in 2009 and 2010, bringing together government officials, raw material suppliers, cup manufacturers, retail and beverage businesses, recyclers, competitors, conservation groups, and academic experts. The collaboration revealed a fundamental need to improve recycling infrastructures while continuing to explore materials and design. (See Figure 2.2.)

FIGURE 2.2 Making recycling clear and easier at Starbucks stores.

At the 2011 Cup Summit in Boston, more than 150 industry leaders, including competitors such as Dunkin' Donuts, McDonald's, and Tim Horton's, continued to build on the learnings and efforts from past summits to build plans for continued collaboration toward a solution. At the 2011 meeting it was announced that the Food Packaging Institute had created the Paper Recovery Alliance—a move to take this initiative industry-wide.

Cause-Related Marketing: Ethos Water Fund

Ethos Water was founded in 2002 to help children around the world get clean water, as well as raise awareness of the world water crisis. In 2005, Starbucks acquired the company, with an intention to raise funds to support water access, sanitation, and hygiene programs around the world. For every bottle sold from Starbucks stores, Starbucks contributes five cents to the Ethos Water Fund, which is part of the Starbucks Foundation. By 2011, more than $6 million has been granted for projects in water-stressed countries, benefiting more than 420,000 people.[7]

Corporate Social Marketing: Grounds for Your Garden

Introduced in 1998, the Grounds for Your Garden initiative began offering customers complimentary five-pound bags of used coffee grounds to enrich garden soil. The program, in fact, was inspired by customers expressing interest in coffee grounds for their backyard compost efforts, providing a rich source of nutrients. *Spent* coffee grounds are complimentary and available upon request at many of their retail locations. Grounds are packaged in reused coffee bean bags and sealed with the Starbucks® Coffee Grounds as Compost sticker. (See Figure 2.3.) Several websites promote use of the compost, including Sustainable Enterprises, where detailed composting instructions and testimonials to the effort can be found. One testimonial came from a Starbucks employee:

> Hi, I work for Starbucks and am the environmental specialist for my district. I have had an overwhelming response from people wanting used coffee grounds for composting and fertilizer . . . . So don't be shy . . . ask for grounds and if a store has not implemented this program, ask who their green team representative is and get in touch with them![8]

FIGURE 2.3   Free coffee grounds for backyard composting.

And the U.S. Composting council "applauds Starbucks for their environ-mentally responsible donation and encourages consumers to take advantage of this generous opportunity."[9]

Furthermore, Starbucks recognizes the impact that individuals can make through simple, eco-conscious choices and encourages customers to use tumblers or reusable travel mugs in their daily routine to reduce their own environmental impact. To further enforce this commitment, Starbucks offered customers a complimentary brewed coffee or tea of their choice if they brought in their own reusable mug to a participating store on Earth Day 2010 and 2011. Every day Starbucks offers a 10-cent discount at participating stores in the United States and Canada to encourage customers to use their own reusable mugs or tumblers for their beverages. Customers staying in a store can also request that their beverages be served in a ceramic mug. Every paper cup saved helps keep our forests intact.

Corporate Philanthropy: Environmental Education for Youth in Malaysia

In 2010, Starbucks Corporation and the Starbucks Foundation gave a total of $22.4 million, with the Corporation giving $10.3 million in cash and

$6.7 million in in-kind contributions toward community-building programs. The Starbucks Foundation made more than 100 grants to nonprofit organizations in 2010, including $1.6 million for Starbucks Youth Action Grants.[10]

One of the grant recipients was the Children's Environmental Heritage Foundation in Kuala Lumpur, Malaysia, a nonprofit organization founded in 1990 to "instill a love of and care for the environment in young people."[11] In 2010, a grant to the YAWA Eco Youth program supported outreach efforts to youth living in low-income communities, programs that educate the youth on the importance of taking care of the environment and nurturing interest in entrepreneurship through a variety of eco activities.

Workforce Volunteering: Building a *Green* Neighborhood in Minhang, China

In celebration of its fortieth anniversary, Starbucks hosted a global month of community service in April 2011, supporting employees (*partners*, as Starbucks calls them) from around the world to take actions that make a positive difference in the neighborhoods where they live and work.

One of those neighborhoods was in Shanghai, China, where 750 Starbucks partners from the region rolled up their sleeves with other local volunteers to rejuvenate the environment, as well as share practices on environmentally friendly lifestyles. The event, organized in partnership with Charyou, a Shanghai-based NGO, and the Sub-District Office of Gumei Community, Minhang District, completed a wide range of projects including gardening, repainting walls, and setting up a rubbish management system. Attendees engaged in educational games and activities that promoted environmentally friendly lifestyles in a fun way. Volunteers also worked with residents to help install simple devices in their homes to help save energy and water.[12]

Socially Responsible Business Practices: Green Buildings

With more than 17,000 locations around the word, it is not surprising to see the company's focus on green building initiatives to help reach environmental targets. To guide their efforts, they use the U.S. Green Building Council's Leadership in Energy and Environmental Design (LEED®) Standards, and established a goal that all new, company-owned stores would be built to achieve this certification.

To achieve this goal, Starbucks collaborated with the USGBC LEED®
Volume Certification pilot program, enabling the company to reduce the
environmental impact of its stores on a global scale with significant cost and
time efficiencies. Once the pilot stores' environmental strategies are audited
and approved, they can be replicated elsewhere. This capability supports
Starbucks' goal of achieving LEED® certification for all new company-owned
stores worldwide beginning in late 2010.

One of their first LEED®-certified stores was a nostalgic choice. The First &
Pike store is located at the gateway to Seattle's historic Pike Place Market
where the original Starbucks opened in 1971. (See Figure 2.4.) The design of

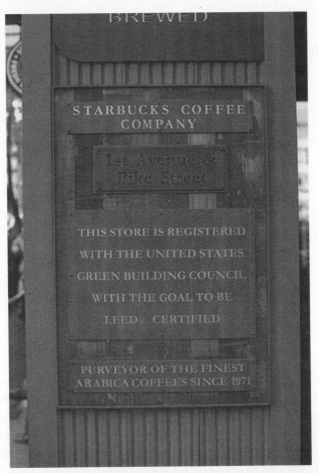

FIGURE 2.4   One of Starbucks' first LEED® -certified stores was a
nostalgic choice.

this new coffeehouse evokes its heritage with warm-colored woods and many other notable green elements:[13]

- Leather on the bar's outer facing was made from the scrap of local shoe and automobile factories.
- Walnut used on tables and doors was salvaged from a nearby farm.
- A large community table was previously located at a Seattle restaurant, and before that, in a private home.
- Restroom partitions are made from recycled laundry detergent bottles.

Target Corporation

A Strategic Focus on Education

Education is a longtime, top-priority social issue for Target, and certainly the fact that it is a priority for their customers, as well, is no coincidence. Target believes, "Every child deserves the opportunity to graduate from high school and reach his or her full potential. That's why we're on track to reach a total of $1 billion in education-related giving by the end of 2015."[14]

FIGURE 2.5   Target logo.

As you will read, a significant portion of these contributions funds programs and partnerships dedicated to an even more focused goal—helping more U.S. children read proficiently by the end of third grade. And this, they say, is because, "Research shows that at the end of third grade, school curriculum shifts from learning to read to reading to learn, and that students who can't read at grade level by this time have trouble keeping up, and often fall behind." Table 2.2 summarizes these education-oriented initiatives, with more detailed descriptions following.

TABLE 2.2 Examples of Social Initiatives for Target

| | Marketing Social Initiatives | | | Corporate Social Initiatives | | |
	Cause Promotion	Cause-Related Marketing	Corporate Social Marketing	Corporate Philanthropy	Workforce Volunteering	Socially Responsible Business Practices
Description	Supporting social causes through promotional sponsorships	Linking monetary or in-kind donations to product sales or other consumer actions	Supporting behavior change campaigns	Making direct contributions to a charity or cause	Supporting employees to volunteer in the community	Adapting and conducting discretionary business practices and investments that support social causes
Example	Hosting book festivals for families to increase excitement about reading	Making a donation to a public school of choice based on purchases using a Target credit card	Supporting a worldwide reading day where parents and children around the world read the same book	Providing grants for school field trips	Contributing employee time and talent to complete library makeovers	Reimbursing employees for tuition for MBA courses

Cause Promotion: Book Festivals

Book festivals sponsored by Target are intended to create the same fun and enthusiasm for reading that children associate with county fairs, water game days, and even Disneyland! Numerous festivals across the country each year feature live, free, family-focused entertainment.

In 2011, for example, the Los Angeles Times Festival of Books at the University of Southern California offered celebrity book readings and signings on the Target Children's Stage by Jamie Lee Curtis, R.L., Stine, and Mo Willems, as well as performances by the popular music group Coo-Choo Soul and Grammy Nominee Justin Roberts.[15]

Cause-Related Marketing: The REDcard®

Take Charge of Education® is a school fundraising initiative created in 1997 to enhance educational opportunities for children in communities across America, and for parents to direct dollars to their own child's school. It works like this. For cardholders enrolled in the program, Target donates 1 percent of all Target Visa Credit Card and Target Credit Card purchases made at a Target Store or at Target.com and 1 percent of all Target Debit Card purchases

FIGURE 2.6   Jamie Lee Curtis in Target's Big Red Reading Chair at a Book Festival.

Source: Target Corporation

made at a Target Store to an eligible K-12 school of their choice. Target also donates 0.5 percent of all Target Visa Credit Card purchases made outside of Target. Schools can use the undesignated funds for anything from books and other classroom supplies to technology improvements.

At Adams Elementary in Corvallis, Oregon, for example, this program was said to have been a life changer for one eight-year-old in the third grade. She was the only one in her class who couldn't read and felt labeled as "the dumb one." An Art@Adams program, funded almost entirely by donations including ones from Target's REDcard, created the breakthrough for her. It turned out that she was an incredibly talented artist, and the praise she received from her classmates helped her begin to enjoy coming to school—and learning.[16]

Since the program's inception, Target has donated more than $298 million to K-to-12 schools (2011), well on the way toward their goal of $425 million by 2015.[17]

Corporate Social Marketing: Read Across America

Given their focus on education, it is not surprising to learn that Target supports a variety of activities that specifically support reading.[18]

Each year, they join the National Education Association in Read Across America festivities to encourage young readers. In 2011, one of their more exciting events took place in New York City where Target unveiled a 26-foot-tall installation of 25,000 Dr. Seuss classics, which were then donated to New York City schools. (See Figure 2.7.) And building on this theme across the country, kids and parents were invited to come to Target Stores for Dr. Seuss Storytime, where they received goodie bags and listened to team members read Dr. Seuss favorites.

In 2010, Target partnered with Jumpstart's Read for the Record event, a celebration of reading that brings children and adults together to read the same book, on the same day, in homes, schools, and communities all over the world.[19] That year they broke the world's record with more than 2 million children and adults around the globe reading *The Snowy Day* by Ezra Jack Keats.[20]

Corporate Philanthropy: Field Trip Grants

Target's grants for school field trips is a program that recognizes that learning opportunities extend beyond the classroom, as well as the fact that schools

FIGURE 2.7   25,000 Dr. Seuss classics create a 26-foot-tall installation in New York City.

Source: Target Corporation

are finding it more and more difficult to fund trips to museums, cultural events, civic experiences, and historical sites. Field Trip Grants help give more children this firsthand learning experience. Interested schools can apply for a grant online, and local organizations create increased visibility for these opportunities, as well as goodwill for Target. In North Carolina, for example, the Office of Environmental Education's website encourages schools to apply for a nature awareness field trip, providing a link to Target's website for ease of application for a grant.

Since launching the program in 2007, Target has provided 1.6 million students the opportunity to take 17,400 field trips and enabled 1 in 25 schools throughout the U.S. to send a classroom on a field trip.

Workforce Volunteering: School Library Makeovers

The Target School Library Makeover program, launched in 2007 in partnership with The Heart of America Foundation, leverages Target's design and construction expertise, as well as the time and talents of Target team members. Since the program's inception, volunteers have transformed a total of 118 K-12 school libraries across the country. In 2011 alone, 42 schools received complete library makeovers. A typical makeover costs $200,000 and features

FIGURE 2.8 A school library with a recent makeover thanks to Target employees.

Source: Target Corporation

light construction, new furniture, shelves, carpets, and technology, as well as 2,000 new books. Each student also recieves 7 new books to take home. (See Figure 2.8.) In May of 2011, at the Library of Congress in Washington, DC, Target announced that 42 new schools were on the list to receive complete makeovers by the end of the year, with all 42 principals present to hear the good news.[21]

Socially Responsible Business Practices: MBAs for Employees

Not all of Target's education initiatives are focused on students in grades K to 12. Their employees are also beneficiaries, with one program offering $5,250 per year tuition reimbursement for MBA courses.[22] Perhaps that contributed to being voted one of the Best Places to Launch a Career, ranking eighth out of 69 companies in 2009.[23]

Johnson & Johnson

A Strategic Focus on Nurse Recruitment and Retention

In 1943, Robert Wood Johnson wrote a credo for the company, a one-page document that outlined responsibilities to customers, employees, the community, and shareholders. The first paragraph of their credo begins with the statement: "We believe our first responsibility is to the doctors, nurses, and patients, to mothers and fathers and all others who use our products and services." And the final paragraph begins with the statements: "Our final responsibility is to our stockholders. Business must make a sound profit."[24] We think the company's strategic focus on social initiatives that support nursing careers has helped the company fulfill on each of these commitments. (Figure 2.9.)

THE CAMPAIGN FOR NURSING'S FUTURE

Johnson&Johnson

FIGURE 2.9   Campaign for nursing future logo.

Andrea Higham, Director of Corporate Equity, reports that "Since the campaign launched in 2002, according to the American Academy of Colleges and Nursing (AACN), there have been significant increases in nursing school enrollment estimating that more than 750,000 people had entered the profession. A 2003 survey of United States nursing schools found that 84% of those institutions that received this campaign's recruitment materials experienced an increase in applications and enrollment. And according to a 2002 Harris Poll, campaign commercials have successfully motivated more young people to think about nursing as a career, including 24 percent of 18 to 24 year-olds.[25]"

In 2010, the National League for Nursing (NLN) bestowed its prestigious *President's Award for Transforming the Image of Nursing* to the campaign for its continued work to provide a positive image of nursing. Prior to receiving the award from NLN, the campaign earned the 2004 to 2005 Ron Brown Award for Corporate Leadership for demonstrating a deep commitment to innovative initiatives that empower employees and communities. These are just two of over 150 awards that the campaign has received to date.

J&J's marketing and corporate social initiatives supporting nursing careers are summarized in Table 2.3, with a more detailed description of each program on the next several pages.

Cause Promotion: Campaign for Nursing's Future

In 2012, Johnson & Johnson will celebrate the tenth anniversary of their *Campaign for Nursing's Future*, a nationwide effort to enhance the image of the nursing profession, recruit more nurses and nurse educators, and retain existing nurses and nurse educators. Promotional elements of the campaign are pervasive:[26]

- *Television* spots launched in 2011, spotlighting real nurses and the important role they play both medically and emotionally: Nurses truly do *heal*. The "Nurses Heal" spots air commercially as well as on the Johnson & Johnson Health Channel.
- *Videos,* with one series highlighting a "Day in the Life" of nurses such as Laurie, an emergency room nurse; Ed, a visiting nurse; and Susan, a nurse educator.
- *Recruitment materials* (over 30 million distributed to date) giving visibility for opportunities beyond acute care nursing, with separate brochures on being a public health nurse, a visiting nurse, school nurse, long-term care nurse, or nurse educator.
- *Website* providing online continuing education, refresher courses, events to celebrate nurses, and links to online resources including information for foreign nurses.
- *Promotional materials* including "Be a Nurse" T-shirts, with 75,000 to date (2011) distributed to nursing programs for students and faculty at graduation ceremonies and 300,000 stickers for cars with the message *Nurses Save Lives.*
- *Social media* elements include a Facebook fan page—Nursing Notes by Johnson & Johnson—where Facebook users who *Like* the page have access to fresh, exclusive content. This Facebook page is now the number one most popular destination for nurses with over 50,000 fans (as of September 15, 2011).

TABLE 2.3 Examples of Corporate Social Initiatives for Johnson & Johnson

	Cause Promotion	Cause-Related Marketing	Corporate Social Marketing	Corporate Philanthropy	Community Volunteering	Socially Responsible Business Practices
Description	Supporting social causes through promotions to increase awareness, fundraising, volunteers	Donating a percentage of revenues to a specific cause based on product sales or related consumer actions	Supporting behavior change campaigns	Making direct contributions to a charity of cause	Providing volunteer services in the community	Adapting and conducting discretionary business practices and investments that support social causes
Example	Developing and sponsoring a multi-media campaign to enhance the image of the nursing profession	Donating $1 for nursing scholarships for every photo uploaded to a website	Developing a free app for nurses to help with handling stress	Supporting fundraising events for nursing scholarships and continuing education	Encouraging nurses to volunteer to mentor potential nurses and advocate with policy makers	Surveying nurses to determine recommended changes to workplace environments

A special section on their website debunks common myths regarding a nursing career:[27]

Myth #1: It's hard to get a job. *Reality*: By the year 2020, there will be an estimated shortage of 800,000 nurses.

Myth #2: Nursing doesn't pay well. *Reality*: Starting salaries range from $30,000 to $45,000 per year plus benefits.

Myth #3: Nurses do the same job every day. *Reality:* There are more than 100 nursing specialties, from infusion nursing to occupational health nursing to nurse legislators.

Myth #4: Nurses only work in hospitals. *Reality*: Legal nurse, consultant, forensic nurse specialist, and school nurse are just some of the many jobs held.

Cause-Related Marketing: A Mosaic Project

The Art of Nursing: Portrait of Thanks Mosaic Project is intended to help inspire the next generation of nurses, as well as raise funds for nursing student scholarships. Nurses from around the world are encouraged to upload a photo on Johnson & Johnson's nursing website—campaignfornursing.com. It can be a photo from on the job, a social event, or even a family outing. Photos will then be compiled to create a single (mosaic) image, one intended to become a symbol of pride for nurses everywhere. For every photo uploaded between August 15, 2011, and February 1, 2012, the campaign will donate $1 to the Foundation of the National Student Nurses Association, a membership organization that mentors the professional development of future nurses and provides educational resources and opportunities. In less than a month, 377 photos were uploaded, and by February 21st, 2012, there were 7600.[28]

Corporate Social Marketing: Techniques for Reducing Stress

Over the years, the campaign has heard countless times from nurses that stress management is one of the greatest obstacles to nurse retention and recruitment. One of many online continuing education modules offered is the "From 'Distress' to 'De-Stress' with Stress Management," designed to teach nurses valuable stress relief skills. *Happy Nurse*,™ the campaign's first

FIGURE 2.10 A mobile app intended to encourage fun, de-stressing breaks.

Source: www.discovernursing.com/happynurse/

mobile app, is also part of the strategic solution mix. This free game includes tips for de-stressing and encourages breaks for well-being while having fun. Promotional messages emphasize that "being a happy nurse means taking care of yourself so you can provide the best possible care to others."[29] (See Figure 2.10.)

For the game, players create a customized nurse avatar they control as it runs an obstacle course in multiple settings from home care to the hospital. For the home healthcare version, for example, the player has 1 minute and 20 seconds to find a homebound patient in distress and is met with multiple obstacles along the way to the home including a trash can, a fire extinguisher, and a park bench they must "jump over."

One user shared his experience online. "So, while it seems more than a little counterintuitive to enter a race against the clock in order to slow down a little and take a break, I encourage you to give the game a try—and then come back here and let me know what you think about it."[30]

Corporate Philanthropy: Nursing Scholarships and Workshops

Helping future nurses earn their degrees and build their skills is a priority philanthropic activity of Johnson & Johnson (J&J), sponsor of the *Promise of Nursing* regional gala fundraising events that have raised over $17.5 million since 2002 for undergraduate student nursing scholarships, faculty fellowships, and nursing school grants.[31] In 2009, for example, the program funded a workshop program for nurses in the Mississippi Gulf Coast area most impacted by the trauma of Hurricane Katrina. The program provided information about trauma, post-traumatic stress disorder, and coping skills to address the effects of natural disasters.[32]

Community Volunteering: Encouraging Nurses to Spread the Word

One strategy J&J uses to help recruit more nurses is to encourage current nurses to volunteer their time in one of many activities that make a difference. Options promoted include volunteering at a school's career day, mentoring a new nurse, and sending letters and e-mails to elected officials asking for funding for nursing schools. Persuasive messages include ones highlighting the statistics that "If each nurse recruited just one person, we'd have 2.5 million new nurses—essentially ending the shortage!"; and another, "Sixty-eight percent of nursing students surveyed said that another nurse was their number one influence to join the ranks of nursing."[33]

Socially Responsible Business Practices: Influencing the Workplace

J&J's ongoing attitudinal surveys of RNs help evaluate and inform their strategic efforts, as well as the business practices of their healthcare partners. In 2008, for example, findings indicated that hospital RNs providing direct patient care reported several improvements over the 2006, 2004, and 2002 results, including higher ratings for job satisfaction, ability of nurses to maintain patient safety, staff communications, and time for collaboration with teams. Increased concerns, however, were reported for musculoskeletal injuries and opportunities to influence decisions on the organization of the work environment and decisions about clinical care.[34]

BOX 2.1   SOCIAL MEDIA SPOTLIGHT

In May 2010, during National Nurses Week, the Campaign for Nursing's Future took a big step into the social media world, launching Nursing Notes by J&J, a Facebook fan page for the monthly newsletter *Nursing Notes*. Prior to this launch, the newsletter was distributed by e-mail each month to 50,000-plus subscribers, featuring news and trends on issues impacting the profession. With the Facebook site, readers could now easily share newsletter content with their colleagues, as well as post comments. In addition to the latest edition of *Nursing Notes*, the Facebook page includes a section for photos and videos, an events section, polls that relate to content presented in the newsletter, and links to scholarships with upcoming deadlines.

The campaign has also launched "Amazing Nurses" on their Facebook page, an initiative that invites the public to submit nominations for nurses who really make a difference. "Amazing Nurses" engages consumers, patients, and the healthcare community to nominate outstanding nurses who demonstrate their love for the profession and inspire others to care.

In Summary

Most social initiatives under the *corporate social responsibility* umbrella fall within one of the following distinct categories: cause promotion, cause-related marketing, corporate social marketing, corporate philanthropy, community volunteering, and socially responsible business practices.

Though there are commonalities between each of the initiatives (i.e., similar causes they are supporting, partnerships that are formed, and communication channels that are used), each has a characteristic that makes it distinct. *Cause promotion* is distinguished by the fact that it supports a cause by increasing community awareness and contributions. *Cause-related marketing* is unique in that donations are linked to product sales or other consumer actions. *Corporate social marketing* is always focused on a goal of influencing a behavior change. *Community volunteering* involves employee and related franchise and retail partners' donation of their time in support of a cause. *Corporate philanthropy* is writing a check or making a direct in-kind contribution of corporate services and resources. And *corporate socially responsible business practices*, as implied, relates to the adaptation of discretionary business practices and investments that then contribute to improved environmental and community well-being.

Why is it important to develop these distinctions? As with most disciplines, awareness and familiarity with the *tools in the toolbox* increases the chances they will be considered, and then used. As noted in Chapter 1, traditional corporate giving and citizenship focused primarily on one of these initiatives: philanthropy. As we have seen in the examples presented in this chapter, a more strategic and disciplined approach involves selecting an issue for focus and then considering each of the six potential options for contributing to the cause.

Based on the in-depth examples for Starbucks, Target, and Johnson & Johnson, a few observations are noteworthy at this point:

- **A corporate theme for social responsibility can be expressed in all six of the initiatives**. Starbuck's environmental focus is reflected in each of the initiatives described. Based on reviews of many corporate social responsibility programs, this model can be very effective for connecting the corporation to a cause, as will be described in our chapter on best practices. It is, however, currently quite unusual.

- **It is more common for a corporation to have several themes**, and for themes to be reflected by only a few initiatives. Although Target has a priority emphasis on education, the company also contributes significant funds and volunteer activities to initiatives related to safe communities, healthy living, and sustainable practices.

- **One campaign may integrate several initiatives**. For example, Ben & Jerry's Lick Global Warming campaign has a *cause promotion* component (e.g., a tool on their website that highlights warming trends), a *corporate philanthropy* component (e.g., with contributions to organizations building wind-turbines), and a *corporate social responsibility* component (e.g., working with scientists to reduce the energy consumption of their freezers).[35]

Finally, it is useful to note other terms that are used to label these initiatives, to underscore the distinctions. Cause promotion may be most similar to programs sometimes described as *cause marketing*, *cause sponsorships*, *cause advertising, co-branding,* or *corporate sponsorships.* Cause-related marketing is included by some when describing *cause marketing* or *co-branding* programs. Corporate social marketing may be considered a subset of *cause marketing.* Corporate philanthropy may be expressed as *corporate giving, community giving, community development, community involvement, corporate social investing,* or *community outreach.* Community volunteering is often covered when referring to *community service, community development, community relations, community involvement, community outreach, community partnerships,* and *corporate citizenship* programs. And socially responsible business practices is synonymous for some with *corporate social responsibility, corporate citizenship,* and *corporate commitment.*

As noted, we suggest that by creating these distinct subcategories, consideration of these initiatives is increased and understanding and application of keys to success for a particular initiative is more likely. As will be described in the following six chapters, each initiative has unique and recommended circumstances for consideration and keys for successful development and implementation.

Marketing Driven Initiatives: Growing Sales and Engaging Customers

3

Cause Promotion: Persuading Consumers to Join Your Company in a Good Cause

The amount of money we can give philanthropically is very limited, but we can produce a great deal for charity—and ourselves—through access to our brands, consumers and the Marks & Spencer machine.[1]

—Richard Gillies
Plan A Director
Marks & Spencer

The first wave of marketing social initiatives in the 1980s was dominated by programs that linked donations to consumer actions. In the past 20 years, cause promotion has grown increasingly popular as a strategy for achieving marketing and social goals.

Cause promotion leverages corporate funds, in-kind contributions, or other resources to increase awareness and concern about a social cause or to support fundraising, participation, or volunteer recruitment for a cause. Well-conceived and executed cause promotions can improve attitudes toward a company; generate consumer traffic, sales, and increased loyalty; and motivate employees and trade partners.

Cause promotion most commonly focuses on the following communication objectives.

- *Building awareness and concern* about a cause by presenting motivating statistics and facts. Examples include publicizing the number of children who go to sleep hungry in the United States each night or the number of dogs that are euthanized each year; sharing real personal stories of people or organizations who have been helped by the cause, such as a poor middle-aged man who gets much needed eyeglasses for the first time in his life; or presenting educational information, such as a brochure on preparing for a healthy pregnancy.

- *Persuading people to find out more* about the cause. They may learn how to go online to a Facebook page that supplies information on adopting a homeless pet or by calling for an informational brochure.
- *Persuading people to donate their time*. The promotion might attract volunteers to host a fundraising coffee to support cancer care.
- *Persuading people to donate money*. A section of a company's website might show visitors how to donate to animal welfare charities or encourage shoppers to make a donation to support child literacy.
- *Persuading people to donate nonmonetary resources*, such as unwanted eyeglasses or clothing.
- *Persuading people to get involved*, such as participating in a fundraising walk or signing a petition to ban animal testing.

Table 3.1 lists 10 case examples featured in this chapter and illustrates many of the benefits cause promotion can yield for diverse types of businesses. Cause promotions often involve prominently featured nonprofit partners whose mission is related to the company's adopted cause, but in recent years, an increased number of corporations have opted to go it alone with programs that do not highlight a nonprofit organization.

TABLE 3.1   Examples of Cause Promotion Initiatives

Corporation	Cause	Target Audiences	Samples Activities	Major Partners
Chipotle Mexican Grill	Food with Integrity	People concerned with sustainable agriculture, family farming, organic food, and nutrition Customers	In-store promotion Fundraising Social media Online video Created corporate foundation Public Relations	Chipotle Cultivate Foundation Farm Aid Jamie Oliver Food Revolution
PetSmart	Animal adoption	Customers Current and potential dog and cat pet owners	Raising money in stores and online Offering retail space for cats and dogs to be adopted	PetSmart Charities Local animal welfare groups

TABLE 3.1   (*Continued*)

Corporation	Cause	Target Audiences	Samples Activities	Major Partners
First Response	Prenatal care	Women of childbearing age	On-pack promotion Printed materials Publicity Online information March for Babies sponsorship	March of Dimes
Macy's	Child literacy	Customers	Discount with contribution offers in stores Employee engagement Facebook sweepstakes	Reading Is Fundamental
Farmers Insurance	Healthy babies	Customers Potential insurance clients Vendors and associated businesses	Agent fundraising activities	March of Dimes
Food Network	Hunger	Food Network viewers Food Network Magazine readers Foodnetwork.com visitors	No Kid Hungry PSA production Donated TV, magazine, and online advertising exposure Great American Bake Sale fundraising event Greater Good Garden builds Celebrity talent Public relations	Share Our Strength Cable operators Media and service vendors
Pearson	Early childhood education	Educators Students Parents Education officials	Participant recruitment Public relations Online promotion Fundraising	Jumpstart

(*Continued*)

TABLE 3.1 (*Continued*)

Corporation	Cause	Target Audiences	Samples Activities	Major Partners
Marks & Spencer	Cancer care Clothing recycling Fight poverty	Customers	Fundraising recruitment online and in stores Offering incentives for in-kind donations Collecting in-kind donations in stores Public relations	Macmillan Cancer Support Oxfam
Yoplait	Breast cancer	Trade customers Consumers	Event sponsorship Event marketing Public relations Advertising Online activity	Susan G. Komen for the Cure
LensCrafters	Vision care for the poor	Customers Employees	Eyeglass collection Eyecare and eyeglass fitting events Employee volunteering Printed materials Website	OneSight

Case #1: Chipotle Mexican Grill — Strengthening Brand Positioning

Steve Ells, founder, chairman, and co-CEO started Chipotle Mexican Grill in 1993 with the idea that food served fast did not have to be a typical fast food experience. Over time, the company developed the slogan *Food with Integrity* to describe its commitment to using fresh ingredients that, where possible, are "sustainably grown and naturally raised with respect for the animals, the land, and the farmers who produce the food."[2]

The fresh Mexican food chain, which, by 2011, operated more than 1,100 restaurants, has made effective use of cause promotion to strengthen awareness of its Food with Integrity positioning. In October 2010, for example, the company "exposed the horrors of processed food" by encouraging people to visit Chipotle on Halloween night dressed as the worst kind of junk food they could imagine.

"We have a long-standing tradition of rewarding our customers who dress up as their favorite Chipotle menu item with a free burrito on Halloween,"[3] Ells explained in a press release. "It's always been a fun promotion, but we wanted to do more with it this year and use the opportunity to reinforce with our customers our belief in the importance of eating wholesome, unprocessed foods."[4]

In addition to cause promotion, the company employed a cause-related marketing tactic: Costumed customers were invited to purchase a burrito for the discounted price of $2 with Chipotle contributing that money (up to a $1 million cap) to Jamie Oliver's Food Revolution, a campaign run by the celebrity chef's foundation to encourage people to eat healthier foods at home, at school, or when dining out.

To document and extend the in-restaurant program's reach, Chipotle ran an online costume contest. Customers could compete for prizes by posting photos capturing how they looked in junk food costumes on the Chipotle website.

Evidence of the program's success? The company fulfilled its promise to donate $1,000,000 to Jamie Oliver's Food Revolution.[5] An amazing assortment of Chipotle fans dressed up as toaster pastries, French fries, refined sugar, hot dogs, and other forms of junk food. And the company repeated the program with new beneficiaries in 2011.[6]

Chipotle would not release figures on participation in these promotions, but it was pleased with the outcome, according to spokesman Chris Arnold. "This was the first time we did Boorito as a fundraiser and it worked well," he said. "Attaching the philanthropic component gave us a better opportunity to use Boorito to say something more about who we are and to leverage the popularity of that event to drive an important message."[7] (See Figure 3.1.)

FIGURE 3.1 Collateral promoting Chipotle Mexican Grill's 2011 Boorito program, part of its Food with Integrity initiative.

Case #2: PetSmart—Building Traffic and Customer Loyalty

With nearly 1,200 stores in the United States and Canada, PetSmart is North America's largest specialty retailer of pet products and services.[8] Many of its consumers and employees are passionate about dogs and cats and the company invests heavily in cause promotions that appeal to them.

Early on, PetSmart decided not to sell cats and dogs, but rather to donate space for in-store adoption centers for homeless pets. Local animal welfare organizations maintain the highly visible in-store centers in coordination with PetSmart employees and keep 100 percent of their adoption fees.[9]

The adoption centers generate store traffic on a daily basis from consumers looking for a pet to add to their families. Publicity around national and community adoption events in individual stores, often supported by corporate sponsors, drives traffic even higher.[10] In 2010, more than 403,000 pets were adopted in PetSmart Stores.[11]

The real estate value of the floor space PetSmart provides is approximately $13 million per year, according to Susana Della Maddalena, executive director of PetSmart Charities, a nonprofit the company helped establish to support "programs that save the lives of homeless pets, raise awareness of companion animal welfare issues and promote healthy relationships between people and pets."[12]

It's a big job. Between 1994 and 2010, PetSmart Charities provided more than $134 million in support to animal welfare organizations and helped save the lives of more than 4.5 million pets.[13] That would not have been accomplished without PetSmart's support: Approximately 80 percent of PetSmart Charities' funding is generated by programs made possible by access the company provides to its customers (e.g., donations solicited at checkout), vendors (e.g., Nestle Purina donates cat litter and food for the in-store adoption program), and an employee payroll deduction campaign.[14]

BOX 3.1   SOCIAL MEDIA SPOTLIGHT

In 2011, PetSmart Charities launched a campaign called People Saving Pets (PSP) to help educate the general public that "Pets bring joy and unconditional love to our lives, but 4 million pets are needlessly euthanized every year—11,000 each day—simply because they don't have homes. . . ."[15]

A Facebook page and other social media and offline promotion drive traffic to the PSP website. There, visitors have access to apps that connect them to local resources to adopt, spay, or neuter a pet, volunteer with an animal welfare organization or donate to PetSmart Charities or a local group. (See Figure 3.2.)

(continued)

(*continued*)

"PetSmart and PetSmart Charities are thinking big. After PSP goes national in 2012, the partners hope People Saving Pets will grow into a social movement, said Della Maddalena."[16]

FIGURE 3.2 An in-store PetSmart Charities adoption center.

Case #3: First Response and March of Dimes—Creating Brand Preference with Target Markets

In 2004, the First Response® Pregnancy Tests brand group arranged to meet with the March of Dimes. They believed that a shared goal of providing childbearing-age women with information on early pregnancy detection could form the basis of a strong cause promotion relationship.[17]

Time has proven them right.

In 2005, Church & Dwight Co., Inc., the maker of First Response pregnancy tests, and the March of Dimes, a leading nonprofit focused on helping mothers have healthy babies, announced a robust partnership focused on "informing women that the sooner they know they are pregnant, the sooner they can start giving their babies a healthy start."[18]

Over the years, the duo has taken advantage of one another's communications channels in numerous ways, including shared joint messaging via packaging, product literature displays, and tagged advertising.

The March of Dimes has collaborated with the maker of First Response on public opinion studies ("National Survey Shows Planned Pregnancies May also Be Healthier Pregnancies"[19]), publications ("Are You Ready?," a free 37-page booklet for moms-to-be[20]), online information (Preparing for a Healthy Pregnancy column by March of Dimes Nurse Advisory Council member Kit Devine on FirstResponse.com[21]), and First Response is a national sponsor of the March for Babies fundraising event series.

Although the relationship is close, program communications have conspicuous disclaimers declaring that the March of Dimes does not endorse specific products or brands.

There are two primary reasons why many nonprofits are careful about appearing to endorse products or services. First, endorsement can trigger unrelated business income tax obligations for a nonprofit. Second, in the mid-1990s, a group of state attorneys general sued the Arthritis Foundation and the McNeil Consumer Products Company over an implied endorsement by the nonprofit of an analgesic product.[22]

First Response is the number-one pregnancy test brand in the United States.[23] It has enjoyed healthy market share growth since 2004, progress attributable to major investments in advertising, technological innovations, new product introductions, and its work with the March of Dimes, according to Stacey Feldman, vice president of marketing at Church & Dwight, the maker of First Response brand pregnancy tests.[24]

"It's a collaboration. We do 360-degree marketing to reach women wherever they are. The March of Dimes is a strategic partner; it's a very important touchpoint," she said.[25]

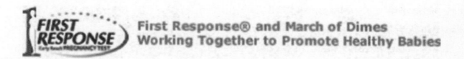

FIGURE 3.3 First Response® and March of Dimes collaborate on many fronts.

Case #4 : Macy's and Reading Is Fundamental—Driving Sales

Macy's has made a science of collaborating with major national nonprofits to field cause promotions that generate millions in customer donations and incremental sales.

Between 2004 and 2011, Macy's partnership with Reading Is Fundamental (RIF) generated nearly $21 million for RIF, the nation's largest children's literacy nonprofit. The funds have been used to purchase millions of books and to support programs that motivate children to read.[26]

The basic program mechanics have been consistent since 2006. Over the course of five weeks, multi-channel promotions invite shoppers at more than 800 Macy's stores to make a $3 donation to receive a voucher good for $10 off a $50 purchase.

The summer 2011 program, Be Book Smart, generated a donation of $4.9 million, up from just over $3 million in 2010[27] and more than four times the total amount raised back in 2006.[28] The 2011 performance is especially impressive considering the challenging economic climate Macy's faced. It was a major shot in the arm for RIF, which had seen its government support slashed by federal budget cuts in March of 2011. (See Figure 3.4.)

Macy's Executive Vice President of Marketing, Martine Reardon, said the program's progress was accelerated by having volunteers from local RIF programs visit stores to educate associates about RIF's local impact.[29] Those interactions helped inspire store personnel to embrace and promote the program.

In 2008, for example, RIF volunteers in 38 target markets made 200 store visits and placed over 300 phone calls. The value of that involvement is reflected in the fact that seven of the 10 top-performing Macy's stores were visited by local RIF volunteers.[30] RIF's local engagement program has grown steadily since. In 2011, local volunteers made approximately 775 store visits to more than 300 Macy's stores.[31]

Macy's continues to invest in this and similar programs with the American Heart Association and other charities because they enhance the shopping experience, engage employees, and help move more product, according to Macy's VP of Media Relations and Cause Marketing, Holly Thomas.[32] In 2008, 70 percent of consumers who received RIF savings vouchers used them—a tremendous redemption rate, according to Reardon.[33]

BOX 3.2   SOCIAL MEDIA SPOTLIGHT

Macy's and RIF have incorporated online tactics to increase awareness of their partnership since its inception, but in 2011, they took their social media efforts to a new level with the creation of a Facebook sweepstakes app.

Designed to encourage supporters to share the Be Book Smart campaign with friends, the sweepstakes, hosted on RIF and Macy's Facebook pages, awarded a $500 Macy's gift card to one winner each week the program ran.[34]

In addition to leveraging Macy's fan base of 2 million users, nearly every campaign-related e-mail, blog post, tweet, Facebook post, and online ad issued by RIF linked to the sweepstakes app.[35]

The sweepstakes app drew 13,001 visitors/views, 4,373 entries, and 3,398 *Likes*, as well as many positive comments from Macy's store associates and local RIF volunteers, according to Thomas.[36]

FIGURE 3.4   Localized creativity helps Macy's and RIF make their national partnership more relevant to shoppers in hundreds of communities.

Case #5: Farmers Insurance, *Be a Hero for Babies Day*—Strengthening Relationships

Since its founding in 1928, Farmers Insurance has had a culture steeped in giving back. "Our founders were really well known for giving and yet they wanted zero recognition for it," explained Community Branding VP Charles Browning, a veteran of three decades with the United States' third largest automobile and homeowners insurance company.[37]

"As public expectations of corporate social responsibility have grown, Farmers' leadership came to see its charitable activity as something to be shared, not hidden," Browning said.[38] In 2005, CEO Paul Hopkins felt it was time to be public about the company's support of March of Dimes, the leading nonprofit organization for pregnancy and baby health. With chapters nationwide, the March of Dimes works to improve the health of babies by preventing birth defects, premature birth, and infant mortality.

"Paul challenged the company's field force—about 15,000 agents and district managers—to raise $1 million (for the March of Dimes) in a single day through grassroots fundraising," said Browning.[39] Thanks to numerous agent-sponsored car washes, golf tournaments, bake sales, and other efforts, the company collectively raised $1.4 million in 2006 in a program that came to be known as Be a Hero for Babies Day®.[40] (See Figure 3.5.)

Through 2011, corporate employees and Farmers' insurance agents and district managers have succeeded in consistently outpacing the previous year's total, creating the type of community ties that help agents build additional business. In 2011, Be a Hero for Babies Day raised $2.75 million.[41] In recent years, the company has published full-page advertisements in *USA Today* announcing its Be a Hero for Babies Day accomplishments and encouraging others to support the March of Dimes.

"We want to be more than just another company that sells insurance," said Browning. "This is a way of differentiating ourselves in a very crowded marketplace while acting on our corporate responsibility to give back."[42]

"Farmers does not have solid quantitative data proving that its efforts for the March of Dimes pave the way for selling more insurance—the grassroots nature of the effort and the infrequent nature of insurance sales make that measurement difficult—but it has enough anecdotal data to feel confident that this is both a good investment and the right thing to do," said Browning.[43]

FIGURE 3.5   Farmers Insurance raised $2.7 million for the March of Dimes in 2011 through Be a Hero for Babies Day activities such as this employee telethon.

Roger Daniel, a third-generation Farmers Insurance agent in Billings, Montana, agrees. He said he's confident that the bowling tournament he organizes each year to support the March of Dimes—$20,000 net raised in 2011—yields a great return on his investment of time and money.[44] "Talking about working together for a good cause with key vendors like attorneys and auto body shops takes our relationship to another level," he said. "They refer people to me big time."[45]

Case #6: Food Network and Share Our Strength—Leveraging Media Assets

Sometimes media companies simply donate unused space or air time to worthy nonprofits and sometimes they build high impact win-win partnerships. In this example, America's leading food cable network provided tremendous support to a nonprofit while enhancing the charitable side of its brand, and strengthening critical industry relationships.

When the national nonprofit Share Our Strength celebrated its twentieth anniversary in 2004, it announced an audacious goal: End childhood hunger in America. Share Our Strength builds public-private partnerships at the state level to connect more children with food and nutrition programs, supports local hunger efforts, teaches families how to cook healthy meals on tight budgets, and mobilizes individuals to take action to fight hunger.

To tackle that challenge, it sought out new corporate partners that could generate funding, awareness, and other resources.

In 2007, one of its top corporate alliance accomplishments was being named the priority pro-social cause of Food Network, a cable television powerhouse distributed to over 100 million U.S. households and known for signature programming such as *Iron Chef America*, *Throwdown! with Bobby Flay*, and Alton Brown's *Good Eats*.

"Initially, Food Network's involvement was largely driven by the passion of a few key executives," said Irika Slavin, the network's vice president for communications and public relations.[46] "Over time partnering with Share Our Strength evolved into a strategic priority and Food Network made major increases in its commitments of senior management attention, funding, in-kind donations, and personnel," she said.[47]

The collaboration publicly kicked off with support for Share Our Strength's annual Great American Bake Sale, a national campaign that mobilizes people to raise money to help end childhood hunger in America by holding bake sales. Food Network produced and aired public service announcements featuring network stars, held an on-air bake sale, and provided a grand prize VIP trip for the nation's top bake sale fundraiser.

A turning point occurred in 2010 when Share Our Strength focused its work and marketing around the theme *No Kid Hungry*. "Previously Share Our Strength had brought us a lot of different projects to get involved with," said Katie Ilch, the network's vice president for on/off air media strategy and planning. "No Kid Hungry really stood for something powerful, it was easy to understand and we were able to get behind it in a big way," she explained.[48]

Reflecting its enthusiasm for No Kid Hungry, Food Network worked with one of their frequent creative agencies, BPG, to donate their creative services in producing a public service announcement used to support the No Kid Hungry initiative. The PSA features the actor Jeff Bridges, a major supporter of Share Our Strength and the face of No Kid Hungry. (See Figure 3.6.)

In the year following the November 2010 launch, Food Network's cumulative support and exposure for Share Our Strength through network airtime, *Food Network Magazine*, an online presence, as well as access to talent and other forms of promotional support, could be valued upwards of $20 million,

FIGURE 3.6   Food Network has provided millions of dollars' worth of air time to broadcast a Share Our Strength No Kid Hungry public service announcement featuring actor Jeff Bridges.

Ilch estimated.[49] "Additionally, Food Network leveraged its media buying to the benefit of Share Our Strength, as our spending resulted in mainstream media opportunities that would otherwise not have been available to No Kid Hungry, gratis," added Ilch.[50]

Food Network also developed its own signature programs to benefit Share Our Strength. The Food Network New York City Wine & Food Festival, for example, has raised millions for Share Our Strength since 2008.

In addition to raising money and awareness for Share Our Strength and increasing consumer participation in its programs, this partnership has benefited Food Network in several ways.

In part to strengthen relationships with cable system operators, Food Network created *Good Food Gardens*, a program that builds edible classroom gardens at schools and community centers. It's very much in keeping with Share Our Strength's goal of surrounding kids with nutritious food where they live, learn, and play.

Food Network and Share Our Strength are now closely tied in the public consciousness, a big change from 2006 when the network's brand was not associated with giving back. "No Kid Hungry, The Good Food Gardens, and other collaborative efforts have provided Food Network with sales, marketing, PR, online, and programming opportunities," said Ilch.[51]

In October 2011, Food Network received Share Our Strength's Great Oak Award, an honor rarely given and reserved for the group's champion partners. As Chief Development Officer Chuck Scofield put it at the award ceremony, "Without Food Network's continued support and unwavering commitment, much of the work we do at Share Our Strength would go unnoticed."

Case #7: Pearson and Jumpstart— Strengthening Corporate Image

Visitors to the Pearson website are greeted by a letter from CEO Marjorie Scardino that begins:

"Welcome to Pearson. Around a decade ago, we set out to make this a learning company."[52]

Since 2006, Read for the Record has been the highest profile initiative positioning the publisher of *The Financial Times*, Penguin books, and numerous learning tools and testing programs as a company dedicated to supporting learning.

Pearson employees and businesses, together with the Pearson Foundation, partner each fall with the nonprofit group Jumpstart to enlist volunteers in setting a world record for the largest number of people reading the same children's book on the same day. (One-to-one reading between adults and children is a core element of Jumpstart's work promoting early childhood education. Since 1993, the Boston-based national education organization has trained tens of thousands of college students and community volunteers to mentor pre-school children in low-income communities.)

From a cause perspective, the goal of Read for the Record is to (1) spread the word that reading with a child before he or she enters kindergarten can improve his or her chances of graduating from high school by as much as 30 percent;[53] (2) draw attention to Jumpstart's work; and (3) generate financial support for the Boston-based nonprofit.

Each year, the Pearson Foundation supplies the featured book (e.g., *The Very Hungry Caterpillar*, *The Little Engine that Could*) to thousands of participating schools. It also raises funds for Jumpstart by contributing all proceeds from sales of a special edition of the featured book. Since 2006, the Pearson Foundation has donated more than 1 million books to young people in conjunction with this program and raised more than $5,000,000 for Jumpstart's work.[54] (See Figure 3.7.)

As the lead sponsor, the Pearson Foundation underwrites many aspects of the campaign including its highly interactive website and engages public relations firms to generate attention. Those efforts have built Read for the Record into the most popular employee engagement program within Pearson.[55]

FIGURE 3.7   Pearson and Jumpstart team up to get millions of people involved in their annual Read for the Record program.

The October 7, 2010, program succeeded in setting a new record by engaging adults to read *The Snowy Day* by Ezra Jack Keats to 2,057,513 children and the 2010 campaign garnered 520,677,372 media impressions, according to Pearson Foundation President Mark Nieker.

"Read for the Record is an ideal way for Pearson people and businesses to lend support to local schools and community organizations that care as much about helping children, and encouraging reading and a love of books, as we do," said Nieker. "Each year, the Pearson Foundation also brings together partners we work with all year long—teachers, education leaders, community leaders and families—to support Jumpstart and to showcase their important work in classrooms year around."

BOX 3.3   SOCIAL MEDIA SPOTLIGHT

Beginning with the 2010 campaign, the Pearson Foundation also made it possible for people to help break the record by reading online via the WeGiveBooks.org website.

E-mails and blog posts recruited volunteers to read online—an important invitation for people who might not have easy access to the physical book. In 2010, more than 65,000 people took part in Read for the Record via We Give Books, according to Nieker.[56]

That digital connection made it possible to continue a conversation with online readers about Jumpstart, and the importance of reading after the one-day event had concluded. Moreover, it created a digital army of volunteers that Nieker said he expected would be "some of the strongest evangelists for the program going forward."[57]

Keys to Success

The following three cases offer perspectives from managers at Marks & Spencer, General Mills, and Luxottica in terms of keys to successful cause promotion initiatives. Their common themes reflect recommendations to carefully select an issue (upfront) that can be tied to your products and your company values. They say it should be a cause that management can commit to long term, is a concern for your customers and target markets, motivates your employees, and has the most chance for media exposure. When developing cause promotion plans, take care to connect the campaign to your products, develop partnerships, incorporate and ensure visibility for your brand, and figure out a way to measure and track results.

Case #8: Marks & Spencer—Deriving Value from Nonprofit Partnerships

In January 2007, Marks & Spencer, a leading British department store chain, launched Plan A, perhaps that country's most ambitious and public corporate social responsibility platforms. Its stated goal: Become the world's most sustainable major retailer.[58]

Since then the company has announced 180 commitments to "combat climate change, reduce waste, use sustainable materials, trade ethically and help our customers to lead healthier lifestyles."[59]

In many cases, M&S has partnered with NGOs to collaborate on issues "that are too large to be tackled by consumers, businesses and even governments alone."[60]

During an interview in his London office, Marks & Spencer Plan A Director Richard Gillies shared background and lessons learned on two such partnerships: Macmillan Coffee Morning and the M&S and Oxfam Clothes Exchange.

Both are emblematic of a major shift in M&S's corporate social initiatives. "In the past our relationships with charities were philanthropic or reactive, small in scale and large in number," said Gillies.[61] We want our relationships with charities to be symbiotic and deliver real value for both parties."

The World's Biggest Coffee Morning

Back in 1990, a local fundraising committee for Macmillan Cancer Support in Kent held a coffee social. The money attendees paid for their morning brew was donated to Macmillan, a well-known British charity that improves the lives of people affected by cancer via practical, medical, emotional, and financial support.

From those modest roots, the annual Macmillan Coffee Morning has grown into the organization's largest grassroots fundraising program and a national institution. In 2009, Macmillan sought out national sponsors for the first time. Marks & Spencer was a logical fit: Its in-store cafes constituted the United Kingdom's third largest coffee chain and its Plan A objectives included, "Help our customers make a difference to the social and environmental causes that matter to them."[62]

When the company's sponsorship of the World's Biggest Coffee Morning launched in 2010, M&S cafes were positioned as perfect sites for anyone to hold a get-together or to support Macmillan through cafe purchases. The company continued to support Macmillan in 2011 and donated 50 pence for every cup of coffee sold in its cafes on the day of the World's Biggest Coffee Morning. For two months leading up to the big day, the company donated 10 pence on a variety of cafe items and contributed all revenue from the sale of promotional items produced by Macmillan: a *little book of treats* baking book with celebrity recipes and pin badges.[63]

Particularly helpful to Macmillan was the company's distribution of registration forms in-store and online, according to Francesca Insole, corporate partnerships account development manager at Macmillan.[64] Those and other promotional efforts led to an increase in the overall number of coffee mornings held inside and outside M&S locations.[65] (See Figure 3.8.)

Two examples:

1. Consumer Incentive: Anyone who registered online to host a coffee morning received a voucher from M&S for a free cup of coffee along with their event planning kit.
2. In 2010, M&S built a media event around the company chairman's use of his M&S Volunteer Day to host a coffee morning and consult with Macmillan executives.[66]

The partnership generated measurable impacts for the company and the nonprofit. For Marks & Spencer, the big payoff of the World's Biggest Coffee Morning is increased *footfall*, the British term for store traffic, Gillies said.[67] "The 50 p[ence] contribution is margin diluting, but the program is a major footfall driver. It creates a stronger connection to our consumer and creates PR value for Macmillan and M&S," he explained.[68]

FIGURE 3.8 Marks & Spencer uses online and offline tactics to help Macmillan Cancer Support recruit people to hold coffee morning fundraisers.

For Macmillan, just over £400,000 was raised in 2010 through the sale of M&S cafe products, pins, and employee and customer fundraising.[69] Both partners benefited from approximately half a million pounds worth of PR, according to Gillies.[70]

M&S and Oxfam Clothes Exchange

One of Marks & Spencer's original Plan A commitments was to "Create partnerships to help our customers reuse or recycle all our products and packaging."

The M&S and Oxfam Clothes Exchange, launched as a trial program in January 2008, has enabled the company to make major progress toward that goal, stimulate additional sales, and generate millions in revenue for Oxfam's work to fight poverty.

Throughout the year, customers who donate M&S clothes in Oxfam's roughly 740 second-hand stores in the United Kingdom and Republic of Ireland receive a voucher worth £5 off a £35 purchase at M&S of clothing, homeware, or beauty products.

The program's initial six-month trial was so successful that it was extended indefinitely, Gillies said.[71] On September 8, 2010, the company took the program a step further by permitting consumers to drop off clothes at M&S stores, a promotion dubbed the "One Day Wardrobe Clear-Out."[72] Although the complex logistics of handling donated clothes in M&S stores initially produced "a bit of a corporate convulsion," according to Gillies, the M&S team learned to cope and now runs the promotion twice a year.[73]

As of September 2011, Oxfam had raised £6.7 million through the sale of donated goods and 8.6 million garments had been recycled instead of going into landfills, according to Richard Gillies.[74]

On the M&S sales side of the equation, consumers are redeeming approximately 50 percent of the give and save vouchers, an "extraordinary" rate compared to the single digit redemption levels M&S experiences for vouchers not tied to a cause promotion, Gillies said.[75] The program is particularly profitable because "there is an above average spend by people who use the voucher," he added.[76]

Richard Gillies offered this strategic and tactical advice to business executives contemplating multifaceted marketing of social initiatives:

> In developing programs, start with a clear business objective and seek charity partners to secure those objectives. In doing so you will ultimately create much greater value for your own organization and the charity involved . . .

> "It is also important that the partnership works with your business model, working with your customers on topics they can associate closely with what you do.[77] (See Figure 3.9.)

FIGURE 3.9   A Marks & Spencer online banner promoting clothing donations to Oxfam.

Case #9: General Mills Yoplait Yogurt—Building Equity, Loyalty, and Passion

Anyone familiar with Yoplait in the United States may find it hard to believe, but the country's leading yogurt was once a brand in search of a promotional identity.

In the early 1990s, brand managers at parent General Mills tried—with little success—to appeal to the product's target market of women ages 18 to 43 by tying into figure skating, women's hockey, and even the science-fiction movie *Jurassic Park*.[78]

The inspiration for what has become one of the world's best-known cause promotion programs started with a 1998 request from employees at Yoplait's California production plant: "Could we sponsor a local breast cancer race?"

Management approved and went on to explore the breast cancer cause further. Time and testing revealed that they had hit upon "an ownable connection," according to Promotion Marketing Manager Berit Morse.[79] It turned out that supporting the fight against breast cancer powerfully appealed to Yoplait's target consumers and to retail partners.

After a short initial partnership with one breast cancer group, General Mills allied itself with the Dallas-based group now called Susan G. Komen for the Cure. The world's largest network of breast cancer survivors and activists, Komen has invested more than $685 million in breast cancer research and $1.3 billion in community health and education programs since its founding in 1982.[80]

Over the years, Yoplait marketers have expanded upon the Komen relationship. It took just three years for Yoplait to become the national presenting sponsor of Komen's Race for the Cure series, the top sponsorship position. Yoplait consistently supports its Komen sponsorship by investing in television, print, and online advertising, sampling at races and fielding public relations programs.

Being a part of the more than 100 race series—and directing contributions to local Komen chapters—provides numerous opportunities for Yoplait to collaborate with the merchants who carry its products, a key element in securing retail merchandising that drives sales.

A cause-related marketing centerpiece of those efforts is the Save Lids to Save Lives program launched in 1998. Each September and October, Yoplait puts pink lids on its products and offers to contribute 10 cents for every lid consumers send in up to a predetermined cap. In 2011, Yoplait promised to contribute up to $2 million through Save Lids to Save Lives.

Over 13 years, Yoplait has donated more than $30 million in financial support for Komen through all of its donations programs.[81] For the business, the positive impacts of this program are clear. Race for the Cure tie-ins and Save Lids to Save Lives consistently create a significant increase in sales during September and October.[82] Consumer passion for the program is evidenced by the growth of the Race for the Cure series (1.6 million people participated in 2010)[83] and the tens of millions of lids that are sent in each year.

Promotion Marketing Manager Berit Morse offered businesspeople the following lessons learned from General Mills' Yoplait experience:[84]

- Connect to a partner who shares your brand's or company's values.
- Unite with a partner who is willing to work with you to develop your own angle on the cause.
- Commit to a consistent long-term relationship.
- Bring your sponsorship to life. Plan to spend two times your sponsorship fee activating.

- Break through. Never underestimate the impact of great design.
- Reach and remind. Make the effort to ensure you have created strong awareness.
- Be where your consumer is— don't expect them to find you.
- Leverage your champions—consumers, customers, partners, and employees.
- Introduce yourself. Find new consumer targets and expand your program in relevant ways (versus creating something completely different).

BOX 3.4   SOCIAL MEDIA SPOTLIGHT

To increase consumer engagement in Save Lids to Save Lives—and reduce the program's carbon footprint—Yoplait launched a new online tool in 2011 that enabled consumers to redeem lids online by entering codes.

To add greater emotional meaning to the data entry process, Yoplait gave consumers the option of dedicating their lids online. The passion the pink lids program ignites and the community it builds is reflected in the thousands of short dedications one could find on savelidstosavelives.com.

Two examples[85]:

- Rachel from Yuma, Arizona, wrote, "I dedicate this to the group of girls dedicated to rallying the whole school to raise money for the fight against breast cancer."
- Tony of Fergus Falls, Minnesota: "I was inspired to collect and redeem these lids by my mother who is currently battling breast cancer. Thank you."

Yoplait also enlisted consumers to spread the word, by liking the Yoplait Save Lids to Save Lives Facebook page (for which the brand pledged to donate 10 cents per *like*, up to $50,000) and by updating their Facebook status with one of a selection of messages such as "I collect pink Yoplait lids for Save Lids to Save Lives" or "I collect pink Yoplait lids for my mom [or sister, friend, aunt, etc.]."[86]

Past test efforts to encourage consumers to participate online instead of sending in lids were not well received (people indicated they liked the

(continued)

(continued)

physical connection of mailing in lids), but preliminary results indicate that this effort may do the trick, Morse said.

FIGURE 3.10   In 2011, Yoplait gave consumers the option of redeeming lids online.

Case #10: LensCrafters—Creating a Point of Differentiation

Established in 1988, OneSight is a family of charitable vision care programs sponsored by the Luxottica Group that provides access to free eye care and glasses to people in need in North American communities and in developing countries. Luxottica Group is a leader in premium eyewear with 7,000 optical and sunglass retail stores around the world, including LensCrafters.

Greg Hare, executive director of OneSight, offered the following insights into the program's structure, as well as its impact, value, and benefit to the company:[87]

"In the realm of cause promotion, LensCrafters and OneSight encourage customers to make cash donations and to donate their gently used glasses to those in need. Promotional materials (print and website) ask customers to 'Please help us continue our international clinic work by donating your old eyeglasses and sunglasses. Often the glasses people receive at our clinics are the first glasses they have ever received.'

"Since 1988, over 2 million glasses have been collected, recycled and hand-delivered to OneSight patients in developing countries. Requests for cash donations emphasize that Luxottica covers more than 95 percent of OneSight's overhead, so donations go directly to deliver glasses to those in need.

"OneSight requires the direct participation of Luxottica employees. Because each person's eyeglass prescription and fit is unique, glasses must be hand-delivered by trained volunteers, capturing the energy and expertise of our people, and this is what makes this program unique. A majority of LensCrafters' 20,000 employees and Luxottica's 60,000 employees worldwide participate in OneSight in one form or another (assisting patients in our stores, on our two Vision Vans, in community outreach programs and on international optical clinics to developing countries). Through OneSight, our employees develop an emotional alignment with our company that's crucial to our competitive context.

"LensCrafters has chosen to differentiate itself from optical competitors with similar products through superior service. While we created OneSight for its social benefits, we maintain and grow it because it helps us build a service-minded culture. Employees involved in OneSight feel proud of the company and remain with us longer.

"We continue to expand OneSight programs because we know they provide terrific teambuilding and leadership training opportunities. What better way to teach teamwork, flexibility, creativity and the power of a positive attitude than to take 25 like-minded adults to a developing country for two weeks and challenge them to deliver quality eye exams and eyeglasses to 10,000 local people—knowing they will face electric outages, equipment held up in customs, unfamiliar food, and strange accommodations. In 200 clinics in 32 developing countries our teams have figured out how to work together to overcome obstacles. This learning is transferable to their jobs and their lives. What better way to teach diversity than to challenge every employee group to partner up with local schools, senior centers, nursing homes, and shelters to help deliver free eye care to more than 200,000 people annually.

"For LensCrafters, building more dedicated employees is a competitive benefit. Through OneSight, we give a higher level of meaning to our jobs so that no employee ever feels he or she is 'just selling glasses.' Delivering glasses to someone who's never seen clearly before brings an immediate improvement. It's a magical moment resulting in tears, hugs and kisses that 'opens the eyes' of our employees as surely as those of our patients.

"We created OneSight, a 501c3 public operating charity, through which we improve the "cost-benefit ratio" of our philanthropy by fundraising from suppliers, employees, customers and local foundations. We raise about $5,000,000 in cash and $3,500,000 in goods annually to supplement Luxottica's commitment of overhead and staff (21 full-time employees plus access to the expertise of every business unit within the company).

"In summary, principles that worked for us and may work for others include the following recommendations:

- Focus your community service on your core expertise/product.
- Involve employees in hands-on giving.
- Push program ownership to the local level.
- Brand the program with a strong, single identity.
- Forge partnerships.
- Set, communicate and track program goals."

FIGURE 3.11   OneSight eyeware collection boxes are placed in LensCrafters and other Luxottica retail locations.

Potential Concerns with Cause Promotion

As with most campaigns and programs that are promotional in nature, several potential downsides for businesses should be kept in mind during the decision-making and planning process.

Visibility for the business can get lost. Most marketing managers considering major engagement with a social issue are interested in ensuring visibility for their company. Jumping on board as a sponsor of a nonprofit event along with a boatload of other companies can yield disappointing results—there's not much brand- or relationship-building value in being included in a line-up of corporate logos on brochures and banners.

The key to success is developing a campaign and tactical elements designed to garner the type of attention the company seeks while remaining true to the cause's mission. As we learned earlier in this section, when Yoplait embraced the fight against breast cancer as the yogurt's cause, they were not satisfied to be just one of many Komen Race for the Cure's sponsors. Yoplait grabbed the national presenting sponsor spot as soon as it became available and has held onto it ever since. Yoplait receives premium level recognition and attention from Komen because of that. Furthermore, Yoplait invests millions each year to activate its sponsorship at the races, through overarching promotional and public relations efforts and via account-specific programs created in tandem with retailers.

Most promotional materials are short term. Brochures, flyers, PSAs, news articles, special events, even another T-shirt, water bottle, or baseball cap can be "here today and gone tomorrow." Managers are encouraged to consider creating long-term components to their campaigns. Pearson's promotional support of early childhood learning peaks each fall with Jumpstart's Read for the Record. Throughout the year, the Pearson Foundation's WeGiveBooks.org website provides interested adults with access to digital versions of classic children's books and the foundation donates a physical book to a child for every book read online.

Tracking total investments and return on promotional investments can be difficult. Many report that not only is it difficult to track results for the company from the promotional effort, it is also difficult to track the actual expenditure of corporate resources, especially non-monetary contributions (e.g., employee time, retail store space, etc.). The intention of many cause promotions is to increase awareness and concern regarding a cause, frequently without a call to action. This is harder and more expensive to measure than changes in behavior or redemption of coupons, for example, which can be accomplished through internal tracking systems. Changes in awareness and levels of concern typically require more quantitative research, adding to the costs of the effort. The need for measurement is a frequent subject of discussion among practitioners, but research budgets are frequently inadequate or are eliminated when budgets are cut.

This approach requires more time and involvement than *writing a check*. PetSmart, for example, invests considerable resources on their in-store adoption centers and collecting donations at checkout stands among many other activities. Cause promotions can pay great business dividends, but—like any marketing program—they require investment, time, and effort.

Promotions can be copied, diminishing their competitive advantage. Successful cause promotions often inspire copycat programs. PetSmart competitor Petco holds frequent pet adoption events in its stores in cooperation with local shelters.[88]

When Should Cause Promotion Be Considered?

Assuming that a cause has been selected that the company wants to support, the following circumstances should lead to considering a cause promotion initiative, either solo or in addition to other initiatives:

- When your company has easy access to the target markets, as PetSmart does for animal adoption or Food Network does for generating interest in No Kid Hungry.
- When the cause can be connected to and sustained by your products and distribution channels, as with Luxottica's collection and dispensing of eyewear and First Response's dissemination of healthy pregnancy information.
- When you have the opportunity to leverage existing business practices or goals, as when Marks & Spencer supported its objective of lengthening the product life of garments it sells by promoting clothing donations to Oxfam.

- When employee or partner involvement will support the cause and create greater esprit de corps, as Be a Hero for Babies Day fundraising activities do for Farmers Insurance employees and agents.
- When there is a co-branding opportunity, as there was for First Response and the March of Dimes in creating and distributing educational materials that support the cause and the brand with target audiences.
- When a potential nonprofit partner has assets such as events, a large supporter base, information or sample distribution channels, access to celebrity supporters, or proprietary technology that will complement and enhance your own.

Developing a Cause Promotion Campaign Plan

Perhaps the most important decision to be made once a social issue has been identified and a cause promotion initiative has been selected is to confirm whether the campaign will include partners, and if so, to identify them. Campaign plans should then be developed together, upfront, as they will include critical decisions on target audiences, key messages, campaign elements, and key media channels.

One of the most effective ways to make these decisions is to develop a document that will provide direction for developing messages, designing campaign elements, and selecting media channels. A useful tool is a creative brief, typically one to two pages in length. It will help ensure that all team members, including external partners, are in agreement on target audiences, communication objectives, and key assumptions prior to the more costly development and production of communication materials. Typical elements of a creative brief to support the development of a promotional campaign include the following sections:

1. Target Audience: This section includes a brief description of the target audience including estimated size, demographics, geographics, psychographics, and behavior variables.
2. Communication Objectives: This is a statement of what we want our target audience to *know* (facts, information), *believe* (feel), and perhaps *do* (e.g., donate or share information via social media) based on exposure to our communications.

3. Benefits to Promise: This is the identification of key factors that will motivate target audiences to participate in volunteer efforts or to make donations—benefits they will experience by taking these steps.

4. Openings: Siegel and Doner describe openings as "the times, places, and situations when the audience will be most attentive to, and able to act on, the message."[89] This information will be key for determining media channels.

5. Positioning and Requirements: This section describes the overall desired tone for the campaign (e.g., serious versus lighthearted), as well as requirements such as the use of corporate logos.

6. Campaign Goals: This is an important section for selection of media channels, as it outlines quantifiable goals for the campaign. These may include process goals (e.g., desired reach and frequency goals) or may include actual outcome goals (e.g., number of people to sign up for the race). This document will then lead to development of campaign elements including slogans, headlines, and copy; graphic images; materials; selection of media channels, evaluation plans, budgets, and implementation plans, including responsibilities and target dates for campaign activities.

In Summary

A marketing social initiative is categorized as a cause promotion when the core element of the effort is promotional in nature. Primary strategies utilized are persuasive communications. Communication objectives focus on building awareness and concern; persuading people to find out more; persuading people to donate their time, money, or non-monetary resources to a cause; and/or persuading people to participate in real or virtual events to benefit a cause. Most commonly, corporations partner with nonprofit organizations, although there has been growth in the number that initiate and implement campaigns on their own. In many cases, the corporation is given visibility on promotional materials and is highlighted in media outreach.

Most corporate benefits are marketing related such as strengthening brand positioning, creating brand preference, increasing traffic, and building customer loyalty. Many corporations experience additional benefits such as increased employee satisfaction and the development and strengthening of nonprofit and business relationships.

There are several potential downsides for the corporation that are inherent in these promotional campaigns: visibility for the corporation can get lost; short-term impact; tracking investments and return on promotional investments is difficult; this approach requires more time and involvement than writing a check; and promotions are often easy to replicate, potentially removing desired competitive advantages.

Keys to success include carefully selecting an issue that can be tied to your products and your company values. It should be a cause that management can commit to long term, is a concern for your customers and target markets, motivates your employees, and has the most chance for media exposure. When developing cause promotion plans, take care to connect the campaign to your products, develop partnerships, incorporate and ensure visibility for your brand, and figure out a way to measure and track results.

This initiative should be given serious consideration when your company has easy access to a large potential target audience; when the cause can be connected and sustained by your products, services, or distribution channels; when you have opportunities to contribute to the campaign by leveraging existing assets; when employee morale can be boosted by the effort; and when there are co-branding or other opportunities that will enable your program to stand out from the crowd.

Developing a plan begins with decisions regarding objectives and strategies. Next comes the critical choice of whether to work with one or more nonprofit partners or go it alone. Then, planning teams identify target audiences and develop key messages, campaign elements, media channels, evaluation plans, budgets, and implementation plans.

4 Cause-Related Marketing: Making Contributions to Causes Based on Product Sales and Consumer Actions

At Sainsbury's corporate responsibility is not an addendum to the business.
We don't do philanthropy, we do investment.

—Jat Sahota
Head of Sponsorship, Sainsbury's Supermarkets Ltd.

Cause-related marketing—linking monetary or in-kind donations to product sales or other consumer actions—dates back to 1983 when American Express contributed to the restoration of the Statue of Liberty each time consumers used or applied for one of the company's charge cards. No complete tally exists summing up funds raised by cause-related marketing programs, but a Cause Marketing Forum review of 10 of the largest programs indicates it easily runs into the billions.[1]

Some cause-related marketing programs operate year-round, but most such offers link a specific product with a specified charity for a designated period of time. Contributions may be in actual dollar or in-kind amounts (e.g., $1.00 donation when a Facebook page is liked or a pair of shoes donated when a pair of shoes is purchased) or a percentage of sales (e.g., 10 percent of revenues from sales of specified products).

Many companies are attracted to cause-related marketing by consumer attitude research that consistently indicates consumers would prefer to purchase products and services that support good causes. For example, 94 percent of consumers surveyed across 10 countries in 2011 indicated they were likely to switch brands to one that supports a cause if both brands were similar in price and quality, according to the 2011 Cone/Echo Global CR Opportunity Study.[2] Nonprofits are attracted to cause-related marketing by the opportunity to receive substantial, often unrestricted, donations from corporations.

Examples in this chapter illustrate that cause-related marketing programs can generate social and financial benefits, but it is not uncommon for these efforts to generate criticism when companies are vague about their contributions (e.g., stating only that "a portion of the proceeds will be contributed"), fail to comply with state regulations, or are otherwise seen as being misleading or opportunistic in their support of a cause.

What most distinguishes cause-related marketing from the five other types of initiatives described in this book is the way it links a corporation's level of giving to consumer action. Because of that linkage, cause-related marketing initiatives often require more detailed agreements and coordination with nonprofit partners involving important activities such as establishing specific promotional offers, developing co-branded advertisements, abiding by state regulations and industry guidelines, and tracking consumer purchases and activities.

Typical Cause-Related Marketing Offer Formats

Typical cause-related marketing offers include one or more products that the corporation will promote, a cause that will be supported, and a charity, charities, or corporate foundation that will benefit from the effort. Although the range of corporations participating in cause-related marketing initiatives is broad, this approach is perhaps most ideal for companies with products that have mass market appeal, large customer bases, and wide distribution channels, especially those in the consumer goods, retail, financial services, transportation, and telecommunications industries.

Several types of product links and contribution agreements are common and considered in keeping with best practices in terms of transparency:

- A *specified dollar amount for each product sold* (e.g., TELUS gave $100 for each new cable television service account opened in participating Canadian municipalities.)[3]

- A *specified dollar amount for every application or account opened* (e.g., Bank of America gives $3 for each new Susan G. Komen for the Cure branded credit card account opened and activated.)[4]
- A *percentage of the sales of a product or transaction* is pledged to the charity (e.g., the eBay Giving Works program enables online sellers to designate 10 to 100 percent of a product's sale price to a nonprofit.)[5]
- A *company makes a specified in-kind donation* in response to a consumer purchase or action (e.g., TOMS Shoes donates a pair of shoes to a child in need with each purchase of TOMS Shoes).
- A *company makes a cash contribution* that underwrites a tangible charitable benefit (e.g., Pampers contributes seven cents to UNICEF from the sale of a disposable diaper package to pay for maternal neonatal tetanus vaccinations).

In addition to being clear on what will be contributed based on a specific consumer action, companies creating cause-related marketing programs should specify what group or groups will receive the contribution, which of its products are participating, the program time frame, any contribution minimum or ceiling, and/or any restrictions on channels of distribution (e.g., a retailer-specific program).

Although cause-related marketing campaigns support a wide range of causes, corporations generally prefer to align themselves with issues that have many supporters, such as major health issues (e.g., cancer, arthritis, heart disease, asthma, AIDS), children's needs (e.g., education, hunger, medical needs), basic needs (e.g., hunger, homelessness), and the environment (e.g., wildlife preservation, nature preserves).

Beneficiaries of funds raised are typically nonprofit organizations or foundations. A foundation is sometimes created by the corporation (e.g., Pedigree Foundation) to collect, manage, and distribute funds. Corporations may award funds to a variety of charities, or may dedicate proceeds from a campaign to one specific organization. Partnerships may include more than one corporation, as well as a public agency (e.g., schools).

Table 4.1 outlines the cause-related initiatives analyzed in this chapter.

TABLE 4.1 Examples of Cause-Related Marketing Campaigns

Corporation	Cause	Apparent Target Audiences	The Offer	Major Partners
TOMS Shoes	Providing shoes to children in need	Shoe buyers	A pair of shoes is given to a child in need for each pair purchased	A variety of nonprofits that distribute shoes
Sainsbury's	Helping disadvantaged people in Africa and the UK	Current and potential shoppers who want Red Nose Day merchandise	A specified portion of the price of Red Nose Day merchandise donated to Comic Relief.	Comic Relief
Avon	Breast cancer	Women who buy cosmetics and care about the breast cancer cause	A specified portion of "pink ribbon" products donated to the Avon Foundation for Women	Avon sales representatives Breast cancer research and patient services
Pedigree	Promoting homeless dog adoption	Current and potential dog owners	$1 donated when consumers upload a picture for the Million Dog Mosaic	The Pedigree Foundation
Pampers	Eliminating maternal and neonatal tetanus	Purchasers of disposable diapers	Each purchase of designated packages of Pampers triggers a donation funding a vaccination	UNICEF
General Mills	Funding for K-8 schools	Parents, teachers, and other consumers who care about kids in school grades K-8	10 cents donated to a designated K-8 school when a consumer redeems a qualifying Box Tops icon from General Mills or products from other participating companies	Public schools Other participating companies
Subaru	Causes favored by its targeted consumers	Car buyers	$250 divided up among participating charities according to a qualifying buyer's preferences	ASPCA Habitat for Humanity and other participating nonprofits
TELUS	Community-based charities	Cable television households	$100 donated to community charity when consumer purchase qualifying services	Local charities in 22 TELUS markets
Kraft Foods	Hunger	Grocery shoppers	Meals donated in response to numerous purchase, online, and other activities	Feeding America

Potential Business Benefits

By design, most business benefits from a cause-related marketing campaign are marketing-related. As the following examples demonstrate, successful initiatives can support company efforts to attract new customers, reach niche markets, increase product sales, and build positive brand identity while raising significant funds for a cause.

Case #1: TOMS—Building Positive Brand Identity

In just four years, TOMS grew from a shoe-selling start-up based in the living room of the owner's shared Santa Monica, California, apartment to a company that had sold more than a million pairs of shoes. Key to its meteoric success was a core cause-related marketing offer: For every pair of shoes sold, TOMS promised to give one pair away to a child in need.

"What we've found is that TOMS has succeeded precisely because we have created a new model," Founder and Chief Shoe Giver Blake Mycoskie explains in his 2011 book *Start Something That Matters*.[6] "The giving component of TOMS makes our shoes more than a product. They're part of a story, a mission, and a movement anyone can join."[7]

Unlike many cause-related marketing offers that briefly add a charitable component to a brand, TOMS' buy-one-get-one proposition is written into the company's DNA and the legend of its founding. Mycoskie recalls the moment he realized that "TOMS was a story as much as it was a product."[8] Just months after starting the company, he was checking in for a flight home to Los Angeles after an unsuccessful selling trip with New York fashion retailers. He saw someone in line wearing TOMS, the first person other than a friend he'd ever seen wearing the company's shoes. Without revealing who he was, he asked her about her shoes.

The woman's eyes widened, her face came alive, and she said boldly, 'TOMS!' . . . and, in an animated voice, she told me the TOMS story. 'When I bought this pair of shoes, they actually gave a pair of shoes to a child in Argentina. And there's this guy who lives in Los Angeles who went to Argentina on vacation who had this idea—I think he lives on a boat and he was once on the Amazing Race TV show—and the company is wonderful, and they've already given away thousands of shoes![9]

That experience helped Mycoskie understand that

[p]eople who tell the TOMS story are more than just our customers, they're our supporters. People who buy TOMS like to talk about their support of our mission rather than simply telling people they bought a nice shoe from some random shoe company. They support the product, and the story, in a way that a casual buyer will never do. Supporters beat customers every time.[10]

In addition to connecting with consumers, the power of TOMS' BOGO offer and story has helped make it "attractive to potential partners who want to attach themselves to something deeper than buying and selling," according to Mycoskie.[11] One example: An advertising agency executive happened to hear a television report on the company in 2008. That started a chain of events that led AT&T to feature Mycoskie and TOMS in a widely aired television commercial about the telecommunications company's usefulness to small businesses in 2009. The tremendous awareness of TOMS that the spot created helped catapult the company's sales.

Hoping to expand its ability to do well and do good, TOMS launched a second product offering in June 2011, TOMS Eyewear, to help save and restore sight to people in need using its trademarked One for One™ concept. (See Figure 4.1.)

FIGURE 4.1   TOMS Shoes Founder Blake Mycoskie puts a pair of new shoes on a child in need.

Case #2: Sainsbury's and Comic Relief—Attracting New Customers

To be competitive, modern supermarkets stock thousands of items, but other than their own house brands, virtually none of them are exclusives. For six weeks every other year, however, Sainsbury's, the United Kingdom's number three grocery chain, is the only place where consumers can find the hottest novelty items in the marketplace: Comic Relief red noses—clever plastic or foam variations on the traditional clown nose that people wear on the charity's enormous, biannual Red Nose Day event. (See Figure 4.2.)

Since 1999, Sainsbury's has been the exclusive, official Red Nose merchandise retailer, a high-profile way of supporting the charity's work on behalf of poor and vulnerable people in the United Kingdom and Africa. Comic Relief's Red Nose Day is a national phenomenon that culminates in a comedy-infused, star-filled fundraising broadcast on the British Broadcasting Company (BBC). Perennially, it is the country's most watched Friday night show.

In the run-up to the March 2011 broadcast, Sainsbury's raised more than 11 million pounds for the charity primarily from the sale of three *monster* red

FIGURE 4.2   English "Mommy Blogger" Emma Brooks posted this self-portrait posing with her daughter wearing red noses purchased at Sainsbury's to celebrate Red Nose Day in 2011.

noses, the Nose that Grows tomato plant, wind-up Runny Noses, and other novelty items.[12]

Red Nose items are sold at no profit, but deliver incremental sales for Sainsbury's "because new customers come to our stores and existing customers come more," said Jat Sahota, Sainsbury's head of sponsorship.[13] In addition, Comic Relief allows Sainsbury's to pass along sponsorship rights to some manufacturers of products sold in its stores. That creates additional in-store excitement and sales, Sahota said.[14]

Sahota's claims about Red Nose Day's impact on footfall and sales are not based on a gut reading of the marketplace. Thanks to the company's Nectar frequent shopper program, Sainsbury's can analyze every shopping basket that contains a Comic Relief item. Tens of millions of pounds in incremental sales more than pays for the company's investment in Red Nose Day sponsorship, Sahota said.[15]

The power of the connection to Comic Relief is further illustrated by consumer awareness of the company's involvement: "80 percent of our customers know we support Comic Relief. Our bananas have been fair trade for four years and only 40 percent of our customers know that even though we say it all the time," he explained.[16]

Case #3: The Avon Breast Cancer Crusade—Building Brand Equity While Raising Funds for a Cause

In 1992, Avon representatives in the United Kingdom tried selling pink ribbon pins to raise funds for a breast cancer charity. From the seeds of that effort grew the Avon Breast Cancer Crusade, a pink juggernaut the direct sales giant has backed to raise and donate more than $700 million to breast cancer programs around the world.[17] The breast cancer cause aligns extremely well with Avon's positioning as *the company for women*. The Avon Foundation awards funds for medical research, screening and diagnosis, clinical care for cancer patients, support services for patients and their families, educational seminars, and early detection programs.

Profits from sales of pink ribbon fundraising products accounted for $266 million of the money the global beauty products company raised for the Breast Cancer Crusade between 1992 and 2010.[18] The bulk of the remaining funds were generated by the Avon Walk for Breast Cancer series plus other events in the United States and around the world.

The product sales total is particularly striking considering that most of the items sell (through Avon representatives) for less than $7 a piece. "We keep the prices low because we need to be very grassroots and accessible," said Avon Corporate Social Responsibility Director Susan Arnot Heaney. "We've always wanted everyone to be able to play a part, every customer, every representative, every employee."[19]

Among the many pink ribbon products marketed by Avon over the years are lipstick, foot cream, pins, pens, mugs, candles, stuffed bears, cosmetic cases, umbrellas, and other items.

Avon is very precise in describing the donation each fundraising product sold generates for the Avon Foundation for Women. (The donation is the difference between the retail price and the cost of goods sold.) For example, the Avon website, in October 2011, stated that Think...Pink! Nailwear Pro Nail Enamel cost $2.99 and yielded a $2.27 donation.[20] (See Figure 4.3.)

FIGURE 4.3 Pink Nailwear Pro Nail Enamel is one of the products Avon sells to raise funds to fight breast cancer. Of the $2.99 price, $2.27 goes to the Avon Foundation for Women.

The company adopted that level of transparency as the Avon Breast Cancer Crusade grew and attracted more critical attention, said Arnot Heaney, who joined the company in 1997.[21] "We tell exactly how much money is donated from each sale and precisely where the money is going."[22]

To further its mission of generating breast cancer awareness and education, Avon includes a flyer with breast health information and resources with every pink ribbon fundraising product sold. Although Arnot Heaney can remember a time when few people associated Avon with breast cancer, she said, "These days it would be very hard to separate our philanthropy from our company."[23]

"We've done research that shows that our consumers and representatives expect Avon to support good causes and that breast cancer continues to rate as a top concern, often #1,"[24] Arnot Heaney said. "That association is a key differentiator over other companies when it comes to the recruitment of representatives, of which Avon has approximately 6.5 million in 100 countries,"[25] she said.

The pride that Avon employees take in the company's efforts to give back runs all the way to the company's top management. Thousands of Avon associates participate as walkers and crew in the Avon Walk events, and "at our latest New York walk, 10 people from our North American Council, the highest level of management, spent an hour and a half on a street corner a mile from the finish line wearing pink T-shirts and waving pom poms to cheer on the walkers. That's how deep this goes,"[26] she said.

Case #4: The Pedigree Adoption Drive—Reaching Niche Markets

Dog food may not be glamorous, but it's a big, competitive business. Dog owners are passionate about their pets and invest billions each year in products and services to care for them. Illustrating that point: 78 percent of dog owners reported buying gifts for their pets in 2011, spending an average of $48 per year.[27]

To solidify its share of the dog food market while maintaining its profitability, Pedigree® brand, owned by Mars Petcare US, began to reposition itself in 2005 as the brand most committed to the proposition that every dog deserves a loving home. While competitors had dabbled with promotions supporting the adoption of dogs in shelters, Pedigree brand "made a commitment to 'own' the cause with fully integrated large-scale, evergreen programming called the Pedigree Adoption Drive."[28]

Every year since, the brand has invested heavily in the Pedigree Adoption Drive and in raising awareness of the plight of homeless dogs via paid television and print advertising, extensive public relations activity, sophisticated digital promotion, and experiential marketing. As of November 2011, Pedigree brand had raised and donated more than $7 million to help dogs find loving homes since 2005; in 2010 alone, it donated more than $2.3 million of product to help feed shelter pets.[29] Much of this is done through the PEDIGREE Foundation, a 501(c)(3) nonprofit organization that provides grants to shelters and rescue organizations nationwide.

In terms of cause-related marketing, Pedigree brand has been a leader in engaging dog lovers online. Two examples:

1. **Million Dog Mosaic:** In 2008, Pedigree recruited consumers to upload pictures of their dogs to help create an online photo mosaic of Oliver, the PEDIGREE® Adoption Drive featured shelter dog. For each photo or video upload, a dollar was donated to PEDIGREE Foundation. More than 2,000 bloggers wrote about the mosaic, helping it become the largest online mosaic ever created with over 50,000 pictures uploaded and more than a million page views.[30]

2. **Facebook Campaign:** In February 2010, the Pedigree brand teamed up with country music star and animal lover Carrie Underwood on the *Become a Fan, Help a Dog* campaign. The brand used multiple media to urge dog lovers to become fans of the PEDIGREE Adoption Drive Facebook page. For each new fan, Pedigree pledged to donate a bowl of food to help feed shelter dogs. The result—growing from 55,000 to 1.2 million fans in a year—set a Facebook record and generated an enormous donation, according to Lisa Campbell, senior brand manager for Pedigree.[31] (See Figure 4.4.)

Overall, the PEDIGREE Adoption Drive has had major positive impacts on Pedigree brand's business as measured by increased retailer engagement with in-store activities, overall sales growth, and enhanced connections with consumers online and in social media communities, said Campbell.[32]

FIGURE 4.4 More than a million people responded when Pedigree offered to donate a bowl of dog food to an animal shelter for each person who liked its Facebook page.

Case #5: Procter & Gamble and UNICEF "1 Pack = 1 Vaccine" — Increasing Product Sales

Disposable diapers are a mature product category in North America and Europe. Category leaders Pampers (Procter & Gamble) and Huggies (Kimberly Clark) and private label brands compete vigorously for market share.

In 2004, an associate product manager responsible for Pampers in Western Europe began testing concepts that tied Pampers purchases during the holiday seasons to contributions to UNICEF that would support child immunizations. His dual goal: create a program that diaper-buying mothers would connect with emotionally and that retailers would support with higher levels of merchandising, a key sales driver.[33]

Impressive sales results from fourth-quarter campaigns in Belgium in 2004 and 2005, linking Pampers to UNICEF donations led Procter & Gamble management to research program refinements that would make this a powerful platform for broader European campaigns going forward.[34]

Focus groups were held in the United Kingdom to explore the reactions of young mothers to a range of cause-related marketing concepts. Consumers voiced skepticism concerning most of the donation ideas presented. There was a very different reaction, however, to the concept of linking the purchase of a package of disposable diapers to a donation that would pay for a single vaccine, according to Yannis Artinos, Pampers marketing director for Western Europe.[35]

"When we showed that concept," Yannis recounted to an Oxford University case study team, "there was silence in the room, silence. And they said, 'Now this is something. It's the first time I've seen something that is worthwhile for me to switch and pay something extra. Because without giving anything that is out of my way, without sacrificing anything, I am just buying a pack of diapers which anyway I need to buy, I will save the life of a baby . . . .' That was how the campaign started."[36]

Armed with that information, Pampers management asked UNICEF to identify a vaccine that could be funded with a donation of 10 cents or less, the amount that could be given while remaining within Pampers' required per unit profit margins.[37] When the research was done, P&G and UNICEF agreed that maternal and neonatal tetanus was a great fit because it enabled mothers buying Pampers to protect other mothers and their babies.[38] (In the developing world, women often give birth in unclean environments, leaving them and their babies vulnerable to life-threatening tetanus infections. Two vaccinations given to an expectant mother can protect her and her offspring for three years.)[39]

The *1 Pack = 1 Vaccine* program was successfully launched in the United Kingdom, Netherlands, Ireland, and Belgium in 2006, spread to 16 countries in 2007, and went global in 2008.[40] In most countries, the campaign has demonstrated impressive and sustained power to grow Pampers sales. In the United Kingdom, for example, donations generated by consumer and trade efforts grew from $287,000 in 2006 to more than $2.5 million in 2010.[41] In Germany, a 2009 study of purchase intent showed a 29 percent lift among consumers who were aware of the campaign.[42]

The funding has been a financial boon to UNICEF's maternal and neonatal tetanus elimination program, but implementing such a major public health initiative in developing countries has presented the organization with many challenges (e.g., high cost of sending personnel to remote areas to vaccinate women).[43] Initially, Procter & Gamble interpreted the wording of its agreement with UNICEF in a way that limited the use of its funding to pay for the vaccine serum. Over time, the company and NGO came to an agreement that the money could be used to fund vaccination delivery costs.[44]

By September 2011, the 1 pack = 1 vaccine campaign had provided funding for more than 300 million vaccines, enough to protect 100 million mothers and their babies.[45] At the 2011 Clinton Global Initiative, Procter & Gamble committed to continue its work with UNICEF to eliminate maternal and neonatal tetanus by 2015.[46]

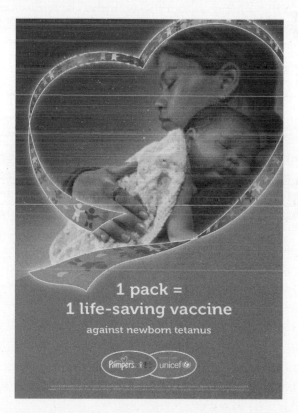

FIGURE 4.5 The "1 pack = 1 vaccine" message has proved powerful for Procter & Gamble and UNICEF.

Case #6: General Mills Box Tops for Education—Building Corporate Partnerships

One of America's best-known school fundraising programs, General Mills' Box Tops for Education (BTFE) program raised over $400 million for more than 90,000 kindergarten to eighth grade schools between 1996 and 2011.[47]

BTFE contributes 10 cents to a consumer's selected school for each proof-of-purchase coupon sent in from more than 240 participating brands. It's a tremendous sales and loyalty driver for General Mills. Fifty-one percent of program participants indicated that BTFE made "me stay more loyal to participating brands than I otherwise would be", and 27 percent said the program influenced them to switch brands, according to a 2011 study.[48]

While highly effective, the program is also expensive to run. In addition to processing hundreds of millions of BTFE coupons, General Mills recruits and supports tens of thousands of volunteer fundraising coordinators with online and offline tools that help them rally parents, faculty, and friends to clip and turn in coupons, said Box Tops for Education Director Zack Ruderman.[49]

To help offset that cost, General Mills began to allow other manufacturers into the program in 2005 on a category exclusive basis in exchange for a licensing fee. "We look for national brands with very strong reputations, that are relevant to families with children in kindergarten through eighth grade, and are interested in making a long-term commitment to the education cause," said Ruderman.[50] For the 2011 to 2012 school year, non-General Mills participation included selected products from Avery Dennison, Boise, Brita, Hanes, Hefty, Kimberly-Clark, Land O'Lakes, Nestle, and SC Johnson.[51]

In addition to defraying costs, these outside partners have helped General Mills obtain retail merchandising support that it would not have been able to obtain on its own, said Ruderman.[52] For example, Sam's Club dedicated the highly coveted cart rail area at the front of its stores during the 2011 back to school season to multi-brand BTFE displays. "They would not do that for a single manufacturer, but they were attracted to this opportunity because of the breadth of brands involved," Ruderman said.[53]

In what Ruderman called a "virtuous cycle,"[54] the more products involved in BTFE, the greater support they receive from retailers, and the more money the program raises for schools. That helps explain why the program raised a record $59.5 million in the 2010 to 2011 academic year, up 21.5 percent from the year before.[55]

BOX 4.1   SOCIAL MEDIA SPOTLIGHT

In October 2011, General Mills announced a pair of firsts: its first automotive partnership and its first program built around eBoxTops. eBoxTops® are electronic credits that are made directly to the BTFE-eligible school by General Mills, equivalent to 10 cents for each eBoxTops credit.

A two-month promotion with Ford rewarded consumers for watching Ford videos (5 eBoxTops each), ordering a brochure online (10 eBoxTops), or purchasing a new Ford vehicle (250 eBoxTops). (See Figure 4.6.) The Ford website made it easy to tell friends about the program via e-mail or Facebook.

FIGURE 4.6   Ford joined the Box Tops for Education program with a major joint promotion in October 2011.

"The partnership with Ford is a major step for Box Tops for Education as we continue to offer new ways to activate the program beyond the packaged goods category," said Mark Addicks, senior vice president and chief marketing officer for General Mills.[56]

Keys to Success

The three cases presented in this section offer success strategies from executives involved in developing and executing cause-related marketing programs. Their experiences are consistent with these best practices:

- Pick a cause your company and your target audience are or can be passion about.
- When selecting a charity partner seek one that has a broad base of engaged supporters that can be activated to stimulate high volumes of activity.
- Target a product offer that has the most chemistry with the cause, looking for the intersection between your customer base, your products, and people who care about the cause.
- Research the idea with targeted customers, or consider a pilot program to gauge general appeal and refine marketing strategies.
- Give the effort considerable visibility with potential buyers. Small mentions on product labels or small type added to existing ads may go unnoticed.
- Keep the offer simple and transparent to ease communication and avoid consumer suspicion. Consider the benefits of disclosing the actual or anticipated amount to be donated to the charity and its potential impact (e.g., the next $1 million raised will be designated to eradicating polio in the world).
- Be willing to recognize errors and make changes.

Case #7: The Subaru "Share the Love" Event—Analyzing and Improving Each Year

More than 40 years after it began importing all-wheel drive cars from Japan, Subaru of America, Inc., remains a niche player with about a 2.1 percent share of the U.S. auto market.[57] Unable to match the mass marketing efforts of larger rivals, its marketing team focused over the years on targeting consumers in niches as varied as outdoor enthusiasts, speech pathologists, and pet lovers.

In 2008, the company leveraged those insights to create the Subaru "Share the Love" event, an end-of-year cause-related marketing program that donates $250 to a new car buyer or lessee's choice of one of five national non-profit organizations. Between 2008 and 2010, Share the Love raised almost $15 million for charity and significantly boosted Subaru sales according to National Advertising Manager Brian Johnson.[58]

"Most car brands have sales events in December, where the main communication is based on incentives like cash back or 0% financing," Johnson explained. "Subaru is not a typical car brand. We define our brand in a way that is a direct reflection of our owners. Subaru owners love to give back. They support good causes and are engaged in philanthropic initiatives. Our consumers inspired us to create this event in 2008. . . . We love it because while our competitors are selling indulgence or are 'yelling and selling,' we're promoting sharing and giving back to our communities as core values of our brand."[59]

Johnson said Subaru used a methodical process to create the Share the Love event and then put substantial marketing resources behind it to raise awareness among target consumers. First, it identified charity partners that would be a good fit with the brand and that were willing and able to promote the campaign to large numbers of followers. Its criteria for selecting organizations included: national in scope, recognizable, high awareness; noncontroversial, nonpolitical; large and active member base; willingness to promote the event with multiple touch points; no competing automotive partnerships; and missions that index high with Subaru owners' interests.[60]

The company selected the ASPCA, Boys & Girls Clubs of America, Habitat for Humanity, Meals on Wheels Association of America, and National Wildlife Federation as its launch partners in 2008.

Next, Subaru produced and fielded promotional creative that explained "how Subaru and its owners were trying to make a difference, the mechanics of this sales event, and the idea that this was a good time to purchase a vehicle," Johnson said.[61] In 2008, the campaign encompassed television and radio commercials, newspaper print and direct mail templates, point of purchase kits, press releases, digital support including a takeover of the

Subaru.com home page, online banner ads, and social media components on Facebook and Twitter. Tag lines included *This holiday help your favorite charity get some real traction* and *Get a great deal, Support a great cause.*[62]

The program was a big success in its launch year of 2008 as measured by numerous metrics. Johnson cited two examples: (1) Sales increased 16.3 percent during the event compared with 5.3 percent for the industry, and (2) 35 percent of first-time buyers reported that their perception of the brand was more positive as a result of the event.[63]

Not only did the program impact purchases and consumer attitudes, but it was more efficient than traditional incentives used at other times of the year. In 2009, Subaru spent $890 on incentives (including the donation) during the Share the Love event as opposed to an average of $1,024 at other times of the year.[64]

Careful post-event analysis led to refinements that have helped the program continue to deliver powerful results. Johnson cited several examples:

The company discovered that greater than one in four consumers had not been told about the program or had been given incorrect information when they visited a dealer. In year two, it provided dealers with handouts covering the ins and outs of the program.

When consumers had to go to Subaru.com to make their charity selection, only 40 percent followed through. Providing dealers with business reply cards that enabled consumers to direct the donation at the time of purchase raised redemption to 65 percent.

In year one, few dealers activated the event in their communities with local charity affiliates largely because they didn't know how or who to talk to. Subaru worked closely with its charity partners to make it easier for dealers to connect with local affiliates and created incentives for local cooperation on events such as pet adoptions at dealerships created in cooperation with the ASPCA.[65]

BOX 4.2   SOCIAL MEDIA SPOTLIGHT

To increase consumer involvement in the 2011/2012 Share the Love event, Subaru leveraged Facebook to engage consumers in selecting one of the participating charities.[66] (See Figure 4.7.)

(continued)

(continued)

FIGURE 4.7 Subaru enables consumers to divide a $250 donation among the nonprofits participating in the Share the Love program.

From August 25 through September 15, 2011, Facebook community members were given the opportunity to vote for one of four charities (Teach for America, The American Red Cross, The Children's Miracle Network, and the Make-a-Wish Foundation). To ensure none of the groups went away empty-handed, each one received 10 cents per vote for each of the first 200,000 votes registered.

In the end, the Make-a-Wish Foundation's outreach to its vast network of supporters via its own online and social media assets and those of corporate and other partners garnered one-third of the 133,068 votes cast[67] and a chance to receive a share of Subaru's Share the Love event millions. Thanks to the campaign, Subaru saw its Facebook community more than double from 79,796 *Likes* to 181,164 *Likes*.[68]

Case #8: TELUS—Maximizing Impact by Localizing Contributions

Strategically giving back is central to corporate culture at TELUS, a leading Canadian telecommunications company. In fact, TELUS was named the most outstanding philanthropic corporation in the world by the Association of Fundraising Professionals in 2010.[69]

The Community TELUS TV (CTTV) campaign exemplifies the company's skill at blending value and values. The 2010 CTTV campaign donated $100 to a local cause for every new TELUS TV customer that signed up in participating communities during a 12-month period. (See Figure 4.8.)

Guided by a *we give where we live* philosophy, the company focused the campaign on 22 smaller communities across Alberta and British Columbia

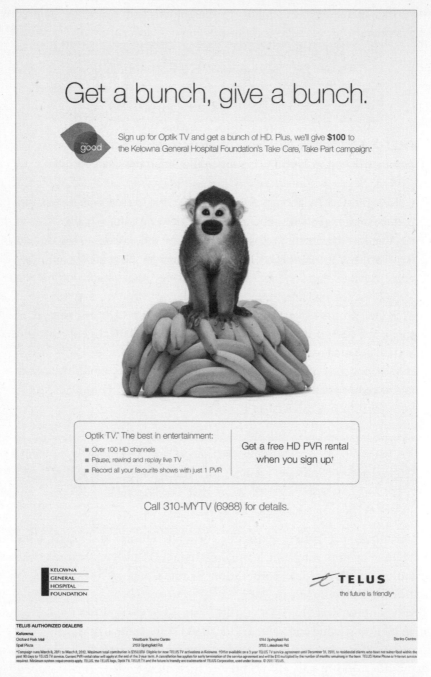

FIGURE 4.8 TELUS offers to make a $100 donation to a local charity when consumers sign up for new services.

with a high percentage of analog TV customers and where the company's donation would have the largest positive impact, according to Vice President of Community Affairs Jill Schnarr.[70] Beneficiaries in each market were chosen with input from local TELUS employees, retirees, and municipal government contacts.

TELUS worked with many of its charity partners to cross-promote this campaign within their communication vehicles such as newsletters, posters, websites, and their Facebook and Twitter accounts, Schnarr said.[71] TELUS often assisted in the creation of these social media messages for the partners.

The CTTV campaign exceeded forecasted results and posted some of TELUS's highest sales increases experienced by the company. Within the CTTV campaign locations, TELUS TV sales were significantly higher, demonstrating the program's effectiveness in attracting customers and driving sales, Schnarr said.[72] On average, sales were 46 percent above forecast in CTTV communities as opposed to 5.4 percent across all cities and communities where TELUS TV was offered.[73] The company attributes the acquisition of 38,690 TELUS TV customers in 2010 and donations of $3,869,000 to the campaign.[74] Based on its strong financial and social metrics, TELUS launched 35 CTTV campaigns in 2011.

TELUS Vice President of Community Affairs Jill Schnarr describes the benefits of its localized approach to cause marketing as follows:

Win for Community

- Builds needed community infrastructure and access for family services, healthcare, technology, literacy, and education.
- Provides a tangible contribution that a customer can see and benefit from.
- Supports local governments and health services projects to make communities more economically viable.
- Provides access to corporate dollars for investment in regional and urban communities.

Win for Corporations Like TELUS

- Gives customers another reason to buy from TELUS.
- Allows senior managers to build relationships in their communities.
- Improves the communities in which employees live.

- Builds strong, stable infrastructure for the company by improving the surrounding community.
- Strengthens a surrounding community's potential workforce through improved access to technology, education, and healthcare.[75]

Case #9: Kraft Foods Huddle to Fight Hunger—Embracing Social Media

When Kraft Foods launched Huddle to Fight Hunger in 2010, it showered consumers with ways to drive meal donations to Feeding America. They could redeem manufacturer or retailer coupons, join a virtual huddle on the campaign website, text the word *meals* and their zip code, *Like* or upload a photo to the Kraft Foods Facebook page, watch a video on YouTube, Tweet #KraftFightsHunger, or play two football- and hunger-themed online games to name just some of the varied options.

When the program ended, consumer actions had generated 21 million meals for Feeding America's national network of food banks as well as healthy sales and brand equity growth for Kraft Foods, North America's largest food manufacturer.[76] Successfully orchestrating such an enormous program rested on three conceptual pillars, said Kraft Foods Senior Director, Consumer Engagement and Marketing Partnerships, Stephen Chriss:

1. Build it on consumer and customer insight.
2. Obtain active support from senior management in terms of involvement, people, and resources.
3. Create a compelling, integrated marketing campaign that has multiple touchpoints.

Consumer Insight

In developing the program, Kraft conducted market research to be sure that the hunger cause resonated with its female consumer target. Kraft's data revealed that its consumers felt that hunger was a real issue, that it was a cause that they would respond to, and that they understood why Kraft and its brands would be involved with it, Chriss explained.[77] The company also determined that consumers would respond positively to mixing the hunger message with the traditional fall retail theme of football and food (as in eating while tailgating or watching a game with family and friends).[78]

Customer Insight

For major packaged goods marketers, obtaining grocery retailer merchandising support (e.g., in-store displays, advertising in store circulars) is essential to commercial success. To win that support, manufacturers must bring trade customers programs designed to generate profitable incremental sales. Kraft sold retailers on the concept that September/October, the window between back-to-school and Thanksgiving holiday promotions, presented an opportunity to combine the message of fighting hunger with the football food theme.

"We brought them the idea that Kraft plus Feeding America plus football equaled Kraft Huddle to Fight Hunger,"[79] Chriss said. The concept was so persuasive that a record 60 major retailers signed on to a program built around 11 major brands including *Planters* nuts, *Oreo* cookies and *Kraft* cheese.[80]

Senior Management Support

Successfully producing such a massive event required tremendous resources and cooperation from numerous areas of the company. Huddle to Fight Hunger's combination of critical business and CSR goals raised its importance to Kraft's CEO, CMO, and North American president. Their high profile and active interest paved the way for the program's robust implementation.

"I've been doing scale marketing campaigns for many years at Kraft," said Chriss. "Some were tremendously successful and others were less so. Senior management support is often the tipping point for mobilizing the organization to do what needs to get done."[81]

A Compelling Integrated Program

In 2010, Kraft went all out to stage this multi-division initiative, the largest in the company's history. It invested in extensive online and offline, mass, and targeted marketing programs including: sponsoring the first charity-themed college bowl game, the Kraft Fight Hunger Bowl; celebrity endorsers such as football Hall-of-Famer Joe Montana; advertising in *People* magazine, Yahoo.com, and ESPN; a 2.5-minute film that ran in 5,100 movie theaters and an online video series; multiple donation promotions on Facebook; in-store campaigns coordinated with 60 retail chains; extensive couponing; Hispanic outreach programs; and brand extensions such as the first football-shaped Oreo cookie.

Kraft's return on investment on Huddle to Fight Hunger was measured in numerous ways. There are hard sales figures: Huddle to Fight Hunger was a significant contributor to base organic revenue gains of more than 4 percent in Q4, performance so significant it was included in the company's quarterly earnings report.[82] Trade spending generated a three-to-one return, exceeding the program's goal of two-to-one.[83] The company also carefully monitors consumer attitudes. Awareness of Kraft as a company combating hunger increased 55 percent from December 2009 to December 2010, according to Chriss.[84] That attitudinal change is key to building the emotional connections that put more Kraft products on shopping lists when consumers go to the store, he said.[85]

BOX 4.3   SOCIAL MEDIA SPOTLIGHT

Based on launch-year insights, Kraft Foods shifted resources away from traditional couponing into social media marketing in the program's second year. Among the lessons Chriss shared:

For the majority of consumers, it's critical to keep the hurdle to engagement online very low. "Keep it simple for the consumer. We make that first point of entry just a 'click here,' a 'press here,' or an 'enter here' because once they do that they're part of our community of engagement," he said. "Then we provide opportunities for you to become more involved like uploading a photo of your family at a Saturday football game or downloading recipes."

The growing popularity and connectivity of social media led Kraft to move the hub of the campaign from a dot-com website to Facebook. "Being on Facebook opens things up to more sharing, discussion about the cause, thanking Kraft, questioning Kraft (although we hope there won't be too much of that) and making emotional connections."

(continued)

(continued)

Many people prefer that donations stay in their community. For many online aspects of the program, Kraft enables consumers to input their zip codes to direct donations to their local food banks.

FIGURE 4.9 Kraft Foods provided consumers with dozens of ways to generate meal donations including this Kraft Huddle to Fight Hunger online game.

Potential Concerns

In an environment in which some consumers and activist groups are skeptical of all corporate claims related to doing good, cause-related marketing programs can provide targets for criticism. The mechanics of properly implementing and communicating cause-related marketing programs can make them more labor and resource intensive than other types of initiatives and can present more potential legal and marketing risks. For example:

- **Contractual agreements** specifying contribution conditions must be drawn up between the corporation and the charity.
- **Legal restrictions and required disclosures** must be investigated and abided by.
- **Reliable tracking systems are needed** to ensure corporate commitments are fulfilled (e.g., a campaign that sends schools funds associated with

proof-of-purchase redemptions will involve recording the number of returns and ensuring the appropriate schools will be credited with the appropriate amount of funds).

- **Substantial promotion is needed to engage consumers.** This often requires an investment in paid promotions such as advertising, point of purchase signage, packaging changes, or social media in order to obtain a reach and frequency threshold with target audiences.
- **Consumers can be especially skeptical** of campaigns like this, as they will be seen (and rightly so) as more than a philanthropic effort. This is especially true for campaigns that do not provide easy access to information regarding what portion of the proceeds of the sale will go to the charity or how much money is expected to be raised from the effort.
- **Some customers may have concerns with the charity the brand is being associated with** and then not want to purchase the product as a result.
- **Charity partner approval will be needed** on promotional executions, which may cause delays or disagreement based on the group's own guidelines and priorities.

When Should Cause-Related Marketing Be Considered?

Although most companies have the potential for developing and implementing a cause-related marketing initiative, those most likely to experience success are those with products that enjoy a large market or mass market appeal, have well-established and wide distribution channels and would benefit from a product differentiation that offers consumers an opportunity to contribute to a favorite charity. It should be considered when increased product sales, visibility, or co-branding with a popular cause would support marketing objectives and goals for a product or products.

It may also be most successful in situations where a company has an existing, ideally long-term, association with a cause or charity and then adds this initiative to the lineup, in an integrated fashion.

Developing a Cause-Related Marketing Campaign Plan

Steps in developing a CRM effort mirror those of traditional marketing plans, beginning with a situation assessment, setting objectives and goals, selecting target audiences, determining the marketing mix, and developing budget, implementation, and evaluation plans. Although this sequential, linear process is not always practical or common, it is recommended by those looking back on successful as well as disappointing efforts.

In the situation assessment phase, many suggest to begin by identifying the company's marketing needs. Does the company want to enter a *new market* with existing products? Is there a *new product* launch that this effort might help fuel? Or is the market becoming crowded with parity products, offered at similar prices in similar locations, with the company in need of a new strategy for *product differentiation*? With this focus, the assessment then moves to identifying a social issue to support. What issues is the corporation already supporting? Would a CRM effort strengthen the company's association and contribution to this cause? What are the major social concerns of target markets? Of these, which one is the most closely aligned with the company's core values and has the strongest potential for connections with products that would support marketing objectives. At this point, potential partners are explored. As this will be a co-branded effort, what charity or foundation would be the right match for the company and product's positioning? How large is their membership or donor base and what is their reputation in the community?

Once a social cause and charity have been selected, a marketing plan is developed to include marketing objectives (e.g., increase in new applications) and quantifiable goals (e.g., desired fundraising levels). Working with the charity, target audiences are identified and a marketing strategy is developed that will include products the campaign will be linked with, purchase incentives, distribution channels, and promotional strategies. At this stage, legal agreements and contracts will also most likely need to be developed, as will promotional budgets and implementation plans. Tracking systems will need to be established, with clear roles and responsibilities for tracking and reporting.

In Summary

Cause-related marketing campaigns are most distinct from other marketing and corporate social initiatives by the link of contribution levels to product sales or other desired consumer actions; the need for more formal agreements and systems for measurement and tracking; and the likelihood that the program will be funded and managed by the marketing department, often the recipient of the most corporate benefits. Contribution agreements with the charity and the consumer vary widely from ones that announce a percentage of revenue will be donated for each product sold to others that promise to make an in-kind donation based on social media activity. The offer may be for only one specific product or it might apply to a line of products. It may be good for only a brief promotional time period, or it may be open ended.

By design, most corporate benefits from a cause-related marketing campaign are marketing-related and include the potential to attract new customers, reach niche markets, increase product sales, and build positive brand identity. In addition, this initiative may also be one of the best strategies for raising significant funds for a cause. Potential concerns and challenges should also be anticipated and addressed, including increased needs (relative to other social initiatives) for promotional funding, staff time for planning and coordination of the campaign with charity partners, and attention to potential legal and marketing risks in comparison to other types of initiatives.

Experts recommend that managers select a major cause that inspires passion in their company and target audience, preferably one the company is already supporting. The ideal scenario is one where the charity partner has a large potential following, the product has good chemistry with the cause, and the incentive (offer) is straightforward and easy to understand. A formal marketing plan should be created that includes considerable promotional effort and resources, recognizing success will most likely depend on high participation levels, especially when contributions per transaction are small.

5 Corporate Social Marketing: Supporting Behavior Change Campaigns

As a company, Levi Strauss & Co. is committed to building sustainability into everything we do.[1]

—John Anderson, CEO
Levi Strauss & Co.

Our research shows that it's important to ask consumers to join this conversation, as a significant environmental impact from our products happens after consumers take their clothes home from the store.[2]

Robert Hanson, President
Levi Strauss Americas

Corporate Social Marketing uses business resources to develop and/or implement a behavior change campaign intended to improve public health, safety, the environment, or community well-being.

Behavior change is always the focus and the intended outcome.

Successful campaigns utilize a strategic marketing planning approach including conducting a situation analysis, selecting target audiences, setting behavior objectives, identifying barriers and benefits to behavior change, and then developing a marketing mix strategy that helps overcome perceived barriers and maximize potential benefits.

Corporate social marketing is most distinguished from other corporate social initiatives by this behavior change focus. Although campaign efforts may include awareness building and educational components or efforts to alter current beliefs and attitudes, the campaign is designed primarily to support and influence a particular public behavior (e.g., not to text and drive) or action (e.g., vote).

Philip Kotler and Gerald Zaltman launched the broader field of social marketing as a discipline more than 40 years ago in a pioneering article in the *Journal of Marketing*.[3] It is more recently described by Kotler/Lee/Rothschild as "a process that applies marketing principles and techniques to create, communicate, and deliver value in order to influence target audience behaviors that benefit society as well as the target audience."[4] Over the past three decades, interest has spread from applications for improving public health (e.g., HIV/AIDS prevention), to increasing public safety (e.g., wearing seatbelts), and now more recently, to protecting the environment (e.g., water conservation) and engendering community involvement (e.g., mentoring).

Most commonly, social marketing campaigns are developed and implemented by professionals working in federal, state, and local public sector agencies such as the Departments of Health, Transportation, and Ecology and in nonprofit organizations. Of interest in this chapter is the application for professionals working in for-profit corporations or their foundations.

Typical Corporate Social Marketing Campaigns

Corporate social marketing campaigns most commonly focus on promoting behaviors that address specific issues such as the following:

- *Health issues* including tobacco prevention, secondhand smoke, breast cancer, prostate cancer, physical activity, fetal alcohol syndrome, teen pregnancy, skin cancer, eating disorders, diabetes, heart disease, HIV/ AIDS, and oral health.
- *Injury prevention issues* including traffic safety, safe gun storage, drowning prevention, suicide, and emergency preparedness.
- *Environmental issues* including water conservation, electrical conservation, use of pesticides, air pollution, wildlife habitats, and litter prevention.
- *Community involvement issues* such as volunteering, voting, animal rights, organ donation, crime prevention, and blood donation.

Selection of issues is most often influenced by a natural connection to a corporation's core business (e.g., Allstate and Texting While Driving). A decision to support a behavior change campaign may then be sparked by some growing, perhaps even alarming trend (e.g., increases in child obesity rates). This interest may be initiated by an internal group or staff member, such as a product manager who monitors specific consumer groups and his or her issues. Or, the corporation may be targeted and approached by a public sector or nonprofit organization to partner in an effort (e.g., a medical center approaches a retail store regarding discounts on lock boxes for safe gun storage).

As outlined in Table 5.1, a wide range of industries participates in social marketing efforts. Major campaign elements include forming partnerships, determining a behavior objective, selecting target audiences, and developing and implementing campaign strategies. More detailed steps recommended for developing a social marketing plan are outlined at the end of this chapter.

Although campaigns may be developed and implemented solely by the corporation, it is more common that partnerships will be formed with public sector agencies and/or nonprofits who provide technical expertise regarding the social issue (e.g., heart disease); extend community outreach capabilities (e.g., access to Boys & Girls Clubs); and add credibility, even luster, to the campaign effort and the brand (e.g., American Heart Association partnering with Subway). In typical scenarios, the corporation provides several types of support: time and expertise of marketing personnel; money; access to distribution channels; employee volunteers; and in-kind contributions (e.g., printing of an immunization schedule). Funding may come from several sources within the organization, although marketing is often an enthusiastic contributor, as many of the benefits support marketing objectives and goals.

As suggested in Table 5.1, typical campaigns focus on behaviors that can be expressed as a single act (e.g., recycle unwanted consumer electronics), ones that enable the target audience to understand what the desired behavior is, and ones that campaign managers can measure. Market segmentation is common, with a desired focus on target audiences that will benefit most from the behavior change, are most open to the idea of change, and can be reached efficiently with available media channels. Typical activities include traditional promotional efforts using a variety of media channels including broadcast, social media, websites, print, outdoor, promotional items, and special events.

TABLE 5.1 Examples of Corporate Social Marketing Initiatives

Corporation	Desired Behavior	Target Audiences	Samples Activities	Major Partners
Subway	Choose healthy food options and exercise on a regular basis	Adults and children eating at fast-food restaurants	Sponsor of American Heart Association's *Start Walking Initiative* Subway Fresh Fit Sandwiches and Subway Fresh Fit for Kids™ Online nutrition calculators	American Heart Association
Levi Strauss & Co.	Wash jeans in cold water Line dry them Donate them to Goodwill	Prospective and current purchasers of Levi's	Tag on jeans with desired behaviors Website Pledge program Social media	Goodwill
Best Buy	Recycle old, unused, or unwanted consumer electronics at Best Buy stores	Customers and potential customers of Best Buy	In-store locations for dropping off electronics Consultations with their Geek Squad to ensure privacy of information	None for this initiative
Energizer	Change smoke and carbon monoxide alarm batteries when changing clocks in Spring and Fall	Heads of households, especially those with children	Toolkits for downloading promotional materials Social media	International Association of Fire Chiefs
Allstate	Teens take a pledge not to text and drive	Teens who are driving and their parents	Pledge form Interactive parent/teen contract with tips for creating	Allstate Foundation

Clorox	To help prevent flu: • Wash hands • Disinfect germ hot spots around the home • Cough into your elbow	Families with children	Special events conducted throughout the United States Educational materials	Centers for Disease Control and Prevention Visiting Nurse Associations of America
Miron Construction	Take actions to reduce energy and water use, improve air quality and reduce waste	Employees	Games and contests with prizes and incentives for taking the most actions	Cool Choices
UK Anglian Water	Properly dispose of kitchen oils, food scraps, and sanitary wipes	Heads of households, especially those in areas with significant water pipe blockages	Special event launch in city square Social media	Sole Sponsor
Lowe's	Adopt water-saving practices and utilize water-saving devices	Customers and potential customers of Lowe's	Workshops Informational in store tips on water conservation Water conservation guide	Local city governments Utilities Department of Water Resources Arizona Municipal Water Users Association
V/Line (a privatized train and freight company)	Make positive choices related to alcohol and drug use	Youth and their parents in Victoria, Australia	Life skill training sessions	Victorian Country Football League Netball Victoria Odyssey House Victoria Beyondblue The Butterfly Foundation

Potential Corporate Benefits

As illustrated in the following brief case examples, many of the potential benefits for the corporation are connected to marketing goals and objectives: supporting brand positioning, creating brand preference, building traffic, and increasing sales. Potential benefits beyond marketing include improving profitability and making a real social impact.

Case #1: Subway® Restaurants and *Healthy Fast Food Options*—Supporting Brand Positioning

If you were in charge of securing a brand positioning for SUBWAY as the healthy fast food option, you would no doubt be grateful for your company's long-term partnership with the American Heart Association (see Figure 5.1).

FIGURE 5.1 SUBWAY Restaurants Headquarter employees team up with the American Heart Association for their annual Heart Walk in Milford, Connecticut.

The company's logo appears front and center on several pages of the Heart Association's website, most recently (2011) as the national sponsor of their social marketing effort, the *Start Walking Initiative*. And this sponsorship doesn't go unnoticed, with 90 percent of Start! Heart Walk participants surveyed in 2006 correctly identifying SUBWAY as being involved with the American Heart Association.[5]

Several additional strategies also help contribute to this competitive positioning.

First are supportive *product* features, which had their beginnings in 1965, when 17-year-old Fred DeLuca made sandwiches for his first customers in a small storefront sandwich shop with an intention to be "a new kind of quick service restaurant—a restaurant without a fryer and where sandwiches were not pre-made."[6] Fast forward to 2011 stores, and you will find at least eight SUBWAY FRESH FIT® six-inch sandwiches low in fat, saturated fat, and cholesterol, with four subs under 300 calories and seven under 350. And beginning in 2012, none of their core six-inch sandwiches will exceed 600 calories, and at least 50 percent of their core six-inch sandwiches will be less than 40 calories.

Integrated *promotional communications* also have their eye on this nutrition-focused positioning. In 2007, they were the first known restaurant system to post calories on hundreds of New York City menu boards. In 2010, they made available a nutrition calculator on their website to provide nutrition facts for customized sandwiches. And any advertising on children's programming features the SUBWAY FRESH FIT FOR KIDS™ meals, which meet stringent nutritional criteria, automatically coming with one serving of a fresh fruit and either 100 percent juice or low-fat milk, and no soda.

Case #2: Levi's® Care Tag for the Planet—Creating Brand Preference

Levi Strauss & Co. is the global leader in jeanswear, with their products in more than 110 countries worldwide.[7] They have a commitment to build sustainability into everything they do, and their social marketing initiative, *A Care Tag for Our Planet*, will no doubt contribute to this brand distinction as well as to creating a more loyal and engaged customer base. (See Figure 5.2.)[8] They

FIGURE 5.2 Levi's "Care Tag for Our Planet."

are the first major retailer to include a tag on their jeans with messaging that encourages people to help the planet by: washing less, washing in cold water, line drying, and (in the end) donating to Goodwill when no longer needed.

Launched in January of 2010, this partnership with Goodwill is designed to reduce the estimated 23.8 billion pounds of clothing and textiles that go into U.S. landfills each year.[9] It is the first of its kind to encourage donation as a way to extend the life cycle of clothing, as well as to reduce their environmental impact.[10]

The Levi's® brand has used the *Care Tag* program to start a long-term conversation with consumers about what they can do to save water and energy after they buy a pair of Levi's® jeans or Dockers® khakis.

Several opportunities to stimulate customer engagement are presented on their website, featuring clear, specific behaviors and information on convenient locations for Goodwill donations. (See Figure 5.3.) An important feature of the website is one to *Take a Pledge*, a best practice strategy that has been used successfully by social marketers to increase the chances that a target audience will actually follow through on a desired action.[11] Social media opportunities are prominent with a link for Facebook sharing, and making it a part of your Twitter profile. In the fall of 2011, the company launched a new consumer action campaign, *Dirty Is the New Clean*. The brand is asking consumers to re-think their washing habits encouraging them to wash their jeans less, and

FIGURE 5.3 Website graphic encouraging the desired behaviors.

recruiting them to tweet how many times they wear their pants before washing (#Care4OurPlanet).

Case #3: Best Buy and *e-Cycle*—Building Traffic

"No matter where you bought it, we'll recycle it" is the headline on Best Buy's *e-cycle* website with information on recycling old, unused, or unwanted consumer electronics including computers, keyboards, monitors, cell phones, TVs, and more.[12] More detail follows, including the fact that all U.S. Best Buy stores, including Puerto Rico, offer this in-store solution for customers, including kiosks just inside the door for easier drop off of ink and toner cartridges, rechargeable batteries, and wires, cords, and cables (see Figure 5.4). And as of November 6, 2011, there are no fees charged to the consumer for this recycling.

FIGURE 5.4 Recycling kiosks inside every U.S. Best Buy store.

A Frequently Asked Questions section and video on their website quickly addresses typical consumer barriers including concerns that these won't end up in landfills or in foreign countries, and that all hazardous materials are disposed of properly. They also advise that in the case of hard drives on laptops or desktop PCs, customers have the option to remove their data themselves, or they can consult with a Geek Squad® Agent about services to remove the hard drive before handing the PC over to be recycled.

Best Buy's 2011 sustainability report, *Our World, Connected*, highlights the impact of their global sustainability strategies including the outcome that they collected 83 million pounds of consumer electronics and 73 million pounds of old appliances for recycling, or approximately 387 pounds of e-waste each minute in U.S. Best Buy stores.[13] Although they don't report on the traffic and sales these customer contacts generated, data from their customer surveys indicates increased likelihood of making purchases. We can imagine it would be substantial, as those bringing their used and unwanted items in were likely looking for replacement.

Case #4: Energizer and *Change Your Clock Change Your Battery"*® — Increasing Sales

Every year, approximately 2,600 Americans die in home fires, with more than half of these deaths (52 percent) occurring between the hours of 10:00 p.m. and 7:00 a.m., when residents are typically sleeping.[14] And the risk of dying from a fire in a home where a smoke alarm is installed, but not working, is twice as high as in a home that has working smoke alarms.[15] Influencing homeowners to ensure the battery in their smoke alarm is functional, and to then replace it if it isn't, is a natural social marketing campaign for a brand like Energizer to support. Linking this action to another routine behavior is an even smarter strategy.

A press release from Energizer on October 19, 2011, provides clear motivations for these behaviors, as well as instructions:[16]

"Whether it's providing a band-aid for a scraped knee or equipping their cars with safety seats, parents are the first line of defense for their children at home. This October, as part of National Fire Prevention Awareness Month, Energizer (NYSE: ENR) and the International Association of Fire Chiefs (IAFC) are asking Moms and Dads to take a vital step to keep their kids safe at home—Change Your Clock Change Your Battery® (see Figure 5.5). Throughout October, Energizer is inviting parents across the country to join the Energizer Bunny® Brigade on Facebook (www.facebook.com/energizerbunny) for a chance to win free smoke alarms and batteries for their home or a grand prize of a home fire safety makeover . . .".

"For 23 years, Energizer, the IAFC and more than 6,200 fire departments have partnered to educate communities on the importance of home fire safety and having working smoke alarms," said Michelle Atkinson, vice president of marketing for Energizer North America. "By having parents and families actively pledge to change the batteries in their smoke alarms and carbon monoxide detectors, we are hoping they

FIGURE 5.5   Energizer's Fire Prevention Campaign Logo.

will share the information with their network of friends and hopefully help other families do this simple and life-saving task—now that's positivenergy™."

Case #5: Allstate and *Teen Driver Pledge*— Improving Profitability

Given the statistics that, according to the Centers for Disease Control and Prevention, car crashes are the number-one killer of U.S. teenagers, it might not be surprising to find that Allstate Insurance is interested in influencing safer teen driving.[17] And given the alarming (some refer to it as an epidemic) increase in teens' texting while driving, it isn't surprising that texting is a focus for their efforts, one with the potential to reduce their claims.

Messages on Allstate's auto insurance website and materials impress parents with the tragic facts that nearly 5,000 teens die in car crashes every year,[18] an average of about 13 every day, and nearly 375,000 are injured, an average of 1,000 every day.[19] And that even though "sex, drugs, and rock 'n' roll" are considered high risks for teen safety, the biggest threat "is parked just outside your home."[20]

Making pledges are part of Allstate's national *X the TXT*[SM] campaign, a national campaign to raise awareness about the dangers of texting while driving, and encourage teens and their families to pledge not to text and drive. The movement began in November 2009 with a 30-city national tour of live pledge events, a Facebook virtual pledge page, and a petition urging congress to address the issue of texting while driving. Upon pledging, participants receive thumb bands with the words TXTNG KLLS to wear as a daily reminder of their commitment. To date (November 2011), Allstate had received more than 250,000 X the TXT pledges.[21]

Case #6: Clorox and the Centers for Disease Control *Say "Boo!" to the Flu*—Attracting Enthusiastic and Credible Partners

Because of the behavior change focus and potential, corporate social marketing initiatives, perhaps more than others, are likely to be welcomed and supported by nonprofit organizations and public sector agencies, one such as the Centers for Disease Control and Prevention (CDC).

Estimates are that every year in the United States, more than 20,000 kids younger than five years old are hospitalized due to the seasonal flu. And, on average, nearly 100 of these kids then die.[22] CDC recommends several preventive actions. One of those recommendations is to use disinfectant products on germ hot spots in homes such as phone receivers, light switches, and TV remotes, so it makes sense that Clorox would be interested in helping to spread the word. It does this through a program called *Say "Boo!" to the Flu*, in partnership with Families Fighting Flu, Inc., Visiting Nurse Associations of America, and Ketchum Communications. (See Figure 5.6.)

The Say "Boo!" to the Flu program was created to increase the number of families vaccinated against the flu nationwide and to influence additional simple prevention behaviors. In its seventh year in 2011, the campaign incorporated a fun Halloween theme and a *boo-mobile* that criss-crossed the country from Boston to San Francisco, hosting events throughout the month of October where families could play fun games and learn how to help prevent the spread of the flu virus. They also provided opportunities for the family to get the seasonal flu vaccine.

Simple tricks (desired behaviors) they promoted at these events, on brochures, and on their website included to *Sing & Scrub, Disinfect Hot Spots*, and *Do the Elbow Cough*. They also encouraged families to take the flu prevention

FIGURE 5.6   Campaign Logo.

pledge to be vaccinated, and those who did were entered into a sweepstakes to win a trip to their favorite wizard-themed amusement park in Orlando, Florida. Additionally, each week five winners received a prize pack.[23]

Between 2006 and 2010, there were 250 separate events, where 38,613 flu vaccines were administered. For Clorox, the events and the promotions associated with them garnered close to one billion impressions of the partnership.[24]

Case #7: Miron Construction Company and Cool Choices—Having a Real Impact on Social Change

More than any other social initiative, social marketing has the potential for impacting positive behaviors of large populations, and thus having an impact on social change.

Miron Construction is one of Wisconsin's largest construction firms and has an environmental ethic and commitment to employee engagement.[25] Cool Choices is a Wisconsin-based nonprofit with a mission to inspire and help "individuals, communities and businesses achieve meaningful reduction in greenhouse gas emissions through voluntary action."[26] A partnership between these two organizations seemed destined to happen.

In 2011, Miron's leadership committed to a partnership with Cool Choices to facilitate increased employee engagement in Miron's corporate commitment to sustainability. Cool Choices worked with Miron to establish a Sustainability Action Team made up of opinion leaders from throughout the company, and that team worked with Cool Choices to create a program that fit Miron's culture. With input from the Action Team, Cool Choices created a game-based competition, called iChoose, in which Miron employees earned points for taking and reporting on environmentally sustainable actions related to energy, water, indoor air quality, waste management, and food. Specific actions included saving energy by using power savers on computers; conserving water by replacing old toilets with low-flow ones; air quality preserving by avoiding idling; and reducing waste by reusing plastic bags. Employees reported their actions via an online database or paper cards and then could earn bonus points by submitting stories or photos regarding their actions.

Cool Choices provided individual prizes to help motivate employee participation in the game and Miron committed to donating sustainability grants to local charities, as selected by the highest-scoring employee teams.[27]

The pilot launched on Earth Day and 75 percent of Miron's 330 office and operations employees signed up to participate in the iChoose initiative. More than 85 percent of those employees reported one or more actions, which translates to a 67 percent participation rate. When the competition ended in October, participants had logged more than 3,500 unique one-time and ongoing actions. In the game, participants got credit for reporting both new actions and actions they were doing prior to the game. Looking only at the new actions, participants were projected to save 463 megawatt hours of electricity, 693,000 gallons of water, 17,500 gallons of gasoline, and 4,300 therms of natural gas annually.[28] Cumulatively, these actions will reduce CO_2 emissions annually by 1.33 million pounds.

In October of 2011, Miron received the 2011 Corporate Citizenship Award from *Corporate Report Wisconsin* magazine and Edgewood College, recognizing the company for "coupling its environmental ethic with the company's commitment to employee engagement, creating a model that benefits the environment, local communities and employees' personal pocketbooks."[29]

Potential Concerns

Several significant potential downsides of social marketing campaigns need to be acknowledged and planned for, especially the following.

Some issues are not a good match for the corporation. Consumers tend to be skeptical about the motivations that a corporation has for promoting or supporting a social issue. It might even be said they have a *nose* for hidden agendas and will be quick to judge the sincerity and authenticity of the effort. For more than a decade, McDonalds, for example, has supported efforts to increase timely childhood immunizations. Compare your reaction to this hypothetical to one where instead, they focused on physical activity for children and handed out brochures in Happy Meals on recommended exercise levels for children at various ages to avoid childhood obesity. Could this gesture be interpreted by many as a way to justify fast food eating habits? Similarly, note the potential difference in acceptance and believability between an initiative where a tobacco company sponsors a campaign to increase the number of receptacles available for cigarette butts and to promote their use versus a campaign to encourage parents to talk with their children about smoking. Will some sincerely doubt the tobacco company's desire to prevent teens from smoking?

For many issues and initiatives, clinical and technical expertise needs to be sought. Many behaviors appropriate for social marketing campaigns need to be grounded and supported by professional opinions (e.g., diabetes prevention and control, reducing cholesterol, natural gardening, and protection from the West Nile Virus). As mentioned earlier, this is the advantage and perhaps necessity of seeking partners in the public or nonprofit sector with expertise in the area of focus.

Behavior change, and therefore impact, does not often happen overnight. Internal publics especially will need to be warned upfront that the campaign will have milestones and that interim measures that indicate progress will need to be established and monitored. A litter reduction campaign, for example, may focus the first year on creating awareness of fines, the second year on convincing citizens that fines will be enforced, with real behavior change not expected until the third year of the campaign.

Be prepared for criticism from those who view social marketing campaigns as *none of your business*. Some citizen groups believe fervently that campaigns that seem to only impact the individual (e.g., smoking) are interfering with personal rights and should not be of concern to governmental agencies or corporations. In states where primary seatbelt laws have been adopted, for example, citizen groups have been known to advocate for reversal of these policies, arguing that if someone wants to kill themselves by not wearing a seatbelt, that's their choice and their right. The best preparation for these situations is to provide facts regarding potential harm to others (e.g., statistics on increased diseases for children living in homes with a parent who smokes) and impact on public tax dollars (e.g., emergency medical costs for injuries that could have been prevented by a seatbelt).

Recognize that developing, even supporting a social marketing campaign, involves more than writing a check. To work well, these campaigns involve more staff time for planning, implementation, and coordination with partners; more integration into current media and distribution channels; increased attention to monitoring and tracking results; and vigilance in keeping updated on trends and events relative to the social issue and related behaviors.

Keys to Success

The following three cases illustrate important principles for successful corporate social marketing campaigns. Highlights include an emphasis on using existing data to identify priority areas for action, using research in the formative phases to keep the needs and wants of core target audience's in mind, supporting desired behavior changes with skill-building programs and services, and taking a long-term view of success.

Case #8: V/Line Life Training in Australia

V/Line is Australia's largest regional privatized public transport operator, serving Victoria with more than 1,400 train and 600 coach services a week. In a 2011 corporate social responsibility report, they demonstrate how they are fulfilling their mission by connecting regional communities, and living their values by addressing important social issues in those communities.[30] A major issue of focus is one that train operators see firsthand: the troubling behaviors among youth associated with binge drinking, illicit drugs, depression, and anxiety disorders. And unfortunately, the isolation of some towns means that many young people miss out on access to prevention and recovery information and services. Their program, V/Line Life Training, aims to bridge this gap.

The training program, launched in 2007 in partnership with the Victorian Country Football League, focuses on providing life skills for youth to make positive choices. With high profile sports ambassadors making presentations at these public sessions, events grew in numbers and by 2011 they had conducted 75 sessions, in 53 towns with over 10,000 participants across Victoria.[31] They are so popular now that they are not able to fulfill all the requests they receive from local communities.

A strong network of additional partners includes nonprofit organizations specializing in alcohol and drug treatment, mental illness, and eating disorders.

The program is supported by a comprehensive promotional effort to both attract participants to events, as well as increase awareness of the issue for the wider community. Media channels include direct mail, social media, posters, websites, and most importantly, over 25 articles in regional papers in 2010 alone and several special features on local television news channels. (See Figure 5.7.)

Living in the country doesn't isolate you from the issues that confront kids.

Binge drinking, drugs, anxiety disorders, depression, issues of body image and self esteem are universal problems. They occur right here in Gisborne and have the potential to cause any kid, including your own, to lose their way.

And in losing their way they can lose a whole lot more – health, motivation, opportunity, ambition, willpower, time, but most importantly they can lose touch with their family.

Don't pretend the problems don't exist here.

Join us for a workshop where binge drinking will be discussed openly. It will be an interactive session led by industry experts aimed at giving everyone some real insights into these problems so that they can make better informed decisions in the future.

where: Gisborne Sports Clubrooms, Gardiner Reserve, Gisborne **when:** Wednesday 27 July at 7.30pm
host: Gisborne Netball Association & Gisborne Rookies Junior Football Club
rsvp: Rebecca Bridgman 0402 085 005 or Colin Rodgers 0417 147 397

Be there, because one kid lost in Gisborne is one too many.

FIGURE 5.7 Direct-mail template encouraging attendance at life skills training event.

Marketing Professor Linda Brennan at RMIT University in Melbourne, Australia, has witnessed numerous benefits of this program for V/Line:[32]

- Developing closer links with their regional communities.
- Establishing their brand as relevant and credible within a previously difficult to reach market (youth).
- Positioning the V/Line company as a responsible regional community centric organization.
- Creating links with partners that had connections to their regional markets thereby increasing their reach in a geographically dispersed marketplace.
- Developing upstream credibility with government and local members of parliament, enabling leverage for other activities.
- Creating downstream brand equity by the extensive publicity and community good will developed by connecting with sports stars as brand ambassadors.
- Developing trust in the brand promise to a high level with 84 percent of local community members indicating that they trusted V/Line to represent their interests in terms of regional prosperity and community.
- Generating a high level of earned media and free advertising normally reserved for community service advertising and not available to the private sector.

Through these activities, V/Line and their partners have managed to gain traction in dealing with difficult social issues in an arena where the target audience is notoriously difficult to reach. Key success factors have been:

- Partnering and collaborating with genuine regard for the synergistic capabilities of the alliance. You do get more than the sum of the parts with these types of collaborative efforts.
- Taking a long-term view of success and having the courage to start something that you may not finish within the scope of a few years.
- Tackling *wicked problems* one step at a time and using research actively in the formative phases of program development: piloting, trialing, taking formative feedback, and using that feedback to inform the next phases.

- Keeping the needs and wants of core target markets clearly in mind as the program develops and ensuring that there are adequate resources to sustain the program over time.
- Taking an organization and community inclusive approach to program development.

Case #9: Lowe's and *Water—Use It Wisely*

For more than 60 years, Lowe's has supported the communities *they call home*.[33] And they believe that "building a healthier business and a healthier environment go hand in hand."[34] The following social marketing initiative in Arizona illustrates this commitment, as well as the benefits of a strong private/public/not-for-profit and media partnership to encourage behavior changes in the way people use water. Lowe's story is provided by Park Howell, president of Park & Co., the marketing firm that created the *Water—Use It Wisely* and the *Lowe's Water Conservation* promotion.

In 2005, Lowe's in Arizona joined a unique private-public partnership to execute one of the most ambitious water conservation events in the state's history. The Water—Use It Wisely Month at Lowe's featured five weeks of ongoing water conservation information and workshops in all 14 of their Arizona stores, in partnership with local city governments, private and public utilities, Arizona Department of Water Resources, and the Arizona Municipal Water Users Association. It combines the technical knowledge and campaign resources of city partners with the marketing muscle and consumer reach of a national retailer.

The event in 2005 was supported by a radio promotional campaign and an aggressive public relations program that featured stories on each week's water conservation topic. As part of the regional radio campaign, the partners scheduled radiobroadcasts every Saturday at prominent Lowe's locations to help drive traffic and purchases of water-saving devices. Lowe's employees presented conservation workshops to their customers on these Saturdays, with the curriculum created by the water conservation experts from the cities. Promotions also include a large exterior entry banner and water-saving tips (in English and Spanish) appearing on aisle, register, and door signs, and in informational bag stuffers. More than 30,000 24-page, color

FIGURE 5.8 More than 30,000 24-page, color water conservation guides were distributed through Lowe's.

water conservation guides were distributed to customers, in addition to the 350,000 color inserts that were featured in the *Arizona Republic* newspaper (see Figure 5.8). A Water—Use It Wisely website enhanced customer engagement, where participants who gave a water-saving tip were automatically entered to win a free washer and dryer.

Water—Use It Wisely Month at Lowe's increased workshop attendance by 50 percent over prior similar workshops; sales of water efficient merchandise increased by an average of 30 percent; and the promotion generated more than 2 million impressions in the stores and in the media. Further, the campaign enjoys recognition among 80 percent of metropolitan residents, with a 30 percent increase in consumer adoption of water-saving behaviors, according to a Behavior Research Center study.[35] In 2009 and 2010, the EPA recognized the company as WaterSense Retail Partner of the Year, and in 2011, for Excellence in Strategic Collaboration.[36]

Howell believes the major key to this success is the *partnership*, one where everyone benefits. The city partners have a forum through Lowe's stores to reach significantly more people in the region with their conservation messaging, while directing them to the products and the water-use behaviors that can have an immediate impact on conservation. Lowe's benefits from an increase in retail sales of low water-use plants, products, and appliances, while generating goodwill with its customers, employees, stakeholders, media, and the towns and cities where its stores are located.

Howell also recognizes that, from a social marketing best practice perspective, the effort was successful in that specific behaviors were not only promoted, but were also supported by the skill-building workshops and availability of related products.

Case #10: United Kingdom—Anglian Water's *Keep It Clear* Campaign

Anglian Water is a private sector company supplying water and wastewater services to more than 6 million domestic and business customers in the east of England and Hartlepool.[37] And although their population has grown by 20 percent in the past 20 years, they still provide the same amount of water as they did in 1990 (almost 1.1 billion liters every day) by minimizing leaks and encouraging more water-wise customers.[38] The success of their *Keep It Clear* corporate social marketing effort is part of the reason. (See Figure 5.9.)

The campaign was designed to change the behavior of what people put down sinks and toilets, behaviors that were causing an estimated 15,000 blockages a year at a cost of over £6 million. They started with a pilot in Peterborough in 2011, targeting neighborhoods with the most frequent blockages with strategies including direct mail, community outreach, and prompts in food service establishments and in homes.

FIGURE 5.9 "Keep It Clear" Campaign logo.

Outcomes of the pilot were impressive:[39]

In homes:

- 100 percent of people were concerned about blockages—up 31 percent from 69 percent.
- 72 percent are making an extra effort to get rid of their waste appropriately, a 21 percent increase.
- People claiming to never flush sanitary protection increased from 25 to 60 percent for panty liners.

In food serving establishments:

- 98 percent claimed they scrape plates before washing, a 25 percent increase.
- 64 percent said they use sink strainers all the time, a 26 percent increase.
- 73 percent use sanitary protection signs in their loos [restrooms], a 13 percent boost.
- Food outlets saying they never dispose of food waste in the sewer rose to 86 percent.

Average number of weekly blockages in the pilot scheme area.

- Before the trial: **3.3**
- During the trial: **1.16**

John Drummond, chairman of Corporate Culture, a social marketing firm in London, England, commented on his blog on October 14, 2011, regarding the secrets to the campaign's success:

Tonight in Peterborough, Anglian Water launched one of the world's leading examples of corporate social marketing . . . or how to work with customers to achieve real behaviour change and measurable social results.... The campaign was created following a rigorous step by step process. Evidence was gathered on the primary material streams that were put into water pipes. Principle areas and neighbourhoods which had repeat blockages were identified. Customer segments were identified and research identified current knowledge, beliefs, behaviours and motivators. Interventions were designed to make it easy for customers to act. Two priority areas for action were then identified as food service establishments putting fats, oils and greases into the water cycle and domestic customers flushing sanitary waste and wipes.... Why is the campaign important?... It is, in my view, a game-changer for utilities: it adds customer behaviour change to the universe of strategies to tackle real issues (in addition to capital investment and fixing problems) and...it once again shows that customers are inclined to act, but there is a need for strategies and interventions that make it easy for them to do so."[40]

BOX 5.1 SOCIAL MEDIA SPOTLIGHT

On October 13, 2011, Anglian Water launched their Keep It Clear campaign across the Peterborough region in Cathedral Square using a dramatic 3D Light Show that was then captured as a video for YouTube and replayed by thousands (www.youtube.com/watch?v=Bs1aDpRWj44). Paul Gibbs, director of wastewater services, said: "This event is going to show, in all its hideous technicolour, the scale of the problem we face when our sewers are clogged up with rubbish that shouldn't be in them."[41]

In keeping with a sound social marketing approach, they first captured three problem behaviors: putting food waste and grease down kitchen sinks and unflushables down the toilet. They then made real the resultant blockage, and quickly followed this with desired behaviors: scraping food waste into the garbage, pouring grease in cans, and putting baby wipeables into a trash can.

When Should a Corporate Social Marketing Initiative Be Considered?

Based on the unique characteristic of social marketing campaigns (a focus on behavior change), the following situations should signal an opportunity to consider the social marketing option:

- *When the primary objectives of an initiative are to support corporate marketing goals and objectives* versus corporate giving or community involvement agendas (e.g., an electronic store wants to build traffic and advertises that according to the public health department, it's time to check your home fire alarm batteries this weekend and then mentions that they're having a discount special on them in all their locations).
- *When the issue the organization wants to support (e.g., healthy children) is one that has the potential for an individual behavior change component* (e.g., a fast-food restaurant then teams up with the local children's hospital and community health clinics to print immunization schedules on tray liners).
- *When the dollars for support of the initiative are coming (primarily) from the marketing department* and can therefore be managed and integrated into marketing communications (e.g., a produce company putting the national 5 A Day logo on packaging, advertisements, and coupons).
- *When the behavior can be tied to one or more corporate products* and then integrated into their features, pricing, distribution channels, and promotions (e.g., a life-vest manufacturer attaching water safety tips to labels and creating retail displays on how to choose a life vest that's right for your child, and then distributing discount coupons via a local children's hospital).

Developing a Corporate Social Marketing Campaign Plan

A planned approach is key to success, with the following steps and principles recommended for developing a strategic social marketing plan.[42] (It is highly recommended that partners be identified prior to this formal planning process and involved in developing each step of the plan.)

1. *Determine a purpose and focus for the effort.* Who is the sponsor of this effort? Why are they doing this? What social issue and/or population will the plan focus on and why?
2. *Conduct a situation analysis*, which initiates an analysis of internal strengths and weaknesses and external opportunities and threats. Special efforts should be made at this step to review past and similar campaigns for lessons learned, as well as potential for replication

(e.g., the Click It or Ticket campaign, adopted by many states across the nation, was initiated by one state: North Carolina).

3. *Select target audiences*, starting with those who have the greatest need, are easiest to reach, are the best match for the organizations involved, *and* are most ready for action (e.g., newly pregnant women as a focus for a tobacco Quitline).

4. *Set behavior objectives (the desired behavior) and behavior change goals.* One key to success at this step is to establish behavior objectives that are single, simple, and doable acts that become the core of the campaign effort (e.g., put an infant on its back to sleep). Quantifiable goals are established in terms of behavior change in the targeted population, similar to sales goals in the corporate marketing model.

5. *Determine barriers and motivations to behavior change.* Identify perceived costs and benefits to the desired behavior, as they provide rich material for developing strategies. In addition, it is at this stage that it is important to also identify the competition, and behaviors in which your target audience is currently engaging or prefers to do (e.g., placing infants on their stomach).

6. *Craft a desired positioning statement*, one that describes how you want target audiences to see the desired behavior.

7. *Develop the marketing mix*, including product, price, place, and promotional strategies, ones that uniquely and strategically address the barriers and motivations that target audiences have to adopting the desired behavior. A few keys to success for each of the 4Ps include:

   1. *Product*: Include a tangible object or service in the campaign, ones that will facilitate the desired behavior (e.g., litterbags handed out by mini-marts in support of a state litter prevention campaign).

   2. *Price*: Look for nonmonetary forms of recognition that add value to the exchange (e.g., Backyard Wildlife Sanctuary plaques for homeowners agreeing to natural yard care practices, provided by a local nursery).

   3. *Place*: Look for ways to make access to performing the desired behavior convenient (e.g., dental care offered in mobile vans sponsored by an insurance company).

   4. *Promotion*: Develop messages prior to selecting media channels. Focus on messages that are clear, vivid, and concrete (e.g., *Don't Mess with Texas*) and media channels that provide constant reminders

and are sustainable over time (e.g., state road signs with litter fines and corporate sponsor names).

8. *Develop a plan for evaluation and monitoring*. Evaluation should be based on measuring behavior change goals established in Step 3, a real outcome measure. In addition, evaluation plans can be developed to measure changes in awareness and attitudes, as well as campaign processes (e.g., reach and frequency of campaigns and dissemination of materials).

9. *Establish budgets and find funding sources*. Opportunities should be explored for corporate partnerships with all sectors: public agencies, nonprofit organizations, foundations, and special interest groups.

10. *Complete an implementation plan*. A three-year plan is ideal, recognizing that behavior change may be slow to come and that time is often needed to educate, change attitudes, and provide infrastructures to support behavior change (e.g., more litter receptacles).

In Summary

Corporate social marketing is most distinguished from other social initiatives by its focus on individual behavior change, as well as changes that will help improve health, prevent injuries, protect the environment, and increase community involvement. Potential corporate benefits are greatest for supporting marketing goals and objectives, including strengthening brand positioning, creating brand preference, building traffic, and increasing sales. Potential and significant additional benefits beyond marketing include improving profitability and making a real social impact.

Several concerns and potential pitfalls with corporate social marketing campaigns are real. Some issues, though important, are not an authentic fit for the corporation. For many issues and initiatives, clinical and technical expertise needs to be sought. Behavior change, and therefore impact, does not often happen overnight and key publics and partners need to be forewarned. Be prepared for criticism from those who view social marketing campaigns as none of your business. And recognize that developing, and even supporting, a social marketing campaign involves more than writing a check.

Corporate managers experienced in these campaigns emphasize several keys to success: pick an issue connected to the organization's core business, employees, and current marketing strategies; focus on an initiative that has the potential for a long-term commitment; gain management support; partner with public sector and nonprofit organizations who can provide expertise, credibility, and extended reach into communities; and develop solid plans (up front) with established funding, measurable goals, and clear roles and responsibilities. Finally, as with any strategic marketing effort, a sequential planning process is fundamental and will involve audience research and utilization of all key 4P marketing tools.

Corporate-Driven Initiatives: Expressing and Advancing Your Company's Values and Objectives

6

Corporate Philanthropy: Making a Direct Contribution to a Cause

By offering their skills, time, financial support, and creativity to causes greater than themselves, generous corporate philanthropists strengthen our communities and enrich our lives.[1]

—President Barack Obama

At its core, corporate philanthropy involves a corporation making a *direct contribution* to a charity or cause, most often in the form of *cash grants, donations,* and/or *in-kind services.* In 2010, corporate giving by funding type broke down as 46 percent direct cash, 35 percent foundation cash, and 19 percent non-cash, according to a study of 184 corporations (including 63 of the Fortune 100 companies) by the Committee Encouraging Corporate Philanthropy.[2]

As recently as the 1980s, many companies equated making cash donations to hometown charities as sufficient to fulfill their social contract.[3] The character of corporate philanthropy has changed, primarily in response to internal and external pressures to balance concerns for shareholder wealth with expectations to demonstrate responsibility for communities contributing to the corporation's livelihood.[4] Perhaps the most consistent response has been to move to a more strategic approach to selecting social issues to support, with an increased tendency to choose an area of focus and to tie philanthropic activities to the company's business goals and objectives.

At the same time, corporate philanthropy has also trended in the direction of building more long-term relationships with nonprofit organizations;

expanding giving to include contributions of excess products, use of distribution channels, and technical expertise; more employee involvement in selecting philanthropic priorities and recipients; attempting to better track and measure business and social outcomes related to contributions; and, as a reflection of globalization, directing more resources to international communities where corporations are also doing business.[5]

In the past few years, the growth of social media has led some companies to experiment with crowd-sourced giving, engaging consumers online to nominate and/or select the recipients of contributions.

Typical Programs

Philanthropic efforts commonly involve selecting a cause that reflects a priority area for the corporation, determining the type of contribution to be made and identifying a recipient for contributions. The range of giving options include:

- **Providing cash donations** (e.g., matching employee donations, providing financial support for a YMCA teen program, or making a donation to provide emergency support for victims of natural disasters).
- **Offering grants** (e.g., providing grants to community organizations to promote water conservation or to schools to underwrite the cost of creating libraries).
- **Awarding scholarships** (e.g., funding for students pursuing careers in restaurant management or for high school students in developing countries to attend college in the United States).
- **Donating products** (e.g., medicine to fight trachoma, toys to entertain children in hospitals, or appliances to reduce the cost of building houses for low-income families).
- **Donating services** (e.g., printing child immunization schedules for a community health clinic, providing call center support for a hotline to report littering on freeways, or offering free dental care for families in a homeless domestic violence shelter).
- **Providing technical expertise** (e.g., sharing strategies for setting up inventory control systems or reviewing health educational materials for technical content regarding nutritional guidelines).
- **Allowing the use of facilities and distribution channels** (e.g., car dealerships that make room for car seat inspections or grocery stores that provide space for the collection of canned goods for food banks).

- **Offering the use of equipment** (e.g., vans for transporting materials for a science exhibit to schools or medical equipment offered for use at a health fair).

Recipients of these contributions are most often existing nonprofits and foundations in the community. They may also be foundations that have been created by the corporation to manage and distribute funds or public entities such as schools. There may also be additional partners in the effort, even ones that also provide funding for the cause.

Guidelines for determining levels of giving vary. Many companies budget their donations based on the prior year's income. Some target a percent of pretax earnings. The Committee Encouraging Corporate Philanthropy reported that in 2010, surveyed companies contributed 0.91 percent of their pre-tax profits in cash plus in-kind donations or 0.69 percent of pre-tax profits when only cash was taken into account.[6] A 2010 *Forbes* article ranked companies based on their cash donations as a percentage of operating income: Topping the list was Kroger at 10.9 percent of 2009 profits followed by Macy's (8.1 percent), Safeway (7.5 percent), and Dow Chemical Company (7.3 percent).[7]

Table 6.1 highlights examples of corporate philanthropy programs highlighted in this chapter.

Potential Benefits

On the surface, involvement in philanthropic activities appears to contribute most to the image and regard for the corporation among its varied publics including customers, channel members, employees, and community organizations, especially ones that track and report on corporate giving. Many managers point to *increased respect* and *community good will* and a stronger *desired brand position*.

In their classic *Harvard Business Review* article, "The Competitive Advantage of Corporate Philanthropy," Michael Porter and Mark Kramer argued that philanthropic activities can and should go beyond generating good will. They cited examples of how activities can enhance a company's *productivity* (Exxon Mobil making substantial donations to improve roads in developing countries where it operates), *expand markets* (Apple Computer donating computers to schools, increasing the usage and appeal of their systems), and ensure a *strong*

TABLE 6.1 Examples of Corporate Philanthropy Initiatives

Corporation	Cause	Major Contributions	Recipient(s)	Major Partners
PepsiCo	Refreshing the world through positive community projects	Funding community projects	Individuals and organizations	Agencies and consultants
Boston Beer Company	Supporting food and beverage small business entrepreneurs	Microloans and mentoring	Small businesses	Accion
Western Union	Economic opportunity for migrant communities	Grants, loans, and training	Migrants around the world and their home communities	Mercy Corps and other nonprofits, Western Union agents
Pfizer	Eradicating blinding trachoma	Medication donations, Program funding	Governmental and nongovernmental organizations around the world	International Trachoma Initiative, World Health Organization
ConAgra Foods	Child hunger	Financial donations, grants, technical support, and in-kind donations	National, regional, and local antihunger organizations	Share Our Strength, Feeding America

future workforce (American Express supporting training for students in careers in travel agencies).[8]

The following examples point to these as well as additional benefits from involvement in corporate philanthropic activities and demonstrate how companies are exploding traditional notions of corporate philanthropy by experimenting with extremely varied approaches.

Case #1: Pepsi Refresh—Creating Community Good Will and National Attention

When Indra Nooyi became CEO of PepsiCo in 2006, she promised herself that she would make PepsiCo "into one of the most responsible companies in the world."[9] The direction she set for the company was captured in three words: *Performance with Purpose*.

Impressed by research that showed, "Consumers liked brands that possessed a soul—brands that had warmth and stood for purpose,"[10] Nooyi encouraged PepsiCo's marketing leaders to explore adding new, socially conscious dimensions to the company's $19 billion-plus brands.

The Pepsi brand marketing team developed a groundbreaking, purpose-driven initiative called the Pepsi Refresh Project born from the concepts that each generation wants to *refresh* the world and that social media presented exciting opportunities to engage consumers.

In the fall of 2009, the company announced that it would forego its traditional multimillion-dollar investment in Super Bowl advertising and redirect those funds into a campaign that would award $20 million in grants ranging from $5,000 to $250,000 to social projects nominated by and voted upon by the public via digital and social media.

Far from a traditional corporate philanthropy effort, Pepsi Refresh was in the vanguard of crowd-sourced giving. Consumers and nonprofit groups were given a central role in nominating pro-social ideas and enlisting others via social media to vote for them. In the case of Pepsi Refresh, the entire program—including all of the grants—was funded out of the Pepsi marketing budget.

As Nooyi explained in a March 2011 TED Talk:[11]

[E]very month we accepted 1,000 projects that people could vote on. During the first month, we were worried whether we were going to get 1,000 projects, but, incredibly, we got it in about 17 hours. In the second month, we got 1,000 projects in 17 minutes. By the third month, 17 seconds after the project lines opened, we had 1,000 videos, and there were tens of thousands of grants waiting to be submitted. We were tapping into something in the world that felt good.

The projects that came in were all so unbelievable and emotionally heart-wrenching because, for $5,000 or $10,000, you could make a huge difference in society. But let me tell you the magnitude of the numbers. There were 183,000 ideas that were started, and $20 million was awarded to 1,000 grantees. There were 84 million votes cast, $65 million of media coverage came from that project; 48 new organizations were started and 108 schools were improved.

The ambitious campaign experienced some technical snafus and generated criticism that it had inadequate safeguards against voting fraud,[12] but it clearly succeeded in getting people talking about Pepsi as a socially conscious brand. Consumers ranked Pepsi number one as a brand "that comes to mind as placing as much or more importance on supporting a good cause as they place on profits" in a fall 2010 survey by Edelman PR.[13]

Some beverage industry analysts dubbed Pepsi Refresh a failure because Pepsi lost market share to Coca-Cola in 2010.[14] Responding to that criticism, Shiv Singh, head of digital for PepsiCo Beverages America, told the *New York*

FIGURE 6.1 The Pepsi Refresh Project sought to attract millennials and retain baby boomers to the Pepsi brand by appealing to their beliefs that they can change the world.

Times that the program was designed to build brand awareness and cultivate a long-term relationship with consumers, not a sales-driving program. "We look at brand equity, brand health and sales—and we have seen movement in all of them."[15]

In 2011, the company refreshed elements of the program to address issues raised in 2010, and expanded it into a number of overseas markets.

Case #2: The Boston Beer Company's Samuel Adams Brewing the American Dream Program—Strengthening the Corporation's Industry

Jim Koch founded The Boston Beer Company in 1984 on a shoestring, brewing the first batch of Samuel Adams Boston Lager in his kitchen, selling his beer bar-to-bar after distributors turned him down. While over time, The Boston Beer Company grew to become the country's largest independently owned American brewer, it makes up just 1 percent of the entire U.S. beer market.[16] Overall, craft beer represents 6 percent of the beer category. In that context, Koch proudly identifies Samuel Adams as the "tallest pygmy" in the craft beer segment, yet he and his team have never forgotten their early struggles.[17]

In 2008, the company launched *Samuel Adams Brewing the American Dream*, a program with the mission of providing low- and moderate-income small business owners in the food and beverage industry with the tools they need to help them grow and succeed. Boston Beer kicked off the program by creating a $250,000 microloan fund and a series of training programs for small business owners in New England. Most notable are speed coaching events, which partner Samuel Adams employees—experts in branding, marketing, sales and distribution, packaging, ingredient sourcing, buzz building, and other disciplines within the food and beverage category—with small business owners for spirited 20-minute coaching sessions over the course of an evening.

Boston Beer knows the beverage business, but the company is not an expert on microfinance, so they turned to ACCION USA, a nonprofit microfinance leader, to oversee that part of the program. Program applicants apply for loans ranging from $500 to $25,000, which can be used for a variety of business purposes including expansion, equipment, and marketing, with all loan payments recycled back into the fund.

Says Koch, "For me, having a program like this when I started Samuel Adams would have made life a lot easier. And not just access to capital, but access to that industry expertise would have made a big difference for me. I would have avoided some pretty significant potholes."[18]

The program's first beneficiary was Carlene O'Garro, a trained pastry chef, who applied for a Samuel Adams Brewing the American Dream microloan as an alternative to financing her catering business with high-interest credit cards. (See Figure 6.2.) Thanks in part to the program's financing and training, O'Garro said her business, Delectable Desires, is making solid progress three years later and she continues to draw from the expertise of the Samuel Adams team as a regular speed coaching participant.[19]

Over time, Boston Beer expanded the program geographically from New England to the New York City, Pennsylvania, Ohio, and Chicago markets. In 2011, it allowed craft brewers nationwide to apply for loans and created an *Experienceship* program that enables selected entrepreneurs to visit the Samuel Adams Boston Brewery and receive mentoring from company experts. The company expected to have funded $1,000,000 in loans by the end of 2011 and to continue expanding the program.[20]

"We really wanted our philanthropy to leverage what we are good at and what we've learned while we've built this business over the last 27 years to deliver even greater value to people who could benefit," said Koch. "At Samuel Adams, we very much identify with our industry's independent 'little

FIGURE 6.2   Boston Beer Company CEO Jim Koch presents the first Samuel Adams Brewing the American Dream micro-loan check to pastry chef Carlene O'Garro.

guy.' This tenacious spirit of following one's dream and doing something that conventional wisdom says should not be possible is really what the company and the brand stand for; it's what our drinkers celebrate; it's why our employees get up and come to work every day. For us, this way of giving back represents the essence of what we stand for."[21]

Case #3: Western Union's *Our World, Our Family* Program—Having an Impact on Societal Issues in Local Communities

Migrants account for roughly 85 percent of the customers of Western Union, the worldwide leader in providing fast, reliable, and convenient ways to send and receive money.[22] In 2010, the company's network of 470,000 agent locations in 200 countries completed 214 million consumer-to-consumer transactions to move $76 billion worldwide.[23]

In 2007, Western Union launched *Our World, Our Family*, a multifaceted corporate citizenship program that focused the Englewood, Colorado-based company on creating economic opportunity, with an emphasis on migrant communities. (See Figure 6.3.) The program is designed "to create global economic opportunities which will help aspiring individuals and their families stay connected, overcome barriers, and realize their dreams."[24]

"These are heroic people who often send 10, 20, 30, or even 40 percent of what they earn back home to support their extended families," said Western Union Corporate Responsibility Director Talya Bosch.[25]

Western Union had long offered matching contributions to encourage local giving by the independent network of agents that enable the company to serve so many different communities. Until 2007, the causes supported by agent giving, like the agents themselves, "had been all over the map," said Bosch.[26]

With the advent of *Our World, Our Family*, the company told agents that it would only match giving that was under the economic opportunity umbrella. "No more healthcare, sports, animals—they are great things, but not related to our cause," said Bosch.[27] Some agents resisted the change, but by 2010, concerted efforts to educate and engage them enabled Western Union to report that 92 percent of its matched giving was supporting economic opportunity, with a focus on migrant integration in their new homes or those in need back in migrants' countries of origin.[28]

FIGURE 6.3   Western Union and its agents support economic development in migrant communities around the world.

For example, many of Western Union's customers are small business owners who understand the challenges of staying afloat in tough times. In Pakistan, the Western Union Foundation partnered with local agent Ravi Exchange to make $60,000 available to struggling entrepreneurs. Business training and microloans of $150 are helping to spur the local economy.[29] In Kenya, five agents came together with the Western Union Foundation to improve education and brighten the economic prospects of the next generation. The Bank of Africa Kenya, Equity Bank, Kenya Commercial Bank, Diamond Trust Bank Kenya, and Postbank (Kenya Post Office Savings Bank) together channeled $50,000 to outfit classrooms with 30 new desks in each of 25 overcrowded schools across Kenya's eight provinces.[30]

In 2011, Western Union offered additional incentives to agents to support the work in their countries of Western Union's preferred NGO partners such as Mercy Corps. This even greater focus will enable the company's "collective giving in each country to roll up into a more significant impact on the issue," Bosch said.[31] That should make it easier for Western Union to increase awareness of the impacts of its giving, which, in turn, should enhance its reputation and relationships with the agents and consumers it serves in communities around the world, she said.

Case #4: Pfizer Trachoma Initiative—In-Kind Contributions

Trachoma, the world's leading cause of preventable blindness, is an infectious eye disease caused by repeated infection by the bacterium *Chlamydia trachomatis*, which is primarily spread by contact with an infected person's hands or clothing. Tens of millions of poor people in 57 countries, mostly in Africa and Asia, have active trachoma infection and need treatment. The poorest of the poor suffer most from trachoma, particularly those with limited access to water and sanitation.

Fortunately, trachoma is treatable and preventable with full implementation of a public health protocol combining surgery, antibiotics, facial cleanliness, and environmental improvement in affected communities.

Since 1998, Pfizer has been working to help end the suffering caused by blinding trachoma by partnering with the World Health Organization's Alliance for the Global Elimination of Blinding Trachoma by the year 2020 (GET2020) and the International Trachoma Initiative (ITI).[32]

Pfizer has committed itself to providing the antibiotic Zithromax® needed in the effort. As of September 2011, Pfizer had donated more than 250 million Zithromax® treatments with an estimated total value of $5 billion across 21 countries with plans to be active in many more.[33] (See Figure 6.4.)

ITI, which Pfizer helped establish, manages the company's global donation of Zithromax® and collaborates with governmental and nongovernmental agencies at the local, national, and international levels to implement the overall initiative. Pfizer also funds a significant portion of ITI's activities worldwide. With the support of Pfizer, ITI, and other partners, Morocco became the first country to reach its trachoma elimination goals and Gambia, Ghana, and Vietnam are on track to eliminate the disease.

FIGURE 6.4 Pfizer donations of Zithromax® have helped fight blinding trachoma.

Pfizer Chairman of the Board Emeritus William C. Steere has written that charitable programs like the trachoma initiative were "instrumental in helping Pfizer become the world's leading pharmaceutical company. Ours is a highly regulated industry, and establishing strong relationships with policymakers is critical to our business success. Our corporate reputation and image are among our most valuable assets, and we work hard to maintain them."[34]

Potential Concerns

Several challenges and concerns associated with philanthropic efforts are similar to those experienced when developing and implementing other social initiatives. Care needs to be given to *selecting a nonprofit charity partner* that has a strong reputation, is easy to work with, and has an existing infrastructure that will assure the effective management and utilization of contributions. As with other initiatives, managers may need to address *shareholder concerns* that the company should not be funding social causes that are or should be within the auspices of governmental agencies. This may be especially true when making large cash contributions.

Many issues, however, are more unique to philanthropic activities. Traditionally, corporate philanthropy had *less visibility* than other types of initiatives, because many leaders espoused the view that corporate philanthropy activities should not be touted. The examples in this chapter—and the swarm of chief executives making public commitments involving corporate philanthropy at the annual Clinton Global Initiative—show how much attitudes have changed. Numerous studies indicate the public expects and watches for a company's philanthropic activities and often makes purchase decisions based on awareness and knowledge of a company's giving.

A corporation can be penalized by the IRS for "self dealing" if donations made by a corporate foundation are deemed to have generated private benefit to the corporation that are more than "tenuous and incidental."[35]

An additional challenge for managers of philanthropic initiatives is to *track activities and measure outcomes*. Philanthropic activities often depend on feedback on outcomes and impact from partners who may lack such measurement systems.

Keys to Success

Several keys to success for corporate philanthropy are similar to those for other initiatives. Choose a cause that has a connection to your business, your employees, and your overall corporate citizenship focus. Make sure leaders in the company are involved from the beginning, especially in major philanthropic efforts. Select the best grantees, find a way to make a concrete and positive difference, and consider multiyear partnerships. Explore opportunities for donations of in-kind services, especially those connected to core products. Finally, don't be shy, but do be appropriate about discussing results and celebrating success.

Case #6: ConAgra Foods—Building a Corporate Philanthropy Logic Model

As the foundation and cause vice president at ConAgra Foods, Kori Reed is focused on integrating the company's corporate social initiatives to maximize societal and business impacts. After years of making contributions to fight child hunger, the company undertook a major evaluation of its efforts built around the concept of a logic model, a process she recommends for other businesses. She shares insights and advice from that process below:

> Innovation, problem solving, leadership, and accountability are common language in a business setting; the key to successful corporate citizenship is to apply those concepts within a social initiative. At ConAgra Foods, working with the ConAgra Foods Foundation, we've been able to advance our social and business impact with input from colleagues in other part of the business as well as our nonprofit partners.
>
> ConAgra Foods aspires to be a leader in the fight against child hunger, an issue that affects more than 16 million U.S. children on an annual basis.[36] As a food company, with brands found in more than 97 percent of America's households, we've taken accountability to help kids have the nourishment they need to flourish. Over nearly 20 years, the ConAgra Foods Foundation invested more than $50 million with anti-hunger nonprofit organizations and contributed 275 million pounds of food. As

leaders, we've concentrated much of our funding on supporting innovation such as expanding after-school feeding programs (*Kids Cafes*), starting up Hunger-Free Summer programs and creating a Child Hunger Corps. In a bottom-line oriented business culture, however, capturing the return on investment of funding program innovation can be tricky.

That issue came to the forefront when a review of our work revealed some discouraging facts. Despite our financial investments and product donations, the numbers had gotten worse (13 million hungry children in 2006 had grown to 16 million in 2010). We challenged ourselves to develop a more focused, long-term, outcomes-oriented approach to tackling the issue.

Leveraging practices used by our supply chain and strategic planning groups, we partnered with outside experts to create a logic model linking strategies to our intended result: reducing food insecurity in the United States (See Figure 6.5).[37] In conjunction with leading hunger nonprofit organizations, we categorized the activities, input and outputs, that ConAgra Foods and the ConAgra Foods Foundation support. To ensure validity and utility related to both program design and measurement, we asked our partners to tell us how and where their organization aligns with strategies funded to date? We also asked what would be appropriate indicators of progress against childhood hunger?

Then, relative to activities and strategies, associated outputs and outcomes were identified. For example, data on the number and type of participants in a feeding program as well as pounds and type of food were associated with the goal of increased food access.

The resulting ConAgra Foods theory of change, read from left to right, identifies five main strategies with two emerging strategies that when integrated, where appropriate, are expected to increase food security.

It is important to note that we know this model is dynamic and incomplete. The logic model, as it stands at the date of this publication, laid the foundation for a plan that has a strong focus on outcomes. The tool created enhanced dialog among partners working in the same space. It gave us a clear snapshot of what we do today and a tool to evolve those efforts over time. Now our attention is focused on the question: Are we supporting *the right stuff* to truly make an impact in this space? How can we develop a plan that prioritizes activities proven to make a bigger impact reducing food insecurity? We continue to evolve the

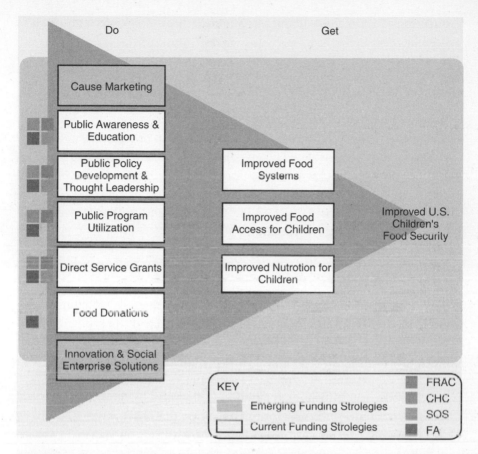

FIGURE 6.5 A simplified graphic representation of ConAgra Foods' theory of change.

Source: Phillips Wyatt Knowlton, Inc.

model. Fortunately, along with the logic model, we've also developed metrics with our grantees that will provide a clearer picture of the value created by our corporate giving.

ConAgra Foods is helping end child hunger, one child, one meal, and one champion at a time. We continue to strive for continuous improvement that leads to better outcomes. Building a logic model and continuing to enhance our program evaluation and management has been an important step forward because, to borrow a phrase from the *Wall Street Journal* article, "Should Philanthropies Operate Like

Businesses?": "Dreams without plans remain dreams. Dreams with plans become reality."[38]

When to Consider

Philanthropic activities are the norm for most corporations and are always a consideration when the corporation has citizenship or philanthropic goals. They should also be considered when community organizations and agencies would benefit from excess or idle corporate resources. Emphasis is placed in this chapter on strategies for developing philanthropic initiatives that are strategic, having the most impact on the social cause, as well as providing the maximum benefits for the corporation.

Developing Philanthropic Endeavors

Major decisions related to philanthropic activities will include selecting a cause to support, choosing a nonprofit charity or other recipient for contributions, determining levels and types of contributions, and developing communication and evaluation plans. Guidelines for each include the following:

- Selecting a cause to support should ideally begin by referring to already established philanthropic priorities, ones that have been chosen by the company as areas of focus based on a variety of factors including business goals, employee passions, and customer concerns. This will help ensure management support for the effort, as well as the possibility that contributions will be connected to causes currently being supported by other types of initiatives. The chances for making a real impact are then increased. Having these areas of focus will also help guide managers at remote or local levels, thereby increasing the likelihood that corporate giving will be integrated throughout its various markets.
- When choosing a nonprofit partner, managers might first look at existing partnerships and build on ones where there is a good working relationship, a history of good fiscal management, and a track record of collaboration. Other criteria that might be used to select a partner include looking for one where there is the possibility for making a meaningful contribution by providing non-monetary resources such as corporate products, use of distribution channels, and technical expertise.

- Determining levels of contributions ideally should also begin with a reference to established corporate guidelines for giving, ones that may specify a percentage of pretax profits, a percentage that varies at different profitability levels, a fixed dollar amount, or may even be based on some other index such as the number of corporate employees.
- With consumers, employees, and other stakeholders hungry for proof that companies are making positive societal contributions, it is critical for companies to effectively communicate about their philanthropic initiatives, a step that some businesses have deliberately skipped in the past.
- Though often difficult, managers are encouraged to establish tracking and measurement tools that will account for total cash contributions, estimate the value of any in-kind services and, ideally, provide information on outcomes and impacts for the social cause.

In Summary

The current range of options for philanthropic giving are broad, breaking from traditions in the past that focused on cash donations alone to more creative giving strategies including donating products and services, providing technical expertise, and allowing the use of facilities, distribution channels, and equipment.

Major strengths of corporate philanthropy include building corporate reputation and good will, attracting and retaining a motivated workforce, having an impact on societal issues (especially in local communities), and leveraging other corporate social initiatives. Of late, experts are challenging corporations to also look at the potential for philanthropic initiatives that will actually increase productivity, expand markets, and ensure a strong future workforce. The greatest concerns expressed by many were the challenges associated with evaluating and choosing a strong cause partner, dealing with shareholder concerns for issues that have been selected, achieving tactful visibility for the corporation for its efforts, and tracking and measuring impact and outcomes.

Strongest recommendations to address these downsides include choosing social issues that have a connection to the corporation's mission and involving other departments in selecting causes, and giving levels. When developing programs, engage employees, secure leadership support, and develop an appropriate communications plan.

7 Community Volunteering: Employees Donating Their Time and Talents

While cash giving declined between 2007 and 2008 for the first time in more than 20 years, the volunteer rate in the United States increased.[1] What's more, the Deloitte Volunteer IMPACT Survey found that skilled volunteerism is increasingly being adopted by corporations." [2]

—2010 Deloitte Volunteer IMPACT Survey

A *community volunteering initiative* supports and encourages employees, retail partners, and/or franchise members to *volunteer their time* to support local community organizations and causes. Volunteer efforts may include employees volunteering their expertise, talents, ideas, and/or physical labor. Corporate support may involve providing paid time off from work, matching services to help employees find opportunities of interest, recognition for service, and organizing teams to support specific causes the corporation has targeted.

Distinguishing community volunteering from other initiatives is not difficult, as it stands alone as the initiative that involves employees of a corporation personally volunteering at community organizations (e.g., Boys & Girls Clubs) and for cause efforts (e.g., picking up litter on roadways). And volunteering in the community is not a new corporate initiative. What is new and noteworthy, however, is an apparent increase in the integration of employee volunteer efforts into existing corporate social initiatives and connecting the volunteer efforts to business goals. Once more, a strategic approach appears to be the norm, where employees are often encouraged to volunteer for causes that are currently supported by other corporate social initiatives, frequently connected to core business values and goals.

Volunteering in the community, and corporate support to do this, is viewed by many (including executives sharing their stories in this chapter) as one of the most genuine and satisfying of all forms of corporate social involvement. In his book *Revolution of the Heart*, Bill Shore shares perspectives and insights that may be contributing to this revival and encourages corporations, as well as individuals, to "contribute through their unique skills and creative abilities," and that by doing this, "they are giving the one thing that is most genuinely theirs and that no one can take away."[3] It means "teaching nutrition and food budgeting to young mothers if you're a chef, tutoring math if you are an accountant, coaching if you are an athlete, examining children if you are a doctor, building homes if you are a carpenter or a builder."[4] He writes about "the yearning people have to be connected both to something special inside themselves and, at the same time, to something larger than themselves and their own self-interest."[5]

Typical Programs

Corporate support for employee volunteering ranges from programs that simply encourage their employees to give back to their communities to those representing a significant financial investment and display of recognition and reward. Examples representing types of support include the following:

- **Promoting the ethic through corporate communications** that encourage employees to volunteer in their community and may provide information on resources to access or explore volunteer opportunities.
- **Suggesting specific causes and charities** that the employee might want to consider and providing detailed information on how to get involved, with causes and charities often being ones supported by other current social initiatives.
- **Organizing volunteer teams** for a specific cause or event, such as a United Way *Day of Caring* event where, for example, employees paint the interior of a child care facility for homeless children.
- **Helping employees find opportunities** through onsite coordinators, website listings or, in some cases, through sophisticated software programs that match specific employee interests and criteria with current community needs.

- **Providing paid time off** during the year to do volunteer work, with typical benefits ranging from offering two to five days of annual paid leave to do volunteer work on company time, to more vigorous programs that provide opportunities for an employee to spend a year on behalf of the company working in a developing country.
- **Awarding cash grants to charities** where employees spend time volunteering; grant amounts are then often based on numbers of hours reported by employees.
- **Recognizing exemplary employee volunteers** through gestures such as mentions in internal newsletters, awards of service pins or plaques, and special presentations at department or annual company meetings.

Types of projects that employees volunteer for range from those that contribute to a local community to ones that improve health and safety for individuals to those that protect the environment.

- *Community projects*, perhaps the most common, include efforts such as building homes, collecting food for food banks, answering phones for public radio pledge campaigns, organizing teams for walk-a-thons, cleaning parks, reading to kids, mentoring youth at risk, volunteering in the classroom, visiting children in hospitals, spending time with seniors in nursing homes, teaching computer skills, befriending people in a homeless shelter, handing out meals at a soup kitchen, building playhouses for orphans, and staffing an adopt-a-pet booth.
- *Health and safety-related projects*, where employees volunteer their time, include ones such as screening kids for dental problems, leading youth physical activity programs, conducting a car-seat safety check, handing out educational brochures on HIV/AIDS, driving seniors to get an annual flu shot, and training children on how to use crosswalks.
- *Environmental volunteering* might involve litter pick-ups, tree planting in areas destroyed by fires, seed propagation for highway beautification, salmon habitat protection, plant identification, weed control, removing alien plants, wetland rehabilitation, cleaning polluted waterways, and clearing storm drains from debris.

Table 7.1 highlights examples of programs of companies featured in this chapter. As you review this list of causes these organizations supported, notice the natural connection to the company.

TABLE 7.1 Examples of Corporate Community Volunteer Activities

Corporation	Example of a Cause Supported	Examples of Employee Activities	Examples of Employee Support
Sellen Construction	Providing hospitalized children recognition and a smile	Painting names of kids in the hospital on steel beams outside their window	Internal recognition and news media visibility
Pfizer	HIV/AIDS prevention	Employee volunteer spending six months helping train sales force	Six months' paid leave
IBM	Children's literacy	Employee volunteer in Bangalore, India, organizing literacy and other fun events	Excellence awards
FedEx	Child pedestrian safety	Sharing best practices with parents and providing hands-on events for kids	Organizing events and time off from work
AT&T Wireless	Disaster relief	Providing mobile phones	Organizing events and providing equipment
Patagonia	Wildlife habitats	Photographs documenting positive impact of organic farming practices	Up to two months of paid leave

Potential Benefits

According to executives contributing to cases and examples in this book, many of the benefits for this initiative reflect its unique capacity to build strong and genuine relationships with local communities and attract and maintain satisfied and motivated employees. This may also be one of the best initiatives for augmenting and leveraging current involvement and investments in other social initiatives. As with several of the other initiatives, additional potential benefits have been experienced, including contributions to business goals, enhancing corporate image, and providing opportunities to showcase products and services.

Case #1: Sellen Construction and Seattle Children's Hospital—Building Genuine Relationships in the Community

First, imagine this: A bunch of construction workers building a new wing of a children's hospital create a game to entertain and distract hospitalized patients. It's something familiar to many of the kids: *Where's Waldo?*™ The workers create a life-sized *Waldo* that looks like the storybook character, all decked out in a red and white striped shirt. Waldo moves around the site every day so that children—and parents and staff—can anticipate searching for him. When they find him, they are eligible for fun prizes.[6] (See Figure 7.1.)

Now, imagine this: same hospital, same project. A group of ironworkers find their own way to cheer up the kids. They spray-paint very visible greetings to individual patients on steel beams before they raise them. They continue this for weeks. One father wrote on the hospital's Facebook page about how his daughter's smile returned after a tough day of treatments when she returned to her room, looked out the window, and noticed "HI KIRA"[7] written on a beam. (See Figure 7.2.)

These caring, voluntary gestures actually happened in 2011, and were made by employees and contractors of Sellen Construction Company in Seattle, Washington, while building a new wing with 80 new beds for cancer and critical care patients. In a *Seattle Times* article featuring the effort, Tim McKey, project superintendent for Sellen, commented, "Every guy out here

FIGURE 7.1 Waldo appears each day in a different location on the Sellen construction site at Seattle Children's Hospital.

FIGURE 7.2 Ironworkers bring cheer to patients.

feels for every kid in the hospital. We're pulling for them, we care about them and we want them to know that."

The story was picked up by at least two local radio stations and four local television stations, including one with the headline "Local iron workers building hope, one beam at a time."[8] Consider the community goodwill for the construction company, as well as the hospital, gained by this visibility.

Also, consider the feelings of pride among the hospital's employees. One nurse said, "This sums up the spirit of Seattle Children's. To see a group of contractors, who are under no obligation to embrace the values and essence of what Children's is all about, turn something mundane into something so joyful and exciting for our kids makes me so proud to be a Children's employee."[9] We imagine it also made employees and subcontractors of Sellen proud, to work for a company that must support, even reward, goodwill gestures such as these.

Case #2: Pfizer's Global Health Fellows Program Contributing to Business Goals

Pfizer, a pharmaceutical company founded by cousins Charles Pfizer and Charles Erhart in 1849, is "dedicated to discovering and developing new, and better, ways to prevent and treat disease and improve health and well-being for people around the world."[10] The company's international corporate volunteer program, Global Health Fellows Program (GHF), is one strategy to fulfill on this commitment. Pfizer colleagues are placed in three- to six-month assignments with international development organizations addressing major health issues and caring for underserved populations. Assignments are focused on those related to Pfizer's core competencies, and include efforts to build health information systems, train health workers, improve service delivery, and enhance management of medicines, vaccines, and technology. One volunteer fellow, Peter Zhang, spent six months in Kenya in 2011, fulfilling a dream to have a positive impact on the people of Africa.[11]

In Kenya, Zhang worked with Population Services International (PSI), one of the world's leading nonprofit social marketing organizations operating in more than 60 developing countries creating demand for essential health

FIGURE 7.3 Peter Zhang training PSI Kenya sales force in increasing retail sales of essential health products.

products and services by using private sector marketing. Zhang, an associate director of public affairs and policy for Pfizer China, helped the PSI team to assess their sales and marketing activities and provide recommendations for improvement; train PSI sales force in sales and marketing techniques; and train the PSI marketing department on a promotional campaign geared to increase retail sales. (See Figure 7.3.)[12]

Consider the benefits, to both Zhang and Pfizer, when he returned:

> The Global Health Fellow experience has helped me in my work at Pfizer interacting with key external stakeholders in China. In sharing my work and learnings gained during my fellowship, I can now personally describe how Pfizer shoulders its corporate responsibilities in an innovative way that contributes to the development of healthcare around the world. This has opened new doors and taken dialogue with long-standing stakeholders in new directions. For example, I recently shared my experience with the head of a major think tank and research institute of the Ministry of Health who is now interested in exploring ways to extend their partnership with Pfizer.[13]

Since 2003, over 270 Pfizer Global Health Fellows, from Pfizer sites around the world, have participated in the program working with over 40 partner organizations and in 40 countries.[14]

Case #3: IBM's On Demand Community—Increasing Employee Satisfaction and Motivation

Stan Litow, vice president of corporate citizenship and corporate affairs and president of the IBM International Foundation, believes the following case example illustrates a principal key to success in increasing employee satisfaction and motivation through volunteering : "Start off with volunteer opportunities that connect to the personal passion of your employees. Then make every effort to build opportunities that take full advantage of [y]our employees' unique and special skills."[15]

In 2011, IBM celebrated a century of employee and retiree volunteers contributing to their communities. One of the top volunteers receiving the IBM On Demand Community Excellence Award was Abhishek Singh, an employee and volunteer in Bangalore, India, with a passion for helping children. The On Demand Community program supports employees like Abhishek, as well as retirees, with leading-edge technology solutions to expand the value and impact of their volunteer work. Each online volunteer kit provides customized materials, including presentations and educational modules that prepare and equip these volunteers for their work in schools or communities.

For the past year, Abhishek and 100 other IBM volunteers he recruited had been working with students on weekends at the Kadesh Children's Home, a nonprofit organization in Bangalore that helps children who have been abandoned or orphaned. To help bridge the knowledge gap between these students attending public schools and those at private schools, Abhishek organized lessons in science, math, and English, and provided a fun-filled learning environment for the children. A summer camp program helped develop interpersonal skills and computer literacy. When he first started teaching, most of the students could not speak English and there was high student absenteeism. After just one year, he saw children improve in attendance, demonstrate better reading fluency, and show more interest in science and technology.[16] (See Figure 7.4.)

On the day before the hundredth anniversary of IBM's establishment, and as part of the company's celebration of service, 300,000 IBMers logged 2.8 million hours of service in 120 countries on just one day. Over 10 million people were served at over 5,000 IBM-led events that day.[17]

FIGURE 7.4 Abhishek with underprivileged students in India, leading a grassroots effort to offer quality education to all children in the country.

As of the end of June 2011, the program passed 12 million hours logged in since its inception, with more than 186,000 employees and retirees from over 84 countries registered to participate and log their hours and best practices.[18]

In June 2011, the Points of Light Institute honored IBM with their prestigious Corporate Engagement Award of Excellence for building strong and effective volunteer programs that build healthy communities and provide a better quality of life for residents.

Case #4: FedEx and Safe Kids Walk This Way—Support for Other Social Initiatives

Supporting employees to volunteer for causes that are a strategic focus for the organization can leverage the contributions already being made through other initiatives such as philanthropy and social marketing. In this example, a corporation has had a long-standing philanthropic focus for contributing to pedestrian safety. It makes real the concept and synergy created when yet one more initiative is integrated into the current strategic mix.

For children ages 10 to 14 in the United States, pedestrian collisions are a leading cause of injury and death. In fact, in 2009, an estimated 13,000 children were injured (over 35 a day), and 244 lost their life (almost one a day).[19]

Safe Kids Worldwide and program sponsor FedEx created Safe Kids Walk This Way in 2000 with a clear intention to reduce this number. And efforts are not only in the United States, enabling FedEx employee volunteers around the world to reach families in their communities with any of several program components, the largest of which is the International Walk to School Day.

On October 5, 2011, millions of children around the world participated in this event, one designed to raise awareness of the benefits of healthy, safe, and walkable neighborhoods for school children. It is also the major opportunity FedEx team members have to provide hands-on education regarding road safety.

In the Philippines, for example, where walking to school is the norm, FedEx volunteers that day shared with parents best practices for maneuvering crowds of children walking to and from school daily. And in New York City, nearly 120 third graders met up with a team of FedEx volunteers who walked with the classes to a place called *Safety City*—a replica of a New York City streetscape created just for kids by the New York City Department of Transportation. (See Figure 7.5.) To impress the kids regarding driver visibility, students were able to board a FedEx delivery truck and get behind the wheel so they could observe the limited visibility of their peers in front of the truck.[20]

Since the beginning of the program, more than 2.2 million students have joined with nearly 14,000 FedEx volunteers in 5,500 schools for this International Walk to School Day in the United States alone. Consider how this hands-on program element supports other FedEx child pedestrian safety initiatives including a grant program for improved infrastructures (philanthropy), funding for materials with safety tips, and giveaways that increase visibility, such as reflective trick-or-treat bags for Halloween (social marketing).[21]

FIGURE 7.5 Showing a child firsthand how limited visibility can be.

Case #5: AT&T Wireless and the American Red Cross—Showcasing Products and Services

Philanthropic initiatives that include donations of products and services can be enhanced through volunteer efforts that provide additional opportunities to associate products with corporate community goodwill. This human, face-to-face gesture provides more memorable connections as illustrated in AT&T Wireless volunteer efforts focused on disaster relief.

AT&T speaks clearly to a commitment to supporting their employees' engagement in the community. "Volunteerism is ingrained in AT&T's culture. For almost 100 years, we have been donating our time and talents to support underserved populations and strengthen our communities. Each year, approximately 300,000 of our employees and retirees take time to enhance their communities. In 2010, employees and retirees donated nine million hours of time to community outreach activities—worth more than $192 million."[22] The company also has focused efforts on community needs with a strategic connection to their products and services.

Back in 2002, the American Red Cross announced an expanded relationship with AT&T Wireless, a longtime supporter of the organization's disaster relief efforts. Additional activities were now to include *corporate volunteerism* to support the over 1,000 Red Cross chapters around the nation. This effort continues today, with 2011 an especially busy year supporting victims of Hurricane Irene on the East Coast and devastating storms in Joplin, Missouri. In addition to providing on-the-ground volunteers and mobile phones, AT&T also incorporated a cause-related marketing effort, helping to raise millions by encouraging customers wanting to contribute to communities impacted by these disasters to send a text to a designated address, with no text message fees applying.[23]

Potential Concerns

Unique benefits can bring unique concerns, as well. Concerns about the types and amounts of corporate support for employee volunteering are real and expressed frequently with challenges and questions such as the following:

- **This can get expensive.** If, for example, a company with 300,000 employees offers 24 hours of paid time off per year for volunteering and 50 percent of employees participate, the company is "donating 3.6 million hours of "productivity." It may be a complex exercise to evaluate against options for giving grants and direct cash contributions and may look riskier than just encouraging volunteer efforts (on your own).

- **With so many employees, efforts may get spread over so many issues that we don't really make a social impact.** This may be of special concern, for example, in corporations that encourage employees to volunteer in the community, but do not offer organized programs or matching services that tend to create more clusters of volunteers for specific causes.

- **Similarly, when efforts among employees are dispersed throughout the market, even the globe, how do we realize business benefits for the company?** If opportunities for economic, as well as social gain from philanthropic initiatives are real, how do we coordinate widespread and diverse efforts so that they are visible and connected with the company and our brand?

- **Being able to track efforts and outcomes for this effort can be the most difficult of all.** This, once more, can be especially true for global companies with volunteers in diverse markets and especially a concern when tracking and reporting systems are not centralized and automated.

- **It is particularly tough with this initiative to find the balance between publicizing our efforts and flaunting them.** Perhaps there is something unique about the personal nature of volunteer efforts that makes communications regarding contributions more uncomfortable than for others. This, then, dampens enthusiasm, perhaps even investments, when a company wants this effort to also help build the brand or enhance corporate reputation.

Keys to Success

Themes for keys to successful corporate volunteer initiatives are familiar. Overall, executives and managers sharing their recommendations tend to stress developing volunteer programs that match real social, economic, and environmental issues with the passion of employees and business needs of the company. They highlight the advantages of connecting volunteer efforts with the company's broader corporate citizenship strategy and with other current corporate social initiatives, such as cause promotions and philanthropic efforts. They stress the need to get management support up front for long-term commitments and to choose strong community partners. They seem to agree that employees should be supported and recognized for their efforts and that tracking and quantifying impact is ideal. And they disagree (somewhat) on if, how, and when these efforts should be made known and publicized. The common ground seems to be that the best visibility is when the messengers are recipients of volunteer efforts sharing the difference that was made or by employees themselves telling personal stories of inspiration and satisfaction with their experiences, as in the following case.

Case #6: Patagonia's Environmental Internships

Patagonia is a $414 million a year, privately owned company based in Ventura, California, offering a wide range of outdoor sports, travel, and everyday wear. It is perhaps best known for innovative designs, quality products, and environmental conscience.[24] Their mission is to "Build the best product, cause no unnecessary harm, and use business to inspire and implement solutions to the environmental crisis."[25] It is the last part of this mission statement that inspired and guides their Environmental Internship Program, created in 1993.

Through this program, employees leave their jobs for up to two months to work for an environmental group of their choice. Patagonia pays their salaries and benefits while they are gone, and environmental groups "get them for free." An expectation is that these ambassadors work to motivate and/or sustain positive change in the environmental practices of these organizations, as Mark Shimahara, an Internet marketer at Patagonia and freelance photographer, did in Guatemala:

> In 2010, I went to a coffee farm in Guatemala, one that had been certified by the Smithsonian Migratory Bird Center as "Bird Friendly," a certification that requires organic farming practices along with the existence of diverse and native shade forestation for a bird friendly habitat. (See Figure 7.6.) To increase coffee production, many coffee farms had converted from "shade grown" plantations, where shrubs are planted amongst trees, to "sun grown" ones, where coffee plants are

FIGURE 7.6 A volunteer mission for Patagonia to provide evidence of bird presence and proof that ecological standards were being met.
Source: Photo by José Luis Zárate/Coffee Kids

planted in plots resembling fields. This method requires trees and the natural forests to be destroyed. Scientists believe that this then led to the decline of bird migration to areas such as Latin America and a loss of habitat of other animals, insects and plants of the tropical forest.

My volunteer "mission" was to perform a "photographic audit" so scientists would have evidence of bird presence and prove that ecological standards on the farm were being met . . . and working. My images were available to scientists at the National Zoo in Washington, DC and posted on Smithsonian's website for the general public, including the coffee buying public, to understand the benefits of bird friendly coffee.

And I feel confident my time, on behalf of Patagonia, helped fulfill our founder Yvon Chouinard's intent to motivate positive change in business practices.[26]

As of 2011, more than 850 employees have taken part in the program, almost 50 a year.[27]

When to Consider

Most large corporations and many smaller ones encourage their employees to volunteer in the community. The dilemma facing most executives centers on the levels and types of support to provide and whether to promote specific volunteer opportunities or to let employees feel free to follow their interests.

Increased and more formalized support for employees and promotion of focused causes are best considered under the following circumstances:

- *When current social initiatives would benefit from a volunteer component* (e.g., home supply retail store promoting natural gardening offers employees an opportunity to help build a native plant garden in a local community park).
- *When a group of employees expresses an interest in a specific cause* that has strong connections with business and corporate citizenship goals (e.g., employees of an outdoor recreational equipment company want to volunteer to help prevent forest fires by removing hazardous brush in threatened mountains).
- *When a community need emerges*, especially an unexpected one that is a good match for the resources and skills of a workforce (e.g., the example presented earlier where American Express helped small businesses in lower Manhattan).
- *When technological advances* make it easier to match employees to volunteer opportunities (e.g., AT&T's tracking of volunteer hours using the program offered by VolunteerMatch.org).
- *When a strong community organization* approaches an organization for support and represents an issue of interest to employees and has a natural connection to strategic corporate citizenship and business goals.
- *When a volunteer effort might open new markets or provide opportunities for new product development and research* (e.g., as presented in the example of Pfizer's activities in Africa).

Developing Community Volunteer Programs

Assuming a company has an interest in developing a formal volunteer program and has decided to go beyond informal communications that simply encourage the workforce to be involved in the community, several steps can then be taken.

1. *Develop guidelines for employee involvement.*
   Decisions will be made regarding whether employees will be encouraged to volunteer for causes that only interest them or whether one or more

specific charities or cause efforts will be promoted. Most commonly, the decision is to adopt a combination of these options. If it is determined that specific causes will be promoted, decisions regarding what causes are best will be made by referencing the company's mission statement, overall corporate citizenship focus, current social initiatives, employee interests, existing community partners, and pressing needs in the community.

2. *Determine types and levels of employee support.*

    Program options include providing monetary incentives such as paid time off and offering cash grants to charities based on the number of volunteer hours spent by individual employees or teams of employees. Non-monetary-related support may include organizing teams of employees to participate in specific events and offering software programs that match employee interests with a database of local volunteer opportunities.

3. *Develop an internal communications plan.*

    Spreading the word to employees at all levels and locations can be critical to fulfillment of a successful companywide volunteer program. Traditional communication planning elements are appropriate including developing a program name and graphic identity and key messages that communicate the company's commitment, the need for community support, and the desire for employee participation.

4. *Develop a recognition plan.*

    Recognition programs may include mentions of volunteer efforts in internal employee communications such as intranet and newsletters, and recognition at departmental and company meetings. Some companies also brand this component of the program, as did Walt Disney with their *EARS to YOU* grant recognition program for volunteerism.

5. *Develop an external communications plan.*

    As a first step, communication objectives are determined, addressing the question of what these communications are intended to support. Is the purpose to simply disclose the corporation's community involvement, leading to targeted communications in annual reports, for example? Or are they also intended to strengthen a corporation's reputation in the community, with implications for broader media efforts? Perhaps it is to support employee recruitment or to provide an additional venue for employee recognition. Once these objectives are clear (and agreed upon), action plans follow.

6. *Develop a plan for tracking and assessment.*

Finally, a plan and system for tracking employ hours and recipients of volunteer efforts is established. Additionally, measures should be agreed upon for assessing communication objectives established in the communications plan.

In Summary

Volunteering in the community, and corporate support to do this, is viewed by many as one of the most genuine and satisfying of all forms of corporate social involvement. *Community volunteering* as an initiative is clearly distinct from others and yet we see trends toward integrating these efforts as an additional component of existing corporate social initiatives.

Support for volunteering ranges from programs that just encourage employees to give back to their communities to ones that have formalized written guidelines and make a significant financial investment over a long period of time.

Volunteer programs are said to have contributed to building strong and enduring relationships with local communities, attracting and retaining satisfied and motivated employees, augmenting and leveraging current involvement and investments in social initiatives, contributing to business goals, enhancing corporate image, and providing opportunities to showcase products and services.

Concerns with developing and managing these programs are real, including concerns with costs, having a meaningful social impact, realizing business benefits appropriately, and tracking and measuring outcomes.

Many keys to success are familiar: match real social, economic, and environmental issues with the passion of employees and business needs of the company; connect volunteer efforts with the company's broader corporate citizenship strategy and other current corporate social initiatives; gain management support up front for long-term commitments; choose strong community partners; support and recognize employees for their efforts; and establish systems for tracking and measurement. Though there is debate regarding the extent and nature of external communications, it seems that the best visibility is when messengers are recipients of volunteer efforts or employees sharing personal, inspirational stories.

Increased efforts for employee volunteer programs should be considered when current social initiatives would benefit from a volunteer component; a group of employees express an interest in a specific cause; a community need emerges; technological advances make it easier to match employees to volunteer opportunities; a strong community organization approaches an organization for support; or when a volunteer effort might open new markets or support new product development. Enhanced programs will benefit from strategic plans that call for developing guidelines; determining types and levels of employee support; and developing plans for internal communications, recognition, external communications, and tracking and assessment.

8 Socially Responsible Business Practices: Changing How You Conduct Business to Achieve Social Outcomes

At the end of the day, it's a team effort. Our customers, buyers, fishermen and fishery managers can all make smart decisions that move us in the direction of greater seafood sustainability. The new color-coded rating system is a transparent way to provide sustainability status information. This new program, along with our promise to phase out red-rated species, deepens our commitment to having fully sustainable seafood departments.[1]

—Carrie Brownstein, Whole Foods Market

A socially responsible business practice is a discretionary business practice that a corporation adopts and conducts to support social causes, to improve community well-being, and/or to protect the environment. Key distinctions include a focus on activities that are *discretionary*, not those that are mandated by law or regulatory agencies or are simply expected, as with meeting moral or ethical standards. *Community* is interpreted broadly to include employees of the corporation, suppliers, distributors, nonprofit and public sector partners, as well as members of the general public. And *well-being* can refer to health and safety, the environment, as well as psychological and emotional needs.

Over the past decade, there has been an apparent shift from adopting more responsible business practices as a result of regulatory citations, consumer complaints, and special interest group pressures, to proactive research exploring corporate solutions to social problems and incorporating new business practices that will support these issues.

177

Why this shift?

- There is increasing evidence being documented and shared demonstrating that **socially responsible business practices can actually increase profits** (e.g., DuPont reporting $3 billion savings from decreased energy use[2]) and has the **potential for increasing revenues** (e.g., what McDonald's is most likely hoping for as a result of a new Happy Meal® that includes locally grown apple slices and low-fat milk options[3]).

- In our global marketplace, **consumers have more options** and can make choices based on criteria beyond product, price and distribution channels. Research presented in Chapter 1 emphasized that consumers are also basing their purchase decisions on reputation for fair and sustainable business practices and perceptions of commitment to the community's welfare (e.g., Whole Foods attracting "green" consumers by labeling the sustainability of fish options).

- Investors and other stakeholders may also be the driving force, with increased public scrutiny and use of sophisticated pressure tactics including use of the technology and **power of the Internet** (e.g., Bank of America reversing its decision to charge $5 a month for its debit card after an online petition gathered over 300,000 signatures).

- An interest in increased **worker productivity and retention** has turned corporate heads to ways to improve employee satisfaction and well-being (e.g., Coca-Cola bottlers in South Africa launching an HIV/AIDS prevention program in the workplace).

- Technology has given **increased visibility to coverage of corporate activities**, especially when things go wrong (e.g., BP and the Gulf oil spill). Recent corporate scandals have made the public more suspicious of business, leading companies to seek new ways to put a positive "shine" on their business activities. This is even more critical today with instant access to 24-hour news channels such as CNN, online news sources, and e-mail alerts.

- The bar for **full disclosure** appears to have been raised, moving potential customers from a "consumer beware" attitude to an expectation they will be fully informed regarding practices including product content, sources of raw materials, and manufacturing processes[4] (e.g., the beverage industry's initiative to print total calories for the entire container in larger type and on the front of cans).

Typical Socially Responsible Business Practices

Most socially responsible business practice initiatives involve altering *internal procedures and policies* related to product offerings, facility design, manufacturing, assembly, and employee support. They can also be reflected in *external reporting* of consumer and investor information and demonstrated by *making provisions for customer access and privacy* and can be taken into consideration when *making decisions regarding hiring practices, facility, and plant locations.* Common activities include the following:

- **Designing facilities** to meet or exceed environmental and safety recommendations and guidelines, such as for increased energy conservation.
- **Developing process improvements**, which may include practices such as eliminating the use of hazardous waste materials or reducing the amount of chemicals used in growing crops or eliminating the use of certain types of oils for deep fat frying.
- **Discontinuing product offerings** that are considered harmful, but not illegal (e.g., McDonald's discontinuing their supersize portions of French fries).
- **Selecting suppliers** based on their willingness to adopt or maintain sustainable environmental practices and supporting and rewarding their efforts.
- **Choosing manufacturing and packaging materials** that are the most environmentally friendly, taking into consideration goals for waste reduction, use of renewable resources, and elimination of toxic emissions.
- **Providing full disclosure** of product materials and their origins and potential hazards, even going the extra mile with helpful information (e.g., including on product packaging the amount of physical exercise needed to burn the calories and fat contained in the candy bar or the number of pounds of pollutants that will be generated from a gas mower).
- **Developing programs to support employee well-being** such as workplace exercise facilities, on-site daycare, and Employee Assistance Programs for those with drug-related addictions.
- **Measuring, tracking, and reporting** of accountable goals and actions, including the bad news as well as the good.

- **Establishing guidelines for marketing to children** to ensure responsible communications and appropriate distribution channels (e.g., not selling products online to children ages 18 and under).
- **Providing increased access for disabled populations** using technology such as assisted listening devices, voice recognition mechanisms, and alternate print formats.
- **Protecting privacy of consumer information**, an area of increasing concern with the sophisticated data collection, recognition, and tracking of individuals and their movements, especially via the Internet (e.g., an online retailer allowing the customer to purchase products without providing demographic profile information).
- **Making decisions regarding plant, outsourcing, and retail locations**, recognizing the economic impact of these decisions on communities.

As represented in Table 8.1, although a wide range of industries participate in incorporating responsible business practices, it appears to be dominated by those in the manufacturing, technology, and agricultural industry categories, where more decisions are made regarding supply chains, raw materials, operational procedures, and employee safety. Those involved in proposing and developing socially responsible business practices most often include operation, facility, corporate social responsibility and other senior managers, and to some extent marketing and strategic planners. Communications regarding the adoption of socially responsible business practices is most often aimed at regulatory agencies, investors, customers, and special interest groups. Although most often the corporation develops and implements practices on their own, they may also do this in partnership with public agencies, nonprofit organizations, suppliers, and distributors.

Potential Corporate Benefits

As will be illustrated in the following brief examples, a wide range of benefits have been experienced by corporations that adopt and implement socially responsible business practices and there appears to be an increasing ability to link these efforts to positive financial results.[5]

Financial benefits have been associated with decreased operating costs, monetary incentives from regulatory agencies, and increased employee productivity and retention. Marketing benefits are numerous as well, with the

TABLE 8.1 Examples of Socially Responsible Business Practices

Corporation	Cause	Target Audiences	Samples Activities	Major Partners/Others
DuPont	Energy conservation	Facility managers, Operations managers	Plant by plant assessments and increased efficiencies	Environmental Protection Agency
Nike	Increased physical activity for Native Americans	Native Americans	Custom designed athletic shoes to accommodate wider and taller feet	Indian Health Services National Indian Health Board Podiatrists
Coca-Cola	HIV/AIDS	Employees of bottling factories in Africa	Education Free testing Counseling Free condoms	Bottling partners
Whole Foods Market	Seafood sustainability	Shoppers at Whole Foods Markets	Labeled fish with stickers: green, yellow, or red	United Kingdom's Department of the Environment, Food and Rural Affairs
Microsoft	Congestion relief	Employees	Free regional bus service	Commuter Challenge
Patagonia	Fair labor practices	Factory managers	Audits of current and prospective factories for working conditions	Fair Labor Association

potential for increasing community goodwill, creating brand preference, build-ing brand positioning, improving product quality, and increasing corporate respect. And, as with other social initiatives, these activities also provide opportunities to build relationships with external partners such as regulatory agencies, suppliers, and nonprofit organizations.

Case #1: DuPont—Decreasing Operating Costs

In a *U.S. News & World Report* article titled "Saving Earth, Saving Money," DuPont was described as a chemical company that "has gone from environ-mental boogeyman to darling of the green movement by voluntarily slashing energy usage as well as greenhouse gas emissions—now 72 percent below 1990 levels."[6] It also reported that conservation steps over the past 15 years had saved the company about $3 billion (billion not million) and that guiding DuPont's green agenda was Linda Fisher, former deputy administrator of the Environmental Protection Agency and vice president and chief sustainability officer for the company.

When asked how they accomplished this reduction in energy consumption, she commented: "There wasn't one big, sexy thing. It was a plant-by-plant, process-by-process assessment of becoming more efficient. We use cogenera-tion when we can, where you produce energy from one source, like a waste stream, and use it to power another."[7]

Fisher still leads this effort in 2011 and remains committed to the com-pany's effort, helping to establish, for example, additional voluntary "footprint reduction goals" with a target date of 2015. She explains,

> "When environmental and safety laws and regulations were introduced in the 1970s and 1980s, our commitment grew to include meeting those new requirements. In the late 1980s and 1990s, we realized that mere compliance was not sufficient, and that our stakeholders expected more from us. So we went beyond regulatory requirements and made voluntary commitments to reduce the environmental footprint of our facilities."[8]

And she acknowledges the need to recognize that more needs to be done and that the "public expects us to deal with them forthrightly, and we are."[9]

The *Sustainability* section of their website is one part of their effort to be transparent in providing progress toward their goals, including one to grow annual revenues by at least $2 billion from products that create energy efficiency and/or significant greenhouse gas emissions reductions for their customers. They estimate these products will contribute at least 40 million tons of additional CO_2 equivalent reductions by consumers. As of 2010, they have grown to $1.6 billion in revenue.[10]

Case #2: Nike's Shoes for Native Americans—Creating Brand Preference

Native Seventh Generation philosophy states that each generation should "look to the three generations preceding them for wisdom and the three generations ahead of them for their legacy."[11] And Nike, through its N7 program, has a longstanding commitment to bringing sport and all of its benefits to Native American and Aboriginal communities in North America. For more than 10 years, N7 has engaged Native communities in the United States and Canada in health promotion and disease prevention through various programs by providing inspiration and tools to help individuals lead physically active, healthy lifestyles. In 2007, this shared vision was realized when Nike unveiled a first of its kind performance athletic shoe designed specifically for Native Americans. They called it the Nike Air Native N7, and Sam McCracken, general manager of Nike's N7 program, commented at the time, "We are stepping up our commitment to use our voice on a local, regional and national level to elevate the issue of Native American health and wellness. We believe physical activity can and should be a fundamental part of the health and wellness of all Native Americans."[12]

Two years before the launch, Nike designers and researchers consulted podiatrists and members of the Indian Health Services and the National Indian Health Board. They examined the feet of more than 200 people from more than 70 tribes nationwide and found that, in general, Native Americans have a much wider and taller foot than the average shoe accommodates. In fact, the average shoe width was three width sizes larger than the standard Nike shoe.[13] As a result of the research, the Air Native has a larger toe box, fewer seams that can cause irritation, and a thicker sock liner. (See Figure 8.1.)

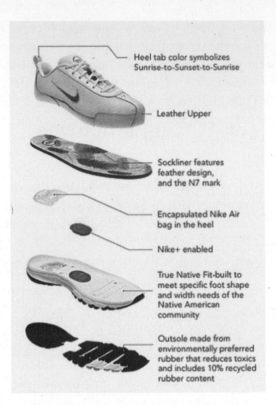

Heel tab color symbolizes
Sunrise-to-Sunset-to-Sunrise

Leather Upper

Sockliner features
feather design,
and the N7 mark

Encapsulated Nike Air
bag in the heel

Nike+ enabled

True Native Fit-built to
meet specific foot shape
and width needs of the
Native American
community

Outsole made from
environmentally preferred
rubber that reduces toxics
and includes 10% recycled
rubber content

FIGURE 8.1   Technical Specifications for the Air Native N7.

Although the Nike Air Native N7 shoes are only available at Native American and Aboriginal Wellness Centers throughout the United States and Canada, in 2009, Nike launched the N7 collection, a selection of performance footwear and apparel for the general public, designed with inspiration from Native American culture and embodying Nike's Considered Design ethos, which creates a performance product that is engineered for superior athletic performance and lower environmental impact. The Nike N7 collection supports the N7 Fund through a portion of profits from sales. The N7 Fund awards grants to Native American and Aboriginal grassroots sport and fitness programs for youth and has raised more than $1 million since it began.

In 2008, Hannah Jones, VP, Sustainable Business & Innovation for Nike, Inc., praised McCracken's efforts:

Intrapreneurship at Nike as led by leaders like Sam McCracken is helping us to develop new forms of value that take into account our ability to innovate for a better world. These projects help to create new lines of sight and unveil opportunities for innovation that benefit communities, drive sustainable design and ultimately contribute to social change.[14]

Case #3: Coca-Cola and HIV/AIDS—Enhancing Employee Well-Being

As we have seen, most corporate social initiatives can contribute to enhanced employee retention and satisfaction efforts, as they engender pride in being associated with a company with a strong reputation for community building and goodwill. Socially responsible business practices can take this even further, offering the additional benefit of actually contributing to improved employee health and safety, as illustrated in the following example.

The Coca-Cola Company believes that the business community can play an important role in battling AIDS by putting into place important initiatives and programs. Since the launch of their HIV/AIDS program in June 2001, one key strategic thrust has been to introduce model workplace programs for their African employees.[15]

Their HIV & AIDS Workplace Program includes: formation of a local AIDS Committee; education on proper condom use; AIDS awareness and prevention material; peer counselor identification and training; employee basic HIV/AIDS training; free testing and counseling on a confidential basis; and access to antiretroviral drugs and prophylactic treatment. Quality condoms are easy to access, available through free vending machines in rest rooms, paycheck envelopes, and in company stores.

Coca-Cola developed an HIV & AIDS corporate policy that commits to: nondiscrimination on the basis of HIV/AIDS status; a right to privacy for employees; encouragement of voluntary disclosure by an HIV-positive associate; voluntary testing; reasonable accommodation; encouragement of prevention practices; identification of community resources; and fostering partnerships with government and NGOs for the implementation of HIV/AIDS programs.

In 2003, The Coca-Cola Africa Foundation turned its attention and resources to its 40-plus bottling partners across Africa, targeting their almost 60,000 employees, including their spouses and children.[16] At the time, only two of the bottlers had HIV/AIDS programs in place. By 2006, 100 percent of bottlers were either participating in existing healthcare programs or had joined their Bottling Partners' HIV/AIDS Workplace Programs.[17] And, importantly, 34,041 employees had engaged in education activities; 13,740 had taken an HIV test; and 1,115 were receiving antiretroviral drug treatment.

Case #4: Whole Foods Market® — Building Influential Partnerships

In 2011, the United Kingdom's Department for the Environment, Food and Rural Affairs published findings from a research study that included a quite actionable opportunity for retailers: 70 percent of shoppers said that buying sustainable fish is important to them, but only 30 percent actually did.[18] The problem for the rest, evidently, is that they aren't sure how to choose sustainable fish products and are confused by labeling. The Department's findings made clear the need for retailers and producers to make sure labels are clear and effective. One retailer did just that, and created influential partnerships in the process.

Whole Foods Market started with one small store in Austin, Texas, in 1980, and by 2011 was the world leader in natural and organic foods, with more than 310 stores in North America and the United Kingdom.[19] Given their mission to provide "Whole Foods" and at the same time take care of the "Whole Planet," their decision in 2010 to empower shoppers to make sustainable seafood choices isn't surprising. They became the first national grocer to provide an easy way for shoppers to know which of the seafood in the case was the "greenest:" they labeled them.

To make this happen, Whole Foods Market has partnered with two organizations—Blue Ocean Institute and Monterey Bay Aquarium—to provide color-coded sustainability status information on all seafood that is not certified sustainable by the Marine Stewardship Council (MSC). Conducting research that is subject to review by scientists, these leading seafood sustainability organizations categorize seafood as being either *green/best choice*, *yellow/good alternative*, or *red/avoid*.[20] With Whole Foods Market's new system (in all their stores including those in the United Kingdom), consumers can walk up to the seafood counter and simply look for MSC-certified products or the green, yellow, and red stickers indicating the sustainability status of each fishery. (See Figure 8.2*a* and 8.2*b*.) It is noteworthy, as well, that each year

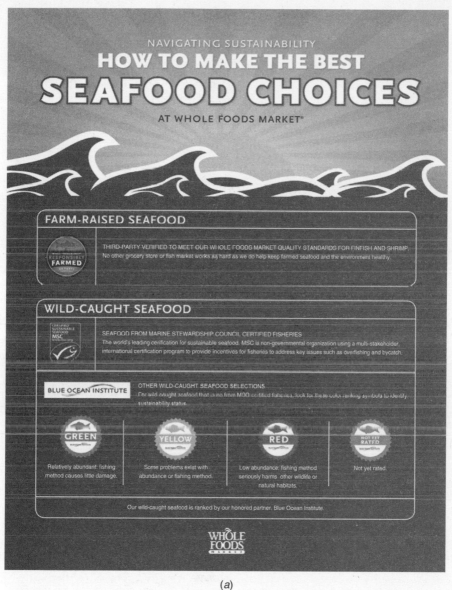

(a)

FIGURE 8.2 Whole Foods Market empowers shoppers to make sustainable seafood choices with their color-coded rating system.[22]

(b)

FIGURE 8.2 (*continued*)

since 2010, Whole Foods Market has eliminated some of the red-rated fish, and has pledged by Earth Day 2012 to eliminate all seafood from red-rated fisheries, with the exception of Atlantic cod and sole, which have an extension until 2013.[21]

Case #5: Microsoft Supporting Alternative Transportation and Generating Community Goodwill

Although Microsoft has operations around the globe and their products touch every corner of the world, the company and more than 40,000 employees call Washington state home.[23] And because this is their home, Microsoft says they have a "huge stake in the state's future and get involved in important community initiatives and public policy issues"[24] that affect not only their employees and their company, but the region as a whole. One of those mutually beneficial issues is to support thousands of employees to commute to their campus in Redmond, Washington, each day, with a goal to reduce the percentage of these that are SOVs (Single Occupant Vehicles).

Employee surveys often reveal the same common barriers to taking alternative transportation: "It takes too much time since I'll have to transfer buses"; "I need my car to go to meetings during the day"; "It's too hard to find a carpool or vanpool partner"; "I have kids and if one of them gets sick, I need to get home right away." The company developed programs to address these concerns. One of those programs is *The Connector*, a free employee transit system that launched in 2007.

The Connector fleet is made up of several types and sizes of comfortable and well-equipped vehicles, many with on-board amenities including Wi-Fi, bicycle storage, overhead storage, cup holders, and in some cases, reclining seats! It has an online reservation tool (of course) and offers e-mail reminders and alerts when there are unexpected route delays. And the program offers a guaranteed ride home in case of emergencies such as a child's illness.

Three years after its launch, nearly 13,500 employees had boarded The Connector, and more than 60 percent of those riders had previously driven alone to work.[25] One employee described how it used to take "anywhere from 25 to 45 minutes to drive from his Seattle home to Microsoft's Redmond campus. Unfortunately, the drive home was much less predictable, occasionally stretching to two hours in the daily backups on Highway 520."[26] Now, The Connector picks him up one and a half blocks from his home and he estimates the commute now takes about an hour each way, time he uses to work on the computer, do crossword puzzles, or just surf the Internet.[27]

In addition to creating this goodwill among employees, the company received the Greater Redmond Chamber of Commerce Way to Go Award in 2010, as well as the 2009 Commuter Challenge Diamond Ring Award, and the 2009 and 2008 Governor's Commute Smart Awards and a Best Workplaces Award.[28]

Potential Concerns

Perhaps more than with any other social initiative, corporate motives for new and more responsible business practices will be questioned, actions will be judged, and results will be scrutinized. Audiences will ask "Is this for doing good or for doing well?" And it will be asked by many, even most, of the company's constituent groups: customers, the general public, employees, investors, regulatory agencies, and the media. Common perceptions include the following challenges:

- **They will be skeptical of the corporation's motives**. They will likely want to believe the news (e.g., decreased use of harmful chemicals in a manufacturing plant) but will wonder whether the news is some type of public relations stunt (e.g., it only applies to one chemical and one type of plant). They'd like to believe this is a real substantial change in the way the company will be doing business going forward, but will wonder if the campaign is just to cover up something that the company doesn't want the public to know or whether it is to distract attention from some impending bad publicity.
- **They will look for actions that back up words and fulfill on promises**. When a company, for example, announces a major program with a renewed emphasis on sustainable building practices, some will want to know if the company will only make changes in new plants, or if they will retrofit and upgrade existing ones as well. When it is written in an annual report that a renewed commitment has been made to recycling in the workplace, what actual changes in infrastructure will be made? Will separate bins for colored paper, glass, and plastic bottles be

provided and conveniently located throughout the workplace, even in conference rooms? Are corporate supplies of paper made from recycled and recyclable materials? Are internal meeting agendas printed on two sides and do staff members get reminders to only print out e-mails they need to file?

- **They will want to know if this is a long-term commitment or short-term campaign.** There will be a big difference in perception between a company that stresses, "This year we want everyone to try to join a carpool, vanpool, or take the bus to work" and one that adapts a program that offers free bus passes, covered bike racks, ride-matching, flexcars for personal use, monthly incentives, increased parking charges for single occupant vehicles, and visible publication of the names of all employees who've joined the effort (or not), including senior managers.

- **They will have questions about whether and how the new practices will make a real difference.** It won't be enough to just say this will improve the environment, increase employee safety, or protect consumers. They will want concrete, measurable facts that demonstrate impact (e.g., number of tons of garbage that are now being recycled and not going into landfills and number of employees no longer coming to work in single occupant vehicles and associated reductions in fuel and air pollutants).

- **They will want to know what you used to do.** When a new practice is announced (e.g., more disclosure of product contents), the next most likely question for many will be "What else haven't you been telling me?" Or when a harmful practice is abandoned (e.g., dumping of pollutants into streams), they will want to know what harm was done all those years before you banned this harmful practice.

- **They will be waiting to hear the results of your efforts.** Once implemented, audiences will be watching for reports on how you did relative to published goals (e.g., in annual reports), and if you didn't achieve the desired results, what further measures will be taken. It will be important to report the bad news as well as the good, externally as well as internally.

Keys to Success

Many keys to success deal with challenges and concerns facing the implementation and reporting of new business initiatives. In summary, corporate managers encourage others to decrease skepticism and criticism by being preemptive; choosing an issue that meets a business as well as a social need; making a long-term commitment; building employee enthusiasm; developing and implementing infrastructures to support the promise; and providing open, honest, and direct communications.

Patagonia's efforts to support volunteer efforts were described in Chapter 7. Their efforts to support fair labor practices are highlighted here.

Case #6: Patagonia and Fair Labor Practices[29]

Some say that Patagonia's success over the years can be attributed in large part to its founder Yvon Chouinard's firsthand knowledge and love of the outdoors. But he also had another passion—fair labor practices—and decided early on that the greatest good his company could do for change was to develop Patagonia as an exemplar for other companies to emulate.[30]

Many people are familiar with the term "sweatshop" and many more were when a human rights group, The National Labor Committee, reported on specific incidents in 1996 in Honduras that gained national attention. Patagonia had heard similar tales of conditions in garment factories from Asia to the Americas—factories with workweeks seeming to have no end, subminimum wages, no overtime pay, unsafe work conditions, and child labor.

Like most clothing companies, Patagonia does not make their own products, nor do they own the more than 70 factories that do. They concentrate on their strengths: designing, testing, and selling their gear. They pay other companies with technical expertise and equipment to produce the fabrics and do the actual cutting and sewing. In the past, they relied primarily on selecting factories that shared their values of integrity and environmentalism, and didn't have to make a lot of extra effort to achieve this. Their demand for high quality and their close relationships with the small number of factories they did business with helped assure this. In the early 1990s, as they expanded, however, they decided to test these assumptions and began regular factory visits that led to a strengthened policy, one that eliminated their working with any factory they couldn't visit for a formal review of both product quality and working conditions.

After the incidents in 1996, and in response to President Clinton's *No Sweat Initiative*, they created an even more formal process, used only third-party auditors, and became a founding member of the Fair Labor Association, an independent multi-stakeholder verification and training organization that audits their factories.

The following perspective on Patagonia's keys to success for their fair labor practices is offered by Joe Starinchak, outreach coordinator for the U.S. Fish and Wildlife Service:

In working for America's only national fish and wildlife conservation agency, we're observing the cumulative impact of 312 million people on the environment. This toll is manifesting itself in many ways, all of which impact fish and wildlife. While consumption and our throwaway mentality contribute extensively, businesses have been implicated as the primary vehicle for our country's destruction of nature. However, even though they are the main culprit because of their economic and societal roles, businesses represent the best chance to solve this crisis. They have the incentives, operational know-how, scalability and ingenuity to respond to the global challenges we face today.

With this perspective, I have sought out and have developed working relations with businesses that have embraced sustainability. As a nebulous and overused concept, sustainability has become operationally defined as a company's ability to produce social, environmental and financial benefits. In six years of working with Patagonia, their operations are unique and amazing. Not only have they elevated the environment into every aspect of their decision-making, they have also elevated the social side of business. By championing fair labor practices, Patagonia is a founding member of the Fair Labor Association and they regularly conduct social audits to ensure that fair labor practices are a part of their supply chain. Whether it is environmental sustainability or the company's fair labor practices, these operational benchmarks can be traced directly to the owner of the company, Yvon Chouinard. His unyielding ethics, belief in the power of business and his willingness to push the limits for sustainability by hiring the best people and allowing them to flourish represent Patagonia's keys to success.[31]

When Should a Corporation Consider a Major Socially Responsible Business Practice Initiative?

Some consider the word *responsibility*, whether at the personal or corporate level, to mean *ability to respond*, as opposed to a focus on blame. Looking at it from this perspective, a corporation should regularly review and consider new or modified business practices that will improve the quality of life, and at the same time, provide some net benefit to the corporation, ideally financial, operational, relationship-building, or marketing in nature. Circumstances that might provide this optimal situation could include the following, with most references to examples cited earlier in this chapter:

- When a company has been **offered a financial incentive** to alter a business practice for the benefit of the environment, most typically from an external public or regulatory agency.
- When the adoption of **a new practice would reduce operating costs**, as well as contribute to a social issue.
- When a **current business practice can be identified (in part) as contributing to an important social problem** and modifications and improvements would help address the issue.
- When there is an **opportunity to improve employee health, safety, or well-being** by altering a business practice or investing in infrastructures and educational experiences.
- When engagement in this practice **can add an important point of differentiation** to target markets in a crowded, undifferentiated marketplace.
- When there are **opportunities for alliances that will strengthen the brand's positioning**.
- When the adaptation of the practice could actually **improve product quality or performance**, providing increased value and points of difference.
- When investments or changes in practices will **strengthen relationships with suppliers or distributors**.

Developing the Initiative

Based on experiences of professionals, including ones contributing to cases in this chapter, major decisions involved in adapting and implementing socially responsible business practices will focus on the process of carefully selecting the social issue that the initiative will support; developing integrated, strategic plans for implementation; and setting and tracking measurable goals.

As is apparent in many of the case examples, most recommend that *business needs should be identified first.* It might be an emerging or current objective for reduced operating costs or improved supplier relations or reduced regulatory oversight, or there may be important marketing challenges such as repositioning of the brand or standing out in an undifferentiated, crowded marketplace. Next, major social problems are identified that the company could contribute to through altered business practices and investments. As with other social initiatives, a cause should be selected that is substantial, consistent with company mission and values, and that key publics care about. The actual initiative (business practice to be adopted or altered) is then selected based on an assessment of potential for meeting business objectives and contributing to the social cause.

Experienced experts have also stressed the need for an *integrated, planned approach for implementation,* one involving and backed by executive management. New or revised business practices should be supported through employee communications and any related needs for education and training. And in many cases, there will need to be important changes to infrastructure to facilitate the adaptation of new practices and to ensure more substance than rhetoric.

And finally, encourage accountability by *setting goals and establishing mechanisms for measuring, tracking and reporting results.* Many recommend developing communication plans that include publishing goals and reporting on progress. And in the event that goals are not met, identifying and then publishing corrective action plans to ensure continued commitment and progress toward the goal.

In Summary

Socially responsible business practice initiatives involve corporations adapting and conducting discretionary business practices and investments that support social causes to improve community well-being and protect the environment. Key distinctions include a focus on activities that are discretionary; community is interpreted broadly; and community well-being can refer to health and safety, as well as psychological and emotional needs.

Over the past decade, there has been a shift from adapting more responsible business practices as a result of regulatory citations, consumer complaints, and special interest group pressures to engage in proactive research exploring corporate solutions to social problems and incorporating new business practices that will support these issues. Several factors may be contributing to this shift: evidence that socially responsible business practices can actually increase profits; a global marketplace with increased competition and consumer options; interest in increased worker productivity and retention; and increased visibility and coverage of corporate socially responsible (or not) activities.

Most initiatives relate to altering internal procedures and policies, external reporting of consumer and investor information, making provisions for customer access and privacy, and making decisions regarding facility and plant locations.

Financial benefits have been associated with decreased operating costs, monetary incentives from regulatory agencies, and increased employee productivity and retention. Marketing benefits are numerous, as well, with the potential for increasing community goodwill, creating brand preference, building brand positioning, improving product quality, and increasing corporate respect. These activities also provide opportunities to build relationships with external partners such as regulatory agencies, suppliers, and nonprofit organizations.

Experts warn that corporate motives for new and more responsible business practices will be questioned, actions will be judged, and results will be scrutinized. Corporate managers encourage others to decrease skepticism and criticism by being preemptive; choosing an issue that meets a business as well as a social need; making a long-term commitment; building employee enthusiasm; developing and implementing infrastructures to support the promise; and providing open, honest, and direct communications.

Major decisions involved in adopting and implementing socially responsible business practices will focus on the process of carefully selecting the social issue that the initiative will support; developing integrated, strategic plans for implementation; and setting measurable goals and establishing plans for tracking and reporting results.

IV

Offense and Defense

9

Offense: Choosing a Social Problem to Alleviate

It is true that economic and social objectives have long been seen as distinct and often competing. But this is a false dichotomy; it represents an increasingly obsolete perspective in a world of open, knowledge-based competition. Companies do not function in isolation from the society around them. In fact, their ability to compete depends heavily on the circumstances of the locations where they operate.

—Michael E. Porter and Mark R. Kramer[1]

This book has been written to support managers to choose, develop, implement, and evaluate marketing and corporate social initiatives such that they will do the most good for the company and the cause. Its purpose is to help guide decision-making in the area of corporate social responsibility, resulting in efforts that do the most social, environmental, and economic good. It is, in the end, intended to help maximize the return on discretionary corporate investments in improving the quality of life, with the hope that future participation in these efforts is increasingly satisfying. We discussed early on that it is no longer just *acceptable* that the corporation does well by doing good. It is *expected*.

So, what can we conclude is *good*?

For the cause that is supported by corporate social initiatives, *good* is the increased realization of several potential benefits. The six marketing and corporate initiatives featured in this book have been seen to provide multiple benefits for a cause and for the charities supporting these causes. As many recipients of corporate contributions to their cause have indicated, these initiatives can:

- *Enhance public awareness and concern for the cause* through support of promotional communication efforts (e.g., Chipotle Mexican Grill's efforts to increase concerns with processed food).
- *Support fundraising* by encouraging customers and others in the community to contribute to causes (e.g., British Airway's 15-year campaign that collected pocket change from passengers for children's charities).
- *Increase community participation in cause-related activities* by providing promotional support and use of distribution channels (e.g., PetSmart providing space in their stores for adopting animals).
- *Support efforts to influence individual behavior change and industry business practices* that improve public health (e.g., Coca-Cola Africa Foundation's HIV/AIDS Workplace initiative) and safety (e.g., FedEx's Safe Kids Walk This Way program) and protect the environment (e.g., Best Buy's effort to support recycling of used computers).
- *Provide increased funds and other resources* that help charities and cause efforts, make ends meet, and/or expand efforts (e.g., General Mills providing grants for projects that improve youth nutrition and physical activity levels).
- *Increase the number of volunteers* donating their expertise, ideas, and physical labor to a cause by promoting volunteerism in the community and supporting employee volunteer efforts (e.g., IBM supporting more than 300,000 employees in 120 countries to contribute 2.8 million hours of service on just one day in 2011).

At the same time, we have seen through examples and perspectives provided by corporate executives how these efforts to give back to the community also give back to the company. They can help:

- *Build a strong corporate reputation*, as key constituents observe actions that support promises of good corporate citizenship and responsibility (e.g., Subway's initiative to help reduce heart disease).
- *Contribute to overall business goals* by opening up new markets or providing opportunities to build long-term relationships with distributors

and suppliers (e.g., Starbucks' initiatives to support farmers that provide shade-grown coffee).

- *Attract and retain a motivated workforce* by being known for involvement in the community and for providing employees with an opportunity to become involved in something they care about and to receive corporate support and recognition for doing so (e.g., the personal story by the Pfizer employee about how volunteering helped him fulfill a dream to have a positive impact on people in Africa).
- *Reduce operating costs* by adopting new socially responsible business practices such as procedures that increase efficiency and reduce costs for materials (e.g., DuPont saving several billion dollars by reducing energy consumption).
- *Reduce regulatory oversight* by working closely with regulatory agencies to meet or exceed guidelines, thereby increasing confidence and building strong relationships for the future (e.g., Patagonia's commitment to fair labor practices, including becoming a founding member of the Fair Labor Association).
- *Support marketing objectives* by building traffic, enhancing brand positioning, creating product differentiation, reaching niche markets, attracting new customers, and increasing sales, especially when products and services are an integral part of program efforts (e.g., Lowe's initiative to support water conservation, including connections of their products to specific conservation practices).
- *Build strong community relationships* with organizations and agencies that can provide technical expertise, extend campaign reach by providing access to members and donors also supporting the cause, and offer credible endorsement for the corporation's effort and commitment (e.g., Tylenol is a national sponsor of the Arthritis Foundation).
- *Leverage current corporate social initiative efforts and investments* by including additional ones that further connect the company to the cause, thus increasing chances for both an impact on the social problem, and a greater return on current investments (e.g., Johnson & Johnson adding *The Art of Nursing: Portrait of Thanks Mosaic Project*, the cause-related marketing initiative that donates $1 to the Foundation of the National Student Nurses Association for every photo uploaded to a website).

Best Practices for Choosing a Social Problem to Alleviate

Social needs seem endless and the options to provide support overwhelming. At a global as well as at a local level, we should have no problem finding a cause that needs corporate support, from those that help ensure basic needs are met in the community to those that improve health, prevent injuries, increase public involvement, improve education, and protect the environment. The problem is in choosing well among the many options. The following six practices help guide strategic decision making.

Choose Only a Few Social Issues to Support

Many executives interviewed for this text stressed the importance of picking only a few major social issues as a focal point for corporate citizenship and giving. As you read in Chapter 2, education is a longtime, top-priority social issue for Target, and a significant portion of their contributions fund programs and partnerships dedicated to helping more U.S. children learn how to read. The benefits of this practice seem obvious now and are reminiscent of benefits a corporation realizes when it selects target markets and develops entire marketing strategies to win them over. It increases chances that the company can actually have an impact on a particular social initiative, as resources are focused and multiple initiatives aimed at one cause. It makes it easier to "say no" to others, as the company can point to their priority areas for giving. It increases chances that the company will be able to develop long-term, often coveted relationships with strong desirable partners, as they, too, will be looking for a partner willing to provide significant resources and make a long-term commitment. Finally, targeting resources in a few areas increases chances that the corporation will be connected to the cause and will therefore leverage potential brand positioning and other desired marketing benefits.

Choose Those That Are of Concern in the Communities Where You Do Business

Improving communities where facilities are located, where future workforces will be recruited, and where customers lives can support both social and economic goals. As noted earlier, Lowe's demonstrated this practice when it focused on the issue of water conservation in a community threatened by drought, and Levi Strauss was one of the first to step forward in the San Francisco Bay area to support HIV/AIDS prevention. Following the terrorist attacks of September 11, 2001, American Express recognized the need for, and committed itself to, being an active part of a revitalization in lower Manhattan, a reflection of the company's commitment to its home community. Focusing on issues of concern in these communities and for those living in them increases chances that efforts will be noticed and valued among key publics. It adds credibility and believability to standard statements in annual reports and sales catalogues proclaiming, "We believe in giving back to the communities where we do business." It may also help solve real problems facing a business, such as ensuring a future trained workforce, quality suppliers, and even a robust economy.

Choose Causes That Have Synergy with Mission, Values, Products, and Services

Just as products and services are offered that are consistent with a company's mission and then promoted and delivered in a way that reflects a company's values, areas of focus for social initiatives should have the same synergy. Often the choice will be obvious, as it must have been for Crest when they learned more about the "silent epidemic" of oral disease in America, especially among low-income children, and as it must have been for the life vest manufacturer Mustang Survival when approached by a regional children's hospital to support a campaign to help reduce the number of drownings among children in this state. For AT&T, the decision to partner with the American Red Cross, which included donations of phones to support the organization's disaster relief efforts, seems easy and the same for General Motors' dealerships to support car-seat safety checks. When corporations contribute to causes that make sense, we find consumers are less suspicious, investors are less likely to judge the effort as peripheral, and employees are more likely to have the needed expertise and passion to volunteer.

Choose Causes That Have Potential to Support Business Goals: Marketing, Supplier Relations, Increased Productivity, and Cost Reductions

Subject experts such as Michael Porter of Harvard Business School and Mark Kramer, managing director of the Foundation Strategy Group, say this simultaneous support for business goals is true strategic philanthropy : "It is only where corporate expenditures produce simultaneous social and economic gains that corporate philanthropy and shareholder interests converge. It is here that philanthropy is truly strategic."[2] Pfizer was clear about the benefits of assigning a volunteer to provide retail sales and marketing techniques to employees of Population Services International, a provider of health products and services in developing countries. In this, as in similar examples, the corporation chose to support a social issue that had potential for contributing to business goals, as well as a connection to the company's mission, values, communities, and products and services.

Choose Issues That Are of Concern to Key Constituent Groups: Employees, Target Markets, Customers, Investors, and Corporate Leaders

Support for social initiatives will be leveraged when the cause is also one near and dear to our key publics, both internal and external. LensCrafters' successful collection of used eyeglasses is a reflection of the involvement and enthusiasm that customer-contact staff have for giving the *Gift of Sight*. Parents were most likely grateful when Pampers starting printing *Back to Sleep* on newborn diapers, a just-in-time reminder of an action that can help prevent SIDS. Potential customers for Silk Soymilk may be motivated to choose this product from the lineup on the shelf when they hear of the parent company's commitment to using 100 percent wind power for all of its operations. Investors were perhaps encouraged if they read reports from Nike about their creation of a new line of shoes expected to appeal to Native American and Aboriginal communities in North America. And corporate leaders are probably pleased, perhaps even relieved, when they receive reports on employee volunteer efforts such as Sellen Construction's effort to bring smiles to hospitalized children. The success of most social initiatives reviewed in this book have clearly relied on the connection and resonance the effort has with one or more of these key constituent groups. Such connection should therefore be factored into decisions on what causes to support.

Choose Causes That Can Be Supported over a Long Term

Achieving maximum benefits for the company (and the cause) often depends on long-term commitments, frequently considered three or more years. As with most communication efforts, it takes numerous exposures to messages and events before an effort is noticed and before targeted audiences for fundraising efforts and especially behavior change campaigns will act. It also most often takes a long period of time to make a dent in a social problem, whether supporting medical research for cancer cures or reducing levels of toxic emissions from manufacturing plants. Long-term commitments can also be more economical, as early years in program efforts are often consumed with steep learning curves and coordination with cause partners, and efforts get more efficient in subsequent years. And finally, those companies who stick with the cause over the years are more likely to be able to own it, as does The Body Shop after staying the course with campaigns Against Animal Testing in the cosmetic industry. Even if a competitor decided to move in on this point of differentiation, many consumers are likely to know that The Body Shop was there first.

Those who practice this principle ask themselves and their partners whether this effort will be one that will be a social concern over the next several years; whether it will have continued connection to the company's mission, values, products, and services; and whether key publics will continue to care. Given these criteria, it stands to reason that the Energizer Battery Company has made a long-term commitment to a *Change Your Clock. Change Your Battery*® campaign; for Target to continue to help local public schools; and for Subway to continue to support the American Heart Association.

10 Offense: Selecting a Social Initiative to Support the Cause

We're all in it together. We're an eclectic collective of environmental advocates along with some innovative ice cream and music-makers, working in concert to tackle the man-made problem of global warming.[1]

—Ben & Jerry's
SaveOurEnvironment.org

Once a social issue has been chosen (ideally as an area of focus for the company), all six initiatives should then be evaluated for potential to contribute to the cause, as well as to the company. Table 10.1 summarizes major strengths associated with each initiative, both for the company and for the cause. As the following guidelines suggest, managers will evaluate initiatives relative to their potential for contributing to specific business and cause-related objectives and goals. These best practices also incorporate additional considerations based on perspectives of managers interviewed for this book, as well as academic and other experts on corporate social responsibility.

Select Initiatives That Best Meet Business Objectives and Goals

Corporate involvement in social initiatives can support a variety of business objectives and goals. At this phase in the planning process, managers should identify priority needs that might be met through supporting cause

TABLE 10.1 Major Potential Benefits from Corporate Social Initiatives

	Cause Promotions	Cause-Related Marketing	Social Marketing	Corporate Philanthropy	Community Volunteering	Socially Responsible Business Practices
For the Cause						
Increased awareness and concern for the cause	Major strength	Major strength	Major strength			
Support for fund-raising	Major strength	Major strength				
Increased participation in cause	Major strength		Major strength		Major strength	Major strength
Changes in public behavior			Major strength		Major strength	
Increased funds and other resources	Major strength	Major strength		Major strength		
For the Company						
Build strong corporate reputation	Major strength		Major strength	Major strength	Major strength	Major strength
Contribute to business goals	Major strength		Major strength	Major strength	Major strength	Major strength
Attract and retain motivated workforce	Major strength		Major strength	Major strength	Major strength	Major strength
Reduce operating costs						Major strength
Reduce regulatory oversight						Major strength
Support marketing objectives	Major strength	Major strength	Major strength			
Build strong community relationships	Major strength	Major strength	Major strength	Major strength	Major strength	Major strength
Leverage current corporate social initiatives	Major strength		Major strength	Major strength	Major strength	Major strength

efforts, considering financial, marketing, corporate reputation, operational, and employee-related goals. Premera Blue Cross, for example, is an insurance company in Washington state with an interest in reducing costs associated with upper respiratory infections. This was one factor that guided their decision to partner with others to support a cause promotion initiative that would increase public awareness and concern with the overuse of antibiotics, as well as a social marketing initiative to encourage physicians to practice more conservative measures when prescribing antibiotics.

Select Initiatives That Meet Priority Needs for the Cause

Initiatives that have the potential to meet business objectives and goals are then evaluated against priority needs that have been identified for a cause, zeroing in on those with the most perceived potential to meet both needs. For example, Safeco, a personal and business insurance company, was interested in helping to reduce damage of property from wildfires. Their first offer to a fire department in Oregon, which was experiencing a series of wildfires, was to donate money to help purchase firefighting equipment—a philanthropic initiative. Further discussions with the fire marshal in Oregon, however, shifted the initiative to supporting a social marketing campaign that would persuade homeowners to establish defensible space around their houses. The reasons were expressed well by the fire marshal, who claimed, "A new piece of equipment might save one more home. But to really save homes, individuals have to take personal responsibility for their property before the fire."[2] This social marketing initiative has the potential to do the most good for Safeco, supporting marketing goals and potential cost reductions, as well as for the prevention of wildfires in this region and in others around the country.

Select Multiple Initiatives for a Single Cause, Adding Ones Missing for Current Cause Efforts

Just as skilled marketers practice a fundamental principle of integrated marketing communications, those involved in selecting social initiatives can benefit from a similar practice. In the case of an integrated marketing approach, a company's communications and media channels are coordinated so that messages regarding the company and its products are "consistent, clear, and compelling."[3] Similarly, when a company engages in a variety of initiatives to support a chosen social issue, it increases the likelihood that the company will be clearly associated with the cause, and at the same time will be able to provide more support for the cause than it might through just one initiative.

Ben & Jerry's global warming campaign *Lick Global Warming* exemplifies this practice. One component of this effort is a cause promotion to increase awareness of the threats of global warming. The effort is integrated into other initiatives, as well. In 2006, it included a cause-related marketing effort, where a percentage of sales of the *One Sweet Whirled* ice cream flavor went to organizations working to fight global warming; a social marketing component, where consumers were encouraged to send letters to congress and to make personal pledges to reduce their carbon dioxide emissions; a philanthropic initiative, where grants have been provided for efforts aimed at addressing global warming; a community volunteer component, in which employees are encouraged to "park your car for a day" and find alternative transportation to work; and socially responsible business practices, one of which was expressed on their website in 2011 :

> Our ongoing commitment to the environment also involves working closely with Efficiency Vermont to target areas for energy improvement within our factories—from reducing waste to installing smaller and shorter pipes to increase production efficiency.... Some people think a warmer planet is good for ice cream sales. We realize it's more than bad for business—it threatens our existence![4]

Select Initiatives Representing the Most Potential for Strong Community Partners

Companies should also evaluate potential initiatives relative to their ability to create relationships with partners in the nonprofit as well as the public sector, ones that will add resources as well as credibility to the initiative. Crest, for example, is interested in improving oral health, especially among children in underserved minority communities. This resulted in a cause promotion and social marketing partnership with the Boys & Girls Clubs of America, which was applauded by the U.S. Surgeon General. And Johnson & Johnson's campaign to enhance the image of the nursing profession built relationships with key publics for the company, including healthcare organizations and nursing associations around the world.

Select Initiatives Where You Have a History of Experience

Each of the six initiatives has its own unique set of keys to success, as well as challenges. One consideration when choosing among potential new initiatives is the company's track record and experience in developing and managing prior initiatives, providing an opportunity to capitalize on lessons learned and to be up and running with greater efficiencies. American Express's campaign to revitalize lower Manhattan after 9/11 no doubt benefited from the company's earlier experiences in cause-related marketing efforts to restore the Statue of Liberty. And looking back at Johnson & Johnson's strategic focus on nursing, adding the volunteer initiative encouraging current nurses to recruit new nurses to the field certainly contributed to their success.

Select Initiatives That Will Leverage Current Abundant Resources

Consider which initiative(s) will leverage current resources, especially those that are both highly valued by the cause and underutilized by the company or that can be provided at a low cost. Resources to support cause promotions, for example, may simply require additional messages on existing communications (e.g., Food Network providing increased exposure for Share Our Strength's *No Kid Hungry* campaign through network airtime, *Food Network Magazine*, and online presence). Cause-related marketing efforts can often piggyback on current paid product advertising (e.g., Avon's Pink Nailwear Pro Nail Enamel promotes the benefits of early detection of breast cancers). Social marketing efforts can benefit from existing distribution channels and product labeling (e.g., food growers' support for the 5-A-Day program that includes efforts such as stickers on fruit and the 5-A-Day logo on vegetable packages). Philanthropic initiatives can include donation of existing resources (e.g., Microsoft providing technology skills training for disadvantaged individuals through community-based technology and learning centers, including grants of software). Community volunteering efforts can be tied to existing research and development activities (e.g., Pfizer's Global Health Fellows Program, where assignments are focused on those related to Pfizer's core competencies including the improvement of health service delivery systems). And socially responsible business practices can be incorporated when designing new facilities and revamping current operational procedures (e.g., Starbucks' goal of achieving LEED® certification of all new company-owned stores worldwide beginning in late 2010).

11

Offense: Developing Social Initiative Programs

When it comes to making buying decisions in this tough economic climate, the customer has many choices. We are seeing greater support for Patagonia through increasing sales in this down market and we believe that much of this stems from high levels of customer loyalty to all of the values embodied by our brand: from our high quality products, to our great employee programs, to our focus on conservation and environmental sustainability.[1]

—Bill Klyn
International Business Development Manager,
Patagonia

Many of the best practices compiled here for developing corporate social initiative programs have been formulated in response to the concerns and challenges identified by those sharing their experiences in this book, as well as by academic and subject experts. We heard of concerns associated with appropriate visibility for the corporation's efforts, coordination with cause partners, staff time for involvement and administration, potential need for external expertise, expenses for promotions, anticipated public skepticism, and tracking resource expenditures. Major concerns associated with each initiative are summarized in Table 11.1, and the following descriptions of best practices are intended to minimize the potential risks and costs associated with development processes and implementation of each initiative.

211

TABLE 11.1 Major Potential Concerns in Undertaking Initiatives

	Cause Promotions	Cause-Related Marketing	Social Marketing	Corporate Philanthropy	Community Volunteering	Socially Responsible Business Practices
Visibility for corporate efforts can easily be lost.	Major potential concern			Major potential concern	Major potential concern	Major potential concern
Coordination with cause partners can be time consuming.	Major potential concern	Major potential concern	Major potential concern			
Staff time and involvement can be significant.	Major potential concern	Major potential concern	Major potential concern		Major potential concern	
Efforts may require external expertise.			Major potential concern			Major potential concern
Promotional expenses can be significant.	Major potential concern	Major potential concern	Major potential concern			
Consumers may be skeptical of corporate motivations and commitment.	Major potential concern	Major potential concern				Major potential concern
Tracking resource expenditures and value can be difficult and expensive.				Major potential concern	Major potential concern	

Form Internal, Cross-Functional Teams to Develop Plans

Program plans often have the most impact and are most efficiently administered when developed by teams with representatives from various departments within the company—teams that may include those from marketing, finance, operations, facilities management, human resources, and executive administration. This is especially important at the beginning of campaign planning, when program objectives and goals are established, as such teamwork can be critical to building internal support for activities as well as setting realistic expectations for program outcomes. Microsoft's effort to support alternative transportation for employees began with surveys to reveal common barriers. This then led to multiple requirements that would rely on a variety of teams, including ones to operate a fleet of mini-buses, an online reservation tool, and a guaranteed ride home in case of emergencies.

Include Community Partners in Plan Development

Similarly, involving community partners early in the planning process will maximize program effectiveness and efficiency. Partners should be included in establishing program goals and objectives, laying the foundation for strategic solutions, and aligning expectations regarding outcomes. They should be included in developing strategic communication plans, especially decisions regarding target audiences, key messages, and key media channels, a process that will help avoid costly and time-consuming reworks of promotional materials. Partner involvement in crafting implementation plans will help avoid misunderstandings and confusion regarding roles and responsibilities. The water conservation campaign that Lowe's participated in, for example, required strategic coordination with all community partners, which included more local city governments, private and public utilities, Arizona Department of Water Resources, the Arizona Municipal Water Users Association, and a communications firm.

Establish Clear Objectives and Measurable Goals (Outcomes) for the Company

The often difficult and elusive task of program evaluation can be eased considerably by taking time in the program planning process to establish clear objectives and measurable goals for the initiative, ones that will then be used to evaluate program success. Corporate objectives may include those related to business needs (e.g., reduce energy costs in new facilities), marketing needs (e.g., increase share of toddlers' life vest sales), employee-related needs (e.g., attract talented, motivated employees), or needs related to corporate reputation and goodwill (e.g., reduce levels of toxic emissions). Goals, in this typology, are ideally specific, measurable, achievable, realistic, and time bound (SMART).[2]

Establish Clear Objectives and Measurable Goals (Outcomes) for the Cause

This same practice holds true for the cause. Quantifiable goals might be related to volunteer hours, equipment that will be donated, media impressions that will be provided, or actual dollars that will be raised. In Chipotle's story, for example, we learned that the company's established clear goal for their 2010 promotion was to raise $1 million for Jamie Oliver's Food Revolution. And they fulfilled their promise.

Develop a Communications Plan

Opinions regarding corporate recognition for social initiatives vary significantly. Some recommend a "don't be shy approach" and others have a company policy to "let others do the talking." Regardless of philosophic perspectives on corporate recognition, developing a communications plan for the initiative is a best practice. Often, it will necessitate separate strategies for several key audiences: target markets for the initiative; external publics, such as investors, regulatory agencies, and suppliers; and employees and other internal stakeholders. Communication plans should identify traditional strategic components including communication objectives, key messages, key messengers, and key media channels for each of the targeted audiences. Communication objectives should signal desired audience outcomes (e.g., increased awareness, concern, participation, and/or individual behavior change). Including a *call to action* as a key message has been show to assist tracking and evaluation efforts, and utilization of existing media channels and distribution outlets can help reduce promotional costs.

Identify and Plan for Additional Strategic Elements

Most initiatives will include additional strategic elements *beyond communications* that are incorporated into the planning process. Cause promotions often rely on employee involvement, benefiting from a coordinated effort, such as the one that was key to the Fed Ex event in New York City where drivers showed kids firsthand how limited visibility can be when driving. Cause-related marketing initiatives involve decisions regarding product ties, timelines, and more complex agreements with cause partners, as must have been the case with the General Mills partnership with Ford that made donations to schools based, in part, on consumers watching Ford videos online. Social marketing initiatives often involve support for public engagement, as Levi's *Care Tag* program did, including messaging encouraging people to help the planet by: washing less often, washing in cold water, line drying, and donating to Goodwill when no longer needed. Philanthropic planning efforts will involve deliberation over specific forms of giving, and then development of programs for implementation, as we can imagine must have taken place when choosing criteria for Starbucks Youth Action Grants, awarding $1.6 million in 2010 alone. Community volunteering will also entail selecting types of employee support and then, in many cases, developing systems for engagement like IBM's On Demand Community that helps connect employees and retirees to programs in their communities. And socially responsible business practices can require plans for significant changes as they may involve new work processes, negotiations with suppliers, and decisions on facility design and locations.

Get Senior Management Buy-In

Most managers seeking support for corporate social initiatives recognize and report that executives express a desire to give back and to care for the communities that support their businesses. The challenge is in getting approval for what will be supported and for how much. Earlier in this chapter, a best practice of involving senior management in choosing causes for focus and agreeing on types of initiative to support the cause was emphasized. The same principle holds true for the development of implementation plans, as this is when important decisions regarding budgets will be made, staff resources will be committed, and current business practices may be altered. Planners most likely recognize the need to be prepared for tough questions and straight answers.

Agreement is especially important prior to finalizing program objectives and goals, budgets, and resource allocation. Some executives are reluctant to make a pledge, at the beginning of the fiscal year, of a certain amount of money for corporate social initiatives that can be tied to earnings. Curt Weeden offers this perspective:

> CEOs need to accept the premise that the level of social investing is largely a by-product of a company's historic profitability. In a nutshell, here's how it works. Corporations invest a percentage of an average of the pretax earnings of their previous three years. There is an emergency brake that can be pulled if needed—the CEO retains the power to stop social investing in its tracks if the current year's profits are in jeopardy.[3]

12

Offense: Evaluating Efforts

How to measure the value and results of corporate philanthropy remains one of corporate giving professionals' greatest challenges. Social and business benefits are often long-term or intangible, which make systematic measurement complex. And yet: Corporate philanthropy faces increasing pressures to show it is as strategic, cost-effective, and value-enhancing as possible. The industry faces a critical need to assess current practices and measurement trends, clarify the demands practitioners face for impact evidence, and identify the most promising steps forward in order to make progress on these challenges.[1]

—Terence Lim, PhD
Committee Encouraging Corporate Philanthropy
Manager, Standards and Measurement

The importance of evaluating efforts and calculating returns on corporate social investments is easily understood. Most recognize it is the right thing to do in order to improve future programs as well as to fulfill commitments for responsible reporting to stakeholders. We know we should practice the same rigorous disciplines that govern our business investments. The challenge is in doing it. Of all best practices related to corporate social initiatives, *evaluation strategies* remains the least fully developed. The following six best practices suggest at least a structure for identifying data collection needs and a framework for organizing information into meaningful categories, those that are *output-oriented* and those that are *outcome-oriented*.

Determine Purpose of Evaluation

As with most research-related projects, we begin with the end in mind, answering the question: "What will the information be used for?" Options range from wanting to improve future efforts, to needing to report back to our partners and stakeholders, to being able to calculate a specific return on our investment, to knowing when we have reached an optimal giving level where further investments have a decreasing rate of return for the corporation as well as for the cause. The answer for many, we suspect, is that we want answers for all of these. But the question should be asked, as resources needed to gather this information have varying monetary implications.

Measure and Report Resource Outputs

The focus at this point is on resources that the corporation contributes to the initiative and the total monetary value of those resources. Basic categories will include cash contributions as well as (ideally) the monetary value of in-kind donations of products and services, staff hours, and retail space. It is important to stress that information gathered from this effort is not intended to measure the impact of these investments. It is intended to establish a total monetary value for the investment, which will then be used as a basis upon which to evaluate the efficiencies and actual costs associated with outcomes produced as a result of these output levels.

Methodologies for collecting this information will include internal record keeping (e.g., number of staff hours), financial reports (e.g., cash contributions), and information provided by cause partners and public relations and advertising firms.

In recent years, progress has been made in developing measurement practices and standards that will assist corporations in calculating and reporting the totality of their giving programs. In 2002, for example, The Committee to Encourage Corporate Philanthropy entered into a strategic partnership with the American Productivity and Quality Center, the Center for Corporate Citizenship at Boston College, and the Corporate Citizenship Company, to build a framework of definitions, processes, and systems that would more effectively measure corporate giving. Included in this effort is the development of a tool kit that will provide users with global standards, measurement frameworks, management tools, and collaborative networks. The intent is to support companies to "effectively and completely capture and communicate their contributions to society according to a common framework."[2] As of December 2011, this benchmarking tool features over $85 billion in corporate giving data, including cash giving, non-cash giving, volunteer program details, management and programs costs, and giving focus areas.[3]

Measure and Report Outcomes for the *Company,* Based on Initiative Objectives and Goals

The focus now turns to measuring outcomes associated with corporate outputs, with an emphasis on measurement of accomplishments relative to corporate objectives and goals established in the early planning stages.

Outcomes associated with *general business goals and objectives* would include tracking and reporting on desired accomplishments most often related to enhanced corporate image, strengthened stakeholder perceptions, reductions in operating costs, increases in employee satisfaction, reduction in expenditures related to employee recruitment and turnover, reduction in regulatory oversight, and receipt of any additional incentives or grants for meeting environmental or community impact guidelines.

Outcomes associated with *marketing goals and objectives* would include tracking and reporting on levels of awareness of the corporation's involvement in the initiative; enhancements to brand identity; and increases in customer loyalty, sales, traffic, and media exposures achieved through the initiative. Special efforts should be made to collect information on total levels of exposure created by corporate expenditures (e.g., total impressions achieved through paid media, publicity, material distribution, special events, and website visits) and the monetary value associated with this. A cause promotion initiative, for example, that included a direct contribution of $35,000 for paid advertising may have actually received $75,000 worth of media exposure due to qualifications by the charity for nonprofit rates, often at a 50-percent discount.

Methodologies associated with measuring these outcomes are often more complex and more expensive than those required for assessing outputs. Some of this information can come from internal records and existing tracking systems (e.g., sales data) and reports from external agencies (e.g., broadcast stations) and community partners (e.g., a charity who reports on the number of people who stopped by their booth sponsored by the corporation at a health fair). However, a majority of these factors will require custom consumer surveys, with sample sizes large enough to be representative and methodologies that can be replicated in the future. They may even require establishing a baseline measure, a measure at specific campaign milestones, and a post survey.

Once outcomes are quantified, attempts should be made to determine return on investment. As a simplistic example, a corporation that contributed $50,000 for promotional expenditures related to a charity walk that hypothetically generated 500,000 impressions in the marketplace would assess the cost for each impression at 10 cents, and then compare this cost with prior similar efforts. A cause-related marketing effort that generated 1,000 more product sales than in prior comparable years and increased awareness of the featured product by 25 percent among target markets would be evaluated against total contributions made to the initiative, and again, compared with prior similar efforts.

As noted earlier, this discipline is in its early stages. Managers are encouraged to become more rigorous in tracking, building historic databases, and creating metrics to guide evaluation and decision making.

Measure and Report Outcomes for the *Cause,* Based on Initiative Objectives and Goals

As with outcomes for the corporation, of interest here are accomplishments relative to objectives and goals that were established earlier for the cause and/or charity, ones specifically supported by the corporation's involvement in the initiative. Basic measures may include one or more of the following, most often supported by cause promotions and cause-related marketing initiatives:

- Changes in awareness of the social issue.
- Changes in levels of concern for the social issue.
- Number of volunteers recruited by the initiative and associated hours.
- Amount of funds raised for the charity or issue.

In some cases, outcomes may be expressed in more tangible terms, such as outcomes associated more often with social marketing initiatives, corporate philanthropy, community volunteering, and socially responsible business practices. Examples that could be connected to a specific corporate initiative include the following:

- Number of children fed in after-school programs.
- Number of homeless people sheltered.
- Rises in test scores.
- Tons of waste diverted from landfills.
- Reduction in toxic emissions.
- Number of low-flow toilets installed.
- Number of computers recycled.
- Number of families provided a home away from home while their children were in hospitals.
- Increase in number of toddlers with life vests on a specific beach.
- Number of homeowners who took recommended steps for fire prevention.

This measurement effort should be conducted in cooperation with cause partners. Ideally, the information is collected by others and then reported to the corporation. Corporate managers are encouraged to negotiate for this arrangement when establishing agreements with nonprofit and public agency partners.

Monitor Status of Social Issues That Initiatives Are Supporting

Managers are encouraged to put systems in place to periodically check on the current status of the social conditions being supported by their initiatives (e.g., number of new cases of HIV in the past year). Most recognize that *impact* on social problems takes time and that many factors beyond a corporation's social initiative will contribute to alleviating problems. Given the ideal of a long-term commitment by the corporation to a social issue, however, it follows that a best practice would be to monitor changes and implications of these changes for future social investments.

Allocate Adequate Resources for Measurement and Reporting

In the end, the major challenge associated with evaluation of corporate social initiatives and calculating returns on investments is an economic one. An ideal budgeting scenario would be to assess costs for evaluation efforts based on agreed-upon purposes and then to present this total as a proposed budget. In reality, this draft amount will likely be adjusted based on current financial considerations and priorities. Managers are then encouraged to explore less costly but still valuable methodologies, such as shared cost studies and ad hoc surveys.

13

Summary of Best Practices

Your ads are obnoxious. Sunny is disgusting in them. We swore we would rather sleep on concrete than buy a bed from you because of her ads. But we came because of your role in the community and we stayed because of the service we received at your store.

— Comment card given to CEO Sunny Kobe Cook
Sleep Country U.S.A.

Best practices for choosing a social issue to support, and then selecting, developing, and evaluating social initiatives are listed in this chapter for ease of reference and sharing with others. We have also included a summary of the major strengths and weaknesses of each of the six initiatives in Table 13.1.

As a brief recap, *social problems* to choose from typically include ones related to basic needs (food, shelter, clean water), health, safety, education, fair labor practices, poverty, employment, the environment, and animal protection. *Initiatives* may be marketing-related (cause promotions, cause-related marketing, corporate social marketing) or corporate-related (philanthropy, volunteering, business practices).

Choosing a Social Problem to Alleviate:

1. Choose only a few social issues to support.
2. Choose those that are of concern in the communities where you do business.

TABLE 13.1 Summary of Strengths to Maximize and Concerns
to Minimize

	Major Strengths to Maximize	Major Concerns to Minimize
Cause Promotions	• Builds corporate reputation • Attracts and retains a motivated workforce • Supports marketing objectives • Builds strong community relationships • Leverages current corporate social initiatives	• Visibility for corporate efforts can easily be lost. • Coordination with cause partners can be time consuming. • Staff time and involvement can be significant. • Promotional expenses can be significant. • Consumers may be skeptical of corporate motivations and commitment.
Cause-Related Marketing	• Supports marketing objectives • Builds strong community relationships • Leverages current corporate social initiatives	• Coordination with cause partners can be time consuming. • Staff time and involvement can be significant. • Promotional expenses can be significant. • Consumers may be skeptical of corporate motivations and commitment.
Social Marketing	• Builds corporate reputation • Contributes to business goals • Attracts and retains a motivated workforce • Supports marketing objectives • Builds strong community relationships • Leverages current corporate social initiatives	• Coordination with cause partners can be time consuming. • Staff time and involvement can be significant. • Efforts may require external expertise. • Promotional expenses can be significant.
Philanthropy	• Builds corporate reputation • Attracts and retains a motivated workforce • Builds strong community relationships • Leverages current corporate social initiatives	• Visibility for corporate efforts can easily be lost. • Tracking resource expenditures and value can be difficult and expensive.

TABLE 13.1 *(continued)*

	Major Strengths to Maximize	Major Concerns to Minimize
Community Volunteering	• Builds corporate reputation • Attracts and retains a motivated workforce • Builds strong community relationships • Leverages current corporate social initiatives	• Visibility for corporate efforts can easily be lost. • Staff time and involvement can be significant. • Tracking resource expenditures and value can be difficult and expensive.
Socially Responsible Business Practices	• Builds corporate reputation • Contributes to business goals • Attracts and retains a motivated workforce • Reduces operating costs • Reduces regulatory oversight • Builds strong community relationships • Leverages current corporate social initiatives	• Visibility for corporate efforts can easily be lost. • Efforts may require external expertise. • Consumers may be skeptical of corporate motivations and commitment.

3. Choose issues that have synergy with your company's mission, values, products, and services.
4. Choose issues that have potential to support business goals such as marketing or supplier relations, increased productivity, or cost reductions.
5. Choose issues that are of concern to key constituent groups such as employees, target markets, customers, investors, and corporate leaders.
6. Choose issues that can be supported over a long term.

Selecting Initiatives to Support Social Issues:

7. Select initiatives that best meet business objectives and goals.
8. Select initiatives that meet priority needs for the cause.
9. Select multiple initiatives for a single cause, adding ones missing for current cause efforts.

10. Select initiatives representing the most potential for strong community partners.
11. Select initiatives where you have a history of experience.
12. Select initiatives that will leverage current abundant resources.

Developing and Implementing Program Plans:

13. Form internal, cross-functional teams to develop plans.
14. Include community partners in plan development.
15. Establish clear objectives and measurable goals (outcomes) for the company.
16. Establish clear objectives and measurable goals (outcomes) for the cause.
17. Develop a communications plan.
18. Identify and plan for additional strategic elements.
19. Get senior management buy-in.

Evaluating Efforts:

20. Determine purpose of evaluation.
21. Measure and report resource outputs.
22. Measure and report outcomes for the *company*, based on initiative objectives and goals.
23. Measure and report outcomes for the *cause*, based on initiative objectives and goals.
24. Monitor status of social issues that initiatives are supporting.
25. Allocate adequate resources for measurement and reporting.

Summary Comments for Best Practices

The final and perhaps most important advice offered by a vast majority of those we interviewed is to take time to develop a formal document that establishes written *corporate guidelines* for social initiatives: guidelines that will inform and ease decision making regarding many of the 25 best practices presented in this chapter and will reflect the unique history, culture, goals, markets, and strategies for your company.

These guidelines should be developed (and updated at least every two to three years) by interdepartmental teams and should include sections describing most of the following decisions:

- Priority social issues to support.
- Desired business outcomes from support of social initiatives.
- Desired social and environmental outcomes from initiatives.
- Preferred types of initiatives.
- Guidelines for determining levels of contribution.
- Preferred types of giving (e.g., cash versus in-kind donations versus volunteering).
- Ideal community partners.
- Expectations regarding interdepartmental involvement in planning.
- A planning template, especially for developing internal and external communication plans.
- Philosophies regarding corporate visibility and recognition for efforts.
- Expectations for tracking, evaluation, and reporting.

This document, or at least components of it, can then be shared with potential community partners, helping to establish early on corporate priorities and expectations.

As always, executive management approval and enthusiasm for these guidelines will be critical to their usefulness. The ultimate scenario would be that they actually own the guidelines and embody a passion for doing the most good, as exemplified by the CEO of Kenneth Cole Productions:

What started organically as a personal effort and a contribution to the community as well as a business strategy has become our trademark. Our cause-related marketing is a process that starts with meetings at the beginning of every season, where we take inventory of what concerns us today and what we believe will still be important in a few months . . . . In the absence of therapy, I rant, I rave, I eventually exhaust myself, and then I listen to everyone else do the same thing. A quiet settles over the room as we ask ourselves how we can appropriately address what is on our minds.[1]

14

No Good Deed Goes Unpunished: Dealing with Cynics and Critics

I t is ironic that marketing and corporate social initiatives, instead of inoc- ulating companies from attacks, have been known to stimulate criticism rather than kudos. Although the opinion research we've shared throughout this book shows that most consumers appreciate corporate social initiatives, there are activists, journalists, and a portion of the population that respond with great cynicism to any communications about corporate good works. Certainly, some poorly conceived and executed programs are deserving of criticism, but negative feedback due to what we've dubbed the *no good deed goes unpunished* phenomenon goes beyond that.

In this chapter, we'll provide examples and analysis of this communications challenge, offer advice on avoiding or minimizing the extent of such problems, and share suggestions on how to respond when they do arise.

Types of Criticisms

There are many scenarios that lead activists, journalists, consumers or others to rightly or wrongly publicly criticize corporate social initiatives. Among the more common ones we've identified are:

- A broader debate on the issue (e.g., should the breast cancer movement focus on finding cures for or identifying environmental triggers of the disease) that turns a company into a target for being on the *wrong side*.

- Pre-existing dissatisfaction with a company or its nonprofit partner on one issue (e.g., labor practices in less developed countries) that leads to criticism when a company makes claims that it is a positive player in another, unrelated arena.
- Perceived hypocrisy between a company's social initiative and its behavior related to that issue (e.g., a fast food marketer that claims to be fighting obesity at the same time it advertises high-calorie, high-fat additions to its menu).
- Failure to abide by regulations (e.g., commercial co-venture filings required in some states for cause-related marketing programs) or to receive permission from a nonprofit that a company promotes as being the beneficiary of an initiative.
- Lack of transparency about the amount, timing, or other aspects of a cause-related marketing program (e.g., stating that a nebulous *portion of the proceeds* from consumer purchases will be donated).
- Technical or other issues that arise during the implementation of a campaign (e.g., allegations of voting fraud impacting a crowd-sourced giving program).

To illustrate, the following sections present five examples that made it into the press.

New Balance and Susan G. Komen for the Cure: Headache Caused by an Oversight

Since 1989, New Balance, the Massachusetts-based athletic footwear and apparel maker, has contributed more than $8.9 million and other forms of support to Susan G. Komen for the Cure through sponsorship of the group's race, walk, and marathon programs and the company's *Lace Up for the Cure*® retail program.[1] An October 2009 article in the *Sunday Boston Globe* magazine revealed that New Balance had failed to register its commercial co-venture activity with the Massachusetts state attorney general's charities division. A New Balance spokesman told the *Globe* that it was an oversight: "I thought legal was doing it, and legal thought I was doing it."[2] The company, which quickly rectified the situation, suffered avoidable if temporary damage to its reputation.

Gap and FEED: A Labeling Snafu Raises a Tangential Issue

In December 2010, Gap, the clothing retailer, fielded a cause-related marketing program linking contributions to child anti-hunger programs in the United States to the sales of a line of bags created by FEED Projects LLC.[3] In-store displays indicated the bags were *Made in the USA*. Unfortunately, that was true for some, but not all of the bags being sold. A shopper spotted the contradiction, took a picture of it, and the story went viral.[4] In response, Gap issued the following statement:

> We regret any misunderstanding caused about Gap's line of FEED USA bags. There are several bags in the FEED USA collection. The Feed USA Canvas Tote Bag and the limited edition one-of-a-kind Bandana Bag are both made in the USA. However, the FEED USA Denim Bucket bags are made in China, and should not have been connected to the Made in the USA signs. The tags in the bags are labeled correctly. The signage in the store is incorrect. We are removing the store signage and our website is being updated. We apologize for any inaccurate messaging. We are proud of our FEED USA partnership. Gap donates $5 toward FEED USA's school lunch program for each bag sold.[5]

The *Made in the USA* manufacturing claim was tangential to this campaign's anti-hunger focus, and this brouhaha could have been avoided.

Pepsi Refresh: Technical Problems Steal the Spotlight

PepsiCo received substantial attention and accolades in 2010 when it channeled major marketing resources into *Pepsi Refresh*, a campaign that empowered people to nominate and vote for community projects that would receive a share of $20 million in Refresh grants. For a while, however, the lead story shifted from the good works being funded to allegations made by some nonprofits that the program had insufficient safeguards against voting fraud.

On January 5, 2011, for example, the *New York Times* ran the headline "New Charges of Cheating Tarnish Pepsi Fund-Raising Contest of Nonprofits"[6] over a story containing quotes from disgruntled nonprofit executives who suspected that some winners had engaged overseas proxy voters to inflate their totals and were not satisfied with PepsiCo's responses to their complaints. PepsiCo countered that its systems had blocked fraudulent votes from being counted, but that for security reasons it could not reveal its methods.

Looking back, PepsiCo executive Anamaria Irazabal, who led the Brand Pepsi team at the time of the program launch and fraud controversy, lamented the position the company had found itself in : "It's a double-edged sword. You want to be transparent, but you can't be because as soon as you [were] players would try to hack the system."[7]

Barneys New York and World Wildlife Fund: Fallout When Third Parties Lack Permission

An article in a December 2007 issue of the *New York Times* took some of the joy out of the holidays for the upscale clothier Barneys New York. It revealed that some nonprofits promoted in the company's holiday catalog as beneficiaries of cause-related marketing offers said they did not have contracts with the products' manufacturers.[8] "Unfortunately, just like Barneys shoppers, we're in the dark as to how Barneys and the manufacturers will fulfill their commitment to donate a portion of the proceeds from these products to W.W.F," World Wildlife Fund Senior Vice President John Donoghue is quoted as saying about the program.[9] A spokesman for Barneys told the *New York Times* that responsibility "to hammer out a deal with a charity was on the manufacturers whose products were featured in the catalog."[10]

Unilever and Palm Oil: Mixing Health and Environmental Issues

Responding to calls to remove unhealthy trans fats from food products, Unilever adopted the socially responsible business practice of substituting palm oil as a healthier, economically viable alternative ingredient. The company's sourcing of palm oil, however, surfaced an entirely different issue.

In 2008, Unilever was targeted by Greenpeace as a killer of Indonesian orangutans because it was a major buyer of palm oil raised on plantations located on land formerly covered with rain forest, the ape's shrinking home environment. In a substantial guerrilla marketing campaign, Greenpeace enlisted such tactics as having protestors in orangutan suits climb Unilever's London headquarters building and fielding what became a viral online video entitled "Dove Onslaught(er)," which parodied the company's

Dove Campaign for Real Beauty advertising.[11] In a matter of months, Unilever joined Greenpeace in calling for an end to rain forest deforestation by palm-oil producers and said it would only use sustainable sources by 2015.[12]

As a Unilever spokesman told *Advertising Age* in 2008, "Most activists of whatever persuasion on whatever issue tend to believe that they get most traction (and news coverage) by aiming at the biggest name rather than the biggest challenge.... In most instances, it seems that the biggest 'name' tends to be the one that has done the most to attack the...problem."[13]

Advice from Communications Experts

For advice on how to avoid fallout from the *no good deed goes unpunished* phenomenon, we queried several communications professionals with deep experience in this area. Taken collectively, their advice summed up as follows: *Fear of potential criticism should not stop companies from engaging in corporate social initiatives. It should make them hyperaware of the need to perform due diligence, properly position communications, anticipate potential issues, and be prepared to effectively engage critics and the press.* In this section, we'll explore those points one by one.

Be Smart, Don't Be Afraid

"Many companies commit an unfortunate sin of omission when it comes to communicating their corporate support for positive social and environmental impact," wrote Craig Bida, executive vice president of cause branding at Cone Communications. He continues:

> They are reluctant to talk about what they are doing—often for fear of coming across as insincere or boastful.
>
> Several decades into its evolution, cause marketing is widely recognized as a powerful and effective tool to drive stakeholder engagement. Yet we still come across companies (and more often than you would think) that are brilliant marketers and occupy leadership positions in their industries, but hold back when it comes to integrating the causes they support into their marketing efforts. This, despite overwhelming evidence in our 2011 research that Americans find it broadly acceptable for companies to involve a cause or issue in their marketing (88 percent, up from 66 percent in 1993).

If you are going to do something to impact the world in a positive way (and if you aren't you should be—this is increasingly a basic stakeholder expectation), you should be prepared to tell the world about it, proudly.[14]

Set the Right Tone

"A successful campaign communicates a higher goal for an organization or brand that goes beyond profit to inspire a greater commitment among stakeholders," wrote cause branding pioneer Carol Cone, now managing director and executive vice president of brand and corporate citizenship at Edelman. She continued:

> This is rooted not simply in what stakeholders think about an organization, but also how they feel about it. Purpose looks necessarily different for each company, industry and market: its greatest impact is achieved when led by the "C" suite and when institutional will, creativity, multi-stakeholder engagement and a long-term commitment are demonstrated.
>
> Finding the right tone for campaign communications is truly about understanding your brand and core values. If a brand is a collection of perceptions about an organization, formed by its every communication, action, and interaction, then a successful campaign will build on those values and be deeply authentic to "who you are" as an organization.[15]

Due Diligence Is Key

Cone went on to explain:

> A significant element to building a well-aligned campaign is finding the right partners to help create the desired impact and engagement. . . In designing an authentic and long-term partnership, both corporate partners and nonprofit organizations must perform adequate due diligence. Critical questions to address include:
>
> - Alignment: Is there strategic alignment with brand values, audience, and mission?

- Structure: Are there internal support systems and dedicated resources towards the partnership and its objectives?
- Financial: Is there clarity surrounding resource utilization and are there legal guardrails in place?
- Marketing & reach potential: Does it build stakeholder preference; heighten awareness and engagement?
- Reputation and risk fit: Does the potential partner enhance and strengthen reputation? Have potential risks been adequately assessed?[16]

While potentially time consuming, due diligence is critical to saving face in the long run, wrote Anne Erhard, SVP, cause marketing and CSR at Schwartz MSL Boston.

It can be the "secret sauce" for protecting against your client's worst fears . . . from a deal falling through just before a program launches to a program launching with unwieldy negative fanfare. . . .

On the corporate side, it is so important when determining what issue makes sense for the company to tackle from a cause perspective. From MSL Group research, we know that consumers expect companies to tackle social issues that make sense for their business and are connected in some way to their brand, their product or their higher purpose. This can be a tricky balance, as the issues integrally linked to a client's business may be the more risky ones to tackle—such as a food company taking on health or obesity. So, you need to do your due diligence and make sure that the company "walks the talk"; both internal practices and external communications, products or services must be in line with their social cause. For example, we would not recommend a client launch a campaign around domestic violence if they didn't have a positive work environment for women!

Due diligence is also critical when researching the perfect partnership that could bring a cause program to life. On the corporate side, you must do all the baseline things like checking into an NGO's financials and their charity ratings and rankings. But, you also need to talk to the appropriate people at the organization, really understand how they work—whether they have worked with companies in a deep way before, if they have the internal controls and checks and balances needed, and whether they have the capacity and resources to do what they say they can do. On the nonprofit side, you need to develop the appropriate guidelines for the types of companies that an NGO can and should do business with and in what ways to truly advance the mission and not just raise funds.[17]

Reacting to Criticism

In today's fast-moving digital communications environment, companies that do not plan in advance for negative reactions to their initiatives are living dangerously. "How organizations react in real time to inevitable criticism and dialogue can define brands and drive loyalty (or the opposite), just as significantly as carefully orchestrated marketing and communication efforts,"[18] wrote Craig Bida.

The first step in responding to criticism is to *analyze the source*, advised Anne Erhard:

First determine whether it is coming from the majority or the outliers . . . For any bold, break-through communication there is going to be some criticism. If it is from the outliers, less can be more when it comes to responding as any communication could simply add "fuel to the fire." If the criticism is more widespread, honesty is the best policy—communications must be authentic and transparent and comprehensive. Otherwise, your enemies will get hold of the information they want and the storm could just get more and more violent.[19]

Next, Bida advised, companies and their initiative partners should *assess*: "Figure out if you actually did something wrong, violating standards, norms or hopefully not, laws." Then, it's time to **engage**: "This is about acknowledging criticism and communicating what you're doing to resolve the problem," Bida continued. Finally, take steps to **advance**: "This means getting out in front of the issue, so you can move on and return the focus to what it is you want the world to experience about your brand,"[20] he said.

Coping with criticism is often painful while it is going on, but it is crucial and in some cases can leave a company and campaign stronger. "Consumers value honesty over perfection," Bida asserted. "When it comes to a company's environmental efforts, for example, Cone research shows that a clear majority of people (75 percent) say it is okay if a company is not perfect, as long as it is honest about its progress and objectives. In our time of radical transparency, it turns out that being real is equally as important as being right."[21]

In Summary

Marketing and corporate social initiatives at times have the unintended effect of engendering criticism—some deserved, some not—rather than simply earning accolades. Program managers who are aware of scenarios that often stimulate negative feedback (e.g., a broader debate on an issue, perceived hypocrisy, or technical issues) are better equipped to avoid or minimize communications crises. Public relations experts advise practitioners to set the right tone, perform due diligence, and be prepared to react appropriately to criticism when it arises.

For Nonprofits and Public Sector Agencies Only

15

A Marketing Approach to Winning Corporate Funding and Support for Social Initiatives: Ten Recommendations

If substantial financial resources are to be raised and sustained over a long period of time, it's essential that supportive partners, especially large corporate partners, get as well as give. To find the intersection of public interest and private interest that will work for your partners, begin by sitting down with them to learn about their needs before telling them about yours. What are their marketing and sales challenges? What specific public relations messages do they hope to convey? Who are their principal competitors and on what playing fields are they competing? How do they hope this partnership will be viewed by their employee workforce? Then go back and brainstorm so that you can return to the table with creative ideas for vehicles that will both raise money for and increase awareness of your cause, but will also meet the business need of your partner.[1]

—Bill Shore
Founder and CEO of Share Our Strength

We think Bill Shore's advice is right on, as it reflects a customer-oriented approach to the exchange process, one that has the best chance for securing corporate support for social initiatives. In fact, a synthesis of recommendations presented in this chapter is reminiscent of steps traditionally used in developing a marketing plan: a process that finds the best fit between an organization's mission, objectives, and capabilities and the needs and wants in the marketplace. It is a process that develops and executes product, pricing, distribution, and promotional strategies based on the unique profile of targeted audiences—a process built to win.

This final chapter is written for executives, directors, and program managers of NGOs and public sector agencies seeking to partner with corporations to develop and implement initiatives intended to support a social cause. Most often, these organizations are seeking financial support for promotional campaigns, program expansion, and outreach efforts. They may find, as we have learned, that corporations are sometimes even more willing to contribute nonmonetary resources—especially those they may consider they have in abundance (e.g., staff expertise, employee volunteers, idle equipment, space in promotional materials, and access to underutilized distribution channels). Although the guidelines presented here are most applicable to organizations initiating proposals to corporations, the fundamental principles also apply to those who have been approached by a corporation to assess a potential partnership.

The following 10 recommendations are based on what we have learned from corporate executives about benefits they are seeking, concerns that can hold them back, circumstances that prompt their interest in participation, how they choose among social initiatives to support, how they evaluate potential proposals, and what they want and expect from their partners. Our focus now turns from the process of selection, development, and implementation of social initiatives to guidelines for approaching and securing corporate support. From this point forward, the corporate decision maker is in the customer seat and the cause agency is a marketer.[2]

Recommendation One

Start by developing a list of social issues that your organization or agency is currently charged with supporting and that would benefit from additional resources. Be specific.

Most nonprofit organizations and many governmental agencies exist to support some social cause and, at any given point in time, are focused on programs and services that will advance their mission. Of interest here are those projects and initiatives that would benefit from additional funding or other resources in order to have a greater impact. Key at this initial step is to identify one or more specific issues that can then be put forth for consideration.

For example, at the mission level, the American Cancer Society works to eliminate cancer as a major health problem through efforts including research, education, advocacy, and service.[3] When considering needs for corporate support and involvement, this step would involve identifying specific priorities for campaigns or programs, such as one for the holidays that warns about the increased risk of liver cancer from high levels of alcohol consumption, or one that urges women and men over 50 to get tested for colon and rectal cancer.

Similarly, the Nature Conservancy, which works to preserve plants, animals, and natural communities by protecting lands and waters, currently lists and focuses on four priority conservation initiatives on its website: climate change, forests and watersheds, invasive species, and marine conservation.[4] This specific delineation will provide direction for identifying potential corporate partners.

Issues for the Boys & Girls Clubs of America, the Positive Place for Kids, range from helping members develop basic computer skills to gang prevention and intervention efforts in the community, to providing family fun nights and single-parent support groups as a part of their family support initiative. As we can foresee, each of these social issues can eventually lead to the discovery of different natural partners in the corporate world—partners like Microsoft, which donated more than $150 million in software and cash, providing a comprehensive package of the latest Microsoft products to clubs throughout the country.[5]

Relative to a marketing model, we could think of these specific social issues as products (offerings) that the nonprofit organization or governmental agency wants to sell in the marketplace (e.g., cancer prevention, marine conservation, and computer skills)—that is, ones whose sales volume would benefit from increased financial and related support. And this is where potential corporate partners come in. In reality, these organizations and agencies are seeking corporate partners who will help design, package, produce, promote, and distribute products to a marketplace. Our first need, as recommended here, is to clarify and prioritize potential products.

Recommendation Two

Identify a short list of corporations that these social issues might have a connection with: something that relates to their business mission, products and services, customer base, employee passions, communities where they do business, and/or their corporate giving history.

We heard frequently from those interviewed for cases in this book that one of the first and most important criteria for selecting a social issue to support is that it has some connection to their business. And we saw examples of how this worked.

Inherent in a business *mission*, whether formally articulated or not, is the company's purpose, or what it wants to provide or accomplish in the larger environment. Given this, it seems natural for the American Red Cross, in need of cellular phones for workers to communicate with each other during times of disaster, to approach AT&T Wireless, a company that wants to connect people "with their world, every where they live and work."[6]

Potential connections to *products* are even easier. It seems an obvious fit for Share Our Strength to think of the Food Network to support their annual Great American Bake Sale; for the Lions Club to consider LensCrafters as a partner to collect old or unused eyeglasses; for an Arizona water coalition to think they had a good chance with a store like Lowe's as a corporate sponsor; and for a children's hospital to imagine that a local life vest manufacturer would be interested in having their brand name featured on drowning prevention program materials.

Some issues will appeal to the corporations because they appeal to their *customer base*. The Arthritis Foundation may have predicted Tylenol would be interested in sponsoring their annual walk, and local humane societies probably thought they would be welcomed to conduct adoption fairs at PetSmart. Similarly, we know that corporations want to attract and retain a motivated workforce and are responsive to issues that their *employees* care about. Nonprofit agencies in the Seattle, Washington, area with a mission to protect the outdoors and promote outdoor recreation probably know that employees at Recreational Equipment Incorporated (REI) are eager to participate in their volunteer activities.

We saw how passionate corporations can be about contributing to issues in their own backyard, as Seattle Children's Hospital discovered with Sellen Construction, and local HIV/AIDS prevention organizations have found with the Coca-Cola Foundation and Coca-Cola bottlers in Africa.

Finally, the strongest connection to a social issue may be through a long corporate history of giving to a particular cause. Safe Kids probably knew they could count on FedEx to help get the word out about International

Walk to School Day, and local AIDS organizations probably know Kenneth Cole Productions will be open to ideas for campaigns to support the use of condoms.

These connections can be found using a variety of relatively simple research techniques, including reviewing corporate giving and citizenship statements on corporate websites, in annual reports, in publications (e.g., *Chronicle of Philanthropy*, the Foundation Center, *the Federal Register*, and the Council on Foundations), and in press releases available online, as well as through discussions with board members and other community leaders involved in local businesses. It would, of course, be advantageous if the community agency has an existing or historical relationship with one of these companies on the short list.

As a final component of this activity, at the same time that a short list of ideal potential corporations is made, it is also important to identify corporations that your agency or organization does not consider a good match and/or activities that would not be acceptable (e.g., a state immunization coalition may have established partner guidelines that exclude certain corporate partners such as pharmaceuticals or a public school may decide that it will limit activities from a soft drink sponsor to promotions of bottled water only).

Recommendation Three

Approach corporations and/or their communication agencies and find out more about their interests and experiences relative to supporting social initiatives.

In the ideal world, an initial contact would begin with a brief meeting or telephone conversation with the CEO of each of your targeted companies. It is this person's perspective that is invaluable at this phase of the process, providing more information about the company's interests, experiences, and preferences relative to supporting social causes, and about current business challenges and opportunities. Entering at this level might be made more likely if someone on the board of your agency, or a community leader associated with your agency or cause, is able to provide an introduction. The initial conversation could even be conducted by one of these VIPs, with a subsequent referral to others in the company.

However, it is more likely that initial contacts will be with department managers or their assistants. Relevant departments include those dealing with community affairs (e.g., public affairs, corporate social responsibility, or community relations), corporate communications, marketing, and/or public relations. If the corporation has a foundation, initial meetings may include their representatives as well. If possible, try to arrange an initial meeting that includes one representative from their community affairs area and one from marketing. It is their combined perspectives and responsibilities that will provide the richest input.

Introductory comments should focus on positioning the meeting as an inquiry. You are exploring opportunities for community partnerships to support initiatives of interest to your organization. Your purpose is to learn more about their company's interests and needs, and if appropriate, to come back with ideas on ways you might work together to benefit the cause, as well as meet some of their business goals. This is an interview, not a proposal. Let them know what research you have done on their company that has led you to them and how it aligns with your agency's mission.

Whether in one meeting or multiple meetings, some of the first questions you want to explore are those related to their interests regarding social issues and their experiences relative to social initiatives. Your questions could include the following:

- What social issues currently interest your organization the most and why? (You can share what issues you are aware of that they supported in the past and ask why those issues were selected.) If current issues differ from those that were of concern in the past, what brought about this change?
- What causes are your employees passionate about, if any? Is this a major consideration for you when considering options for support and involvement?
- What causes are your target markets or customers passionate about? Again, is this a major consideration when you evaluate options?
- What forms of support interest you most? (You could mention the various types of initiatives and ask, in general, which are the most and least appealing.) Do you tend to like to work with community partners or prefer to handle things internally?
- What has worked well in the past? What outcomes did you value most?
- What hasn't worked well in the past? What lessons were learned?

Recommendation Four

Listen to their business needs.

Other initial topics to explore are those related to the company's business goals and objectives. Your interest is grounded in your perspective that social initiatives can and should support economic as well as social and environmental goals; and that when corporations can demonstrate a return on their investment in social initiatives, they are more likely to develop long-term relationships with community partners and focus their giving programs on what is working. You think of them as a potential customer and want to understand what needs they have that a partnership with you might be able to fill. Your conversation will inspire your staff to consider options for initiatives with the best chance for winning their support.

Question areas should touch briefly on most aspects of the business, exploring corporate image, operations, human resources, community relations, public relations, and marketing issues. They might be framed as follows:

- Are there any aspects of your *visibility or reputation* in the community that you are interested in enhancing? It may be something that people don't know about you that you wish they did, or something they think about you that you wish they didn't.
- Are there any *key messages* about your company that you feel a sense of urgency to communicate?
- What about *operational issues*? Are there any guidelines from regulatory agencies that you are trying to meet that would benefit from public support? Are there any relationship issues with suppliers, franchise owners, and/or distributors that would be strengthened by involvement in social issues?
- Are you facing any major challenges relative to *attracting and retaining a motivated workforce* that might be supported by corporate involvement in the community or by volunteer opportunities?
- Are there any *consumer or business markets* that you are pursuing where involvement in a social cause might give you a competitive edge, or where a relationship with a strong community partner might be beneficial?

- In terms of *brand images*, are there any specific products that you are trying to position or reposition? Are there aggressive *sales goals* related to any of these products?

One example presented in this book that might help demonstrate the value of these questions is the case regarding Subway, described in Chapter 5. One could imagine that an interview such as the one outlined above, conducted by a representative from the American Heart Association, might have revealed Subway's interest in being perceived as a healthy fast-food option. The interview may also have shown that Subway wanted to support franchise owners with increased sales, to build pride for their products among employees, to differentiate themselves from others in the fast-food industry, and that they wanted their line of low-fat subs to capture a significant share of the healthy fast-food category, and ideally to launch it. One can further imagine that the American Heart Association representative might be eager to return to the office, confident that he or she might have just found a major sponsor for the annual fundraising walk.

Recommendation Five

Share with them the social issues your organization supports, the initiatives you are considering or engaged in, and your strengths and resources. Find out which, if any, they find most appealing.

Social issues, as we are referring to them here, are the specific problems that your organization is interested in solving—ones that would benefit from additional financial and related support. We have suggested that these issues be considered products you want to sell in the marketplace. At some point in this getting-to-know-each-other process, this list should be shared. It should be limited to those that your research, hunches, and early discussions suggest might be of greatest interest to the corporation being approached and interviewed. This is also when you share your guidelines for acceptable activities.

The American Legacy Foundation's story of finding corporate support for one of its initiatives illustrates this process well. As background, the American Legacy Foundation was established in 1999, funded primarily by funds from the Master Settlement Agreement with the tobacco industry. The organization works to build a world where young people reject tobacco and anyone can quit smoking. Efforts are concentrated on providing grants, technical training and assistance, youth activism, strategic partnerships, counter-marketing and grassroots marketing campaigns, and public relations. The organization has a special focus on helping communities disproportionately affected by the toll of tobacco, including African Americans, Hispanics, and Native Americans. One of the foundation's signature programs is *Circle of Friends: Uniting to Be Smoke-Free*, a national grassroots social movement to highlight the importance of supporting smokers who want to quit, while also educating people about the toll of tobacco-related disease on women, their families, and communities.

Of interest for this illustration is one of the foundation's specific partnerships, designed to reach young women smokers ages 16 to 24. In 2003, the foundation was seeking to help young women who want to quit smoking, but also to educate other young women in this age group so that they never start smoking. Match this interest with the knowledge that Avon, the global cosmetics giant, was planning to debut a new beauty business, called *mark*, targeting the 300 million young women ages 16 to 24 in the United States, who have an estimated spending power of $250 billion, $75 billion of which is spent in the beauty and fashion sectors.[7] Picture Avon mark executives' reaction when the American Legacy Foundation explored a potential partnership with them. Compelling research findings had indicated that among the 25 percent of young women ages 16 to 24 who smoke, 65 percent wanted to quit, but only 3 percent succeeded for at least a year.[8]

The two organizations agreed to work together, through Circle of Friends, to reach young women with healthy lifestyle messages around smoking. In a press release announcing the partnership, Deborah Fine, the president of Avon Future, commented: "Building upon Avon's more than 100-year legacy and leadership in the area of women's health, mark is privileged to continue this commitment with a new generation of women who are eager to make a difference."[9] The 2003 press release announced that mark would be promoting cessation messages, encouraging mark representatives to communicate with their peers about tobacco use, and donating all proceeds from the sale of the Circle of Friends Sunburst Necklace to the American Legacy Foundation.

Recommendation Six

Prepare and submit a proposal to those corporations most interested in your social issues. Present several optional initiatives for potential support, ones that are the best match for their stated business and marketing needs.

At this point, you should be rich with input. Ideally, you know the priority social issues the targeted company or companies are interested in and ones they consider a priority. You understand their current business goals and challenges and have identified ones that you might be able to support. You have a sense of what types of initiatives they prefer most and you have an inside track on what they value in a partnership—and what makes them leery. This should make it easy to take the next step, crafting a proposal.

A proposal should include a clear statement of *purpose,* highlighting the potential impact that proposed initiatives would have on a social issue of common concern : "This initiative is intended to help reduce oral disease among children by increasing access to dental care among low-income populations." It should make clear how this specific initiative would meet *priority needs for the cause*: "Your financial support will enable us to reach the vast majority of underserved youth enrolled in after-school programs at Boys & Girls Clubs across the country." You should also indicate your interest and commitment to help develop evaluation mechanisms to measure this impact.

Identify the *strengths and resources* you intend to bring to the table, including your technical and clinical expertise regarding the issue, staff time you intend to dedicate to the project, involvement of high-visibility board members or elected officials, and actual funds you intend to commit. Talk about your interest in a long-term partnership if at all feasible.

Outline *options for their contributions*, recalling their preferences for direct monetary contributions versus in-kind services or employee volunteering.

Highlight *potential benefits for the corporation*. Include mention of how you believe this new initiative will leverage their current and past efforts in the community. Suggest ways their employees might be involved. Point out the business and marketing goals you believe this may support, and express your interest in working with them to maximize these opportunities. Provide options for visibility for their contributions, remaining open to their preferences for tactical strategies such as logo placement and use of corporate colors. Mention any additional *strong community partners* that are currently involved or that you intend to approach, and what they will also be providing. Offer initial ideas about how you might publicly recognize their contributions, ones that reflect the corporation's business and marketing goals as well as its unique culture and style.

Using these principles, imagine how product managers at Dole might have responded to a proposal from the National Cancer Institute's *5 A Day for*

Better Health program that outlined an opportunity to be a founding member of the *5 A Day* initiative, which would include Dole's presence on nutritional education program materials that would likely reach over 30,000 schools and 100,000 elementary teachers in the United States and would provide multiple co-branding opportunities, including using the *5 A Day* logo stickers on a banana. "Where do I sign?

Recommendation Seven

Participate in developing an implementation plan.

Traditional components of an implementation plan will include setting objectives and goals (desired outcomes) for the company and the cause; selecting target audiences; identifying strategic activities; and determining roles, responsibilities, timelines, and budgets. As we heard from many corporate executives, involvement of cross-functional teams in this planning process (from the corporation as well as the NGO or public agency) is often key to a successful program and should be encouraged early on.

Initial plans should be considered a draft, as there will likely be needs for your agency, as well as the company, to review intended strategies with senior management, and in many cases, to test ideas with other key publics including customers of the corporation, donors to your agency, or citizens in a community. For example, a public agency interested in corporate support for a childhood immunization campaign may learn quickly, by conducting a couple of focus groups with parents, that a partnership that included a drugstore's name on the front of a brochure raised considerable concern with material content. But you may also learn that by adding the phrase "Printing courtesy of" before the name and putting it on the back of the brochure, objections were assuaged. From the corporation's point of view, a quick test with customers in a retail store might reveal that cause promotional messages on grocery bags would not be noticed unless the checkout clerk also mentioned the promotion.

Recommendation Eight

Offer to handle as much of the administrative legwork as possible.

Several initiatives—especially cause promotions, cause-related marketing, and social marketing ones—tend to involve more administrative time and effort than others, such as providing a cash grant or participating in a one-time employee volunteer event. In cases where these initiatives have been identified as ideal relative to desired outcomes, it may be important for the NGO or the public agency staff to facilitate the partnership by offering to take on a variety of administrative tasks, which may range from establishing record-keeping systems to editing copy to coordinating with printers and delivering materials.

Willingness to assume these responsibilities will do more than just relieve the corporate partner. It may make the difference in how much they are able to contribute to the campaign and its duration; it may also influence whether a company is willing to commit to a multiyear campaign or a one-time-only event. This then affects the possibility of exploring additional initiatives in the future.

Consider the partnership between *Family Circle* magazine and Share Our Strength and other sponsors, where partners needed to track and then report on the numbers of people across the country that baked, bought, or sold goods during the Great American Bake Sale, and then distribute funds to qualifying organizations, in part according to geographic locations where funds were raised. We can imagine that an offer by Share Our Strength and other partners to help make this happen may be key to the magazine's high level of program participation.

Recommendation Nine

Assist in measuring and reporting outcomes.

Agency managers should express in early discussions a commitment to program evaluation. Corporate satisfaction and long-term commitment to a partnership may in fact rely significantly on this factor.

Once program goals and strategies have been established, a specific evaluation plan can be developed to assess program processes as well as outcomes. This should be a team effort, as it will be important to measure and report outcomes for the cause relative to established objectives and goals, as well as for the company. This plan should include delineation of roles and responsibilities as well as fund requirements.

Evaluation efforts vary significantly by type of initiative, each presenting its own set of metrics, requirements, and challenges. Red Cross may have simply reported back to AT&T Wireless the number of chapters that received their donated phones, the numbers of times the phones were used, and the types of emergency situations that were ameliorated by this improved access during times of disaster. The task for the water conservation coalition and Lowe's in Arizona would be more daunting with desired process measures, including number of participants in workshops and reach and frequency of advertising messages; and outcome measures would need to attempt to monitor increases in sales of featured products as well as changes in awareness of water conservation techniques and levels of water usage in the region. The effort would clearly need more hands on deck.

Recommendation Ten

Provide recognition for the corporation's contribution, in ways preferred by the company.

Although we found varying levels of enthusiasm for corporate recognition and a range of preferred forms for this recognition, one theme was pervasive: Let the cause partner and those who benefited from the initiative tell the story.

What better acknowledgement could there be than for the March of Dimes to acknowledge First Response® Pregnancy Tests on their website as the market leader,[10] or for the Centers for Disease Control and Prevention to applaud Clorox's support for flu prevention. And imagine the satisfaction for Tylenol to be publicly recognized by the Arthritis Foundation, for Pampers by the SIDS Foundation, for Target by the National Education Association, for Subway by the American Heart Association, for Pfizer by Population Services International, for Dole by the National Cancer Institute, and for Whole Foods by the Marine Stewardship Council. Such kudos are about as good as it gets.

Summary of Recommendations for Those Seeking Corporate Support

This chapter has presented guidelines and principles (listed together below) that we believe offer NGOs and public agencies the best chances for winning support from corporations for social initiatives.

1. Start by developing a list of social issues that your organization or agency is currently charged with supporting and that would benefit from additional resources. Be specific.

2. Identify a short list of corporations that these social issues might have a connection with, something that relates to their business mission, products and services, customer base, employee passions, communities where they do business, and/or their corporate giving history.

3. Approach corporations and/or their communication agencies and find out more about their interests and experiences relative to supporting social initiatives.

4. Listen to their business needs.

5. Share with them the social issues your organization supports, the initiatives you are considering or engaged in, and your strengths and resources. Find out which, if any, they find most appealing.

6. Prepare and submit a proposal to those corporations most interested in your social issues. Present several optional initiatives for potential support, ones that are the best match for their stated business and marketing needs.

7. Participate in developing an implementation plan.

8. Offer to handle as much of the administrative legwork as possible.

9. Assist in measuring and reporting outcomes.

10. Provide recognition for the corporation's contribution, in ways preferred by the company.

We recognize that few have the luxury, the time, the patience, or the perfect-world scenario that might be needed to follow these recommended practices, particularly in a sequential order. We know that the reality looks more like "we need to get more funds to make this campaign work, and we need them soon, so let's apply for a grant from General Mills or ask one of our board members if they'd renew their company's annual commitment." We understand this is asking a lot—from the NGO, the public agency, and the potential corporate partner.

At a minimum, stay focused on an intention to develop a program that will do the most good for the cause as well as the company, and hold close a conviction that the public, nonprofit, and private sectors can and should work together to meet social and environmental goals as well as economic ones. In fact, all of our stakeholders and benefactors are counting on us to do just that.

Notes

Chapter 1 Good Intentions Aren't Enough. Why Some Corporate Social Initiatives Fail and Others Succeed

1. "Surprising Survivors: Corporate Do-Gooders," CNNMoney, http://money.cnn .com/2009/01/19/magazines/fortune/do_gooder.fortune (accessed December 11, 2011).
2. "The Social Responsibility of Business Is to Increase Its Profits," *The New York Times*, http://query.nytimes.com/mem/archive/pdf?res=F10F11FB3E5810718ED DAA0994D1405B808BF1D3 (accessed December 11, 2011).
3. Cone Communications "2011 Cone/Echo Global CR Opportunity Study" (http:// www.coneinc.com/news/request.php?id=1064) accessed April 2, 2012.
4. "Creating Shared Value," *Harvard Business Review*, http://hbr.org/2011/01/the-big-idea creating-shared-value/ar/1 (accessed December 11, 2011).
5. Ibid.
6. Giving USA Foundation, "Giving USA 2011," www.givingusareports.org/products/ GivingUSA_2011_ExecSummary_Print.pdf (accessed December 11, 2011).
7. Ibid.
8. IEG Sponsorship Report, "Sponsorship Spending : 2010 Proves Better Than Expected; Bigger Gains Set for 2011," www.sponsorship.com/About-IEG/Press-Room/Sponsorship-Spending--2010-Proves-Better-Than-Expe.aspx (accessed December 11, 2011).
9. Cause Marketing Forum, "The Growth of Cause Marketing," http://www .causemarketingforum.com/site/c.bkLUKcOTLkK4E/b.6452355/apps/s/content .asp?ct=8965443 (accessed February 24, 2012).Ibid.
10. KPMG, "Corporate Responsibility Reporting Hits All-Time High but Lacks Financial Reporting Rigour," www.kpmg.com/Global/en/IssuesAndInsights/Articles Publications/Press-releases/Pages/corporate-responsibility-reporting.aspx (accessed December 11, 2011).
11. Ibid.

12. Ibid.

13. Ibid.

14. General Mills, "Corporate Social Responsibility 2011," www.generalmills.com/~/media/Files/CSR/2011_csr_final.ashx (accessed December 11, 2011).

15. IBM, "2009 Corporate Responsibility Report," www.ibm.com/ibm/responsibility/report/2009/letter.shtml (accessed December 11, 2011).

16. Nike, "CEO Message," www.nikebiz.com/crreport/content/about/2-1-0-ceo-letter.php (accessed December 11, 2011).

17. John B. Replogle, "Corporate Consciousness Report," Seventh Generation, www.seventhgeneration.com/mission/healthy-company/ceo-letter (accessed December 11, 2011).

18. Howard Schultz, "Starbucks Global Responsibility Report 2010," Starbucks, www.starbucks.com/responsibility/learn-more/goals-and-progress/message-from-howard-schultz (accessed December 11, 2011).

19. Craig Smith, "The New Corporate Philanthropy," *Harvard Business Review,* May–June (1994): 105–107.

20. Ibid., 108.

21. Ibid.

22. David Hess, Nikolai Rogovsky, and Thomas W. Dunfee. "The Next Wave of Corporate Community Involvement: Corporate Social Initiatives," California Management Review vol. 44, no. 2 winter (2002).

23. Business for Social Responsibility,"Introduction," www.bsr.org/BSRResources/IssueBriefDetail.cfm?DocumentID=48809 (accessed March 25, 2004).

24. Cause Marketing Forum, "2010 Cone Cause Evolution Study," www.causemarketingforum.com/site/apps/nlnet/content2.aspx?c=bkLUKcOTLkK4E&b=6412289&ct=8968667 (accessed December 12, 2011).

25. Cone Communications "2002 Cone Corporate Citizenship: The Role of Cause Branding: Executive Summary," 4 (http://www.coneinc.com/news/request.php?id=1085) accessed April 2, 2012.

26. 2011 Cone/Echo Global CR Opportunity Study, 2.

27. 2011 Cone/Echo Global CR Opportunity Study, 21.

28. Edelman, "Citizens in Emerging Markets Outpace the US and Europe as Most Engaged in Social Good," www.edelman.com/news/2010/Edelman2010goodpurposeglobalpressrelease.pdf.

29. PR Newswire, "New Study Reveals: Men Really Do Have a Heart," www.prnewswire.com/news-releases/new-study-reveals-men-really-do-have-a-heart-106647888.html (accessed December 12, 2011).

30. Paul Bloom, Kevin Keller Hoeffler, and Carlos Basurto, "Consumer Responses to Social and Commercial Sponsorship," Working Paper 2003.

31. H. Pringle and M. Thompson, *Brand Spirit: How Cause Related Marketing Builds Brands* (Chichester, UK: John Wiley & Sons, 2001).

32. Ibid., *xxi*.

33. Ibid., *xxii*.

34. CNN Money, "World's Most Admired Companies, Best & Worst in: Social Responsibility," http://money.cnn.com/magazines/fortune/mostadmired/2011/best_worst/best4.html (accessed February 24, 2012).

35. The CRO, "CR's 100 Best Corporate Citizens 2011," www.thecro.com/files/100Best 2011_List_revised.pdf (accessed December 12, 2011).

36. Ibid.

37. David Hess, Nikolai Rogovsky, and Thomas W. Dunfee: 110–125. "The Next Wave of Corporate Community Involvement: Corporate Social Initiatives," *California Management Review* vol. 44, no. 2 winter (2002).

38. 2010 Cone Cause Evolution Study, 8.

39. 2010 Cone Cause Evolution Study, 21.

40. Ibid.

41. Aspen Institute, "Aspen Institute's MBA Ranking Reveals Greater Focus on Teaching Business & Society Issues in Wake of Financial Crisis," www.aspeninstitute .org/news/2011/09/21/aspen-institute-s-mba-ranking-reveals-greater-focus-teaching-business-society-issues (accessed December 12, 2011).

42. AT&T 2006 Cause Marketing Halo Award Entry submission.

43. NewCircle Communications, "Corporate Social Responsibility A New Ethic for a New Economy," CSRWire, SRI World Group Inc., www.csrwire.com/page .cgi/nc1.html (accessed April 2, 2004).

44. Blake Mycoskie, *Start Something That Matters* (New York: Spiegel & Grau, 2011), 34–35.

45. Rajendra Sisodia, *Firms of Endearment* (New York: Pearson Prentice Hall, 2007), 17.

46. Caroline Flammer, Corporate Social Responsibility and Shareholder Value: The Environmental Consciousness of Investors (July 18, 2011). Available at SSRN: http://ssrn.com/abstract=1888742.

47. Social Investment Forum Foundation, "2010 Report on Socially Responsible Investing Trends in the United States," http://ussif.org/resources/research/documents/ 2010TrendsES.pdf (accessed December 12, 2011).

48. Curt Weeden, *Smart Giving Is Good Business* (San Francisco: Jossey-Bass, 2011), 189.

49. Praveen Sinha, Chekitan S. Dev, and Tania Salas. "The Relationship Between Corporate Social Responsibility and Profitability of Hospitality Firms: Do Firms That Do Good Also Do Well?" Working Paper January 15, 2002. 4. Cornell School of Hospitality Management, http://www.hotelschool.cornell.edu/chr/research/working/ (accessed April 2, 2004).

50. McDonald's Corporation, *Social Responsibility Report 2002*.

51. John Gourville and Kash Rangan, http://management.bu.edu/research/ISIMS/presentations/1 (accessed April 2, 2004).

Chapter 2 Six Social Initiatives for Doing Well by Doing Good

1. Starbucks Global Responsibility Report, Goals & Progress 2010, 2.

2. Ibid., 1.

3. CNNMoney, "A Service of CNN, Fortune & Money," http://money.cnn.com/magazines/fortune/fortune500/2011/full_list/(accessed September 16, 2011).

4. Ibid.

5. Ibid.

6. Starbucks 2011 Cup Summit www.starbucks.com/promo/cup-summit (accessed September 12, 2011).

7. Ethos Water Fund www.starbucks.com/responsibility/community/ethos-water-fund (accessed September 12, 2011).

8. Sustainable Enterprises Coffee and Gardening, www.sustainableenterprises.com/Business/coffeefert.htm (accessed September 12, 2011).

9. About.com, Freebies Starbucks Coffee Grounds: A Green Thumbs Up, http://freebies.about.com/cs/free/l/blstarbucks.htm?p=1 (accessed September 12, 2011).

10. Starbucks Global Responsibility Report, Goals & Progress 2010, 8.

11. YAWA, "Committed to Changing Young Lives," www.yawa.org/index.php?option=com_content&view=article&id=48&Itemid=27 (accessed September 13, 2011).

12. Starbucks Newsroom,"Starbucks Helps Build 'Green' Neighborhood in Minhang," April 2011, http://news.starbucks.com/article_display.cfm?article_id=523 (accessed September 13, 2011).

13. Starbucks, "1st & Pike," www.starbucks.com/coffeehouse/store-design/1st-and-pike (accessed September 13, 2011).

14. Target, "Reading Matters," http://hereforgood.target.com/education.

15. Target, "Books Come to Life for Families at the Target Children's Book Festival," Pressroom, August 20, 2009, http://pressroom.target.com/pr/news/PRN-books-come-to-life.aspx (accessed September 11, 2011).

16. Target, "Take Charge of Education," http://hereforgood.target.com/education/programs-partnerships (accessed September 15, 2011).

17. Target, "Investing in Kids, Families and Schools," http://hereforgood.target.com/education/our-goals (accessed September 15, 2011).

18. Target, "Focus on Reading," http://hereforgood.target.com/education/focus-on-reading (accessed September 15, 2011).

19. Ibid.

20. Pearson Foundation, "Jumpstart's Read for the Record Campaign," www.pearsonfoundation.org/literacy/partnerships/jumpstart-read-for-the-record.html (accessed September 15, 2011).

21. "Target Announces 2011 School Library Makeover Program," PRNewswire, May 24, 2011, http://multivu.prnewswire.com/mnr/target/50372/ (accessed September 16, 2011).

22. Target, "Careers," http://sites.target.com/site/en/corporate/page.jsp?contentId=PRD03-000539 (accessed September 16, 2011).

23. Target, "Awards & Recognition," http://pressroom.target.com/pr/news/launch-career with-target.aspx (accessed September 16, 2011).

24. Johnson & Johnson, Our Credo, www.jnj.com/wps/wcm/connect/c7933f004f5563df9e22be1bb31559c7/jnj_ourcredo_english_us_8.5x11_cmyk.pdf?MOD=AJPERES (accessed September 9, 2011).

25. American Association of Colleges of Nursing, Research and Data Center, 2002–2010, www.aacn.nche.edu/Media/pdf/EnrollChanges.pdf (accessed September 15, 2011) and personal e-mail from Andrea Higham on March 5, 2012.

26. Johnson & Johnson, "2010 Progress Report," http://campaignfornursing.com/jnj-sectionID_10003-pageID_10097-dsc-graphic.aspx (accessed September 7, 2011).

27. Johnson & Johnson, "DiscoverNursing.com," www.discovernursing.com/why (accessed August 31, 2011).

28. Johnson & Johnson, "A Portrait of Thanks Mosaic Project," http://campaignfornursing.com/portraitofthanks (accessed September 7, 2011).

29. Johnson & Johnson, "Be A Happy Nurse," www.facebook.com/jnjnursingnotes?sk=app_132911166797599 (accessed September 7, 2011).

30. Chuck Holt, comment on "Happy Nurse Game Launches for Nurses Week," ADVANCE Perspective, comment posted May 9, 2011, http://community.advanceweb.com/blogs/nurses3/archive/2011/05/09/happy-nurse-game-launches-for-nurses-week.aspx (accessed September 7, 2011).

31. The Foundation of the National Student Nurses Association, Press Release, April 8, 2011, www.nsna.org/Portals/0/Skins/NSNA/pdf/FNSNA%20Awards%20Promise%20of%20Nursing%20Regional%20Scholarships.pdf (accessed September 9, 2011).

32. Johnson & Johnson, "2010 Progress Report," http://campaignfornursing.com/jnj-sectionID_10003-pageID_10097-dsc-graphic.aspx (accessed September 7, 2011).

33. Johnson & Johnson, "2010 Progress Report," You Can Make a Difference, 16. http://campaignfornursing.com/jnj-sectionID_10003-pageID_10097-dsc-graphic .aspx (accessed September 7, 2011).
34. Johnson & Johnson, "2010 Progress Report," Research Update, Recession's Effect on the Registered Nurse, 17, http://campaignfornursing.com/jnj-section ID_10003-pageID_10097-dsc-graphic.aspx (accessed September 7, 2011).
35. Ben & Jerry's, "Global Warming," www.benjerry.com/activism/environmental/ global-warming (accessed September 16, 2011).

Chapter 3 Cause Promotion: Persuading Consumers to Join Your Company in a Good Cause

1. Richard Gillies, Marks & Spencer, Interview by author on September 21, 2011 at Marks &Spencer headquarters in London.
2. Chipotle, "What Is Food with Integrity?" www.chipotle.com/en-US/fwi/fwi.aspx (accessed October 13, 2011).
3. Chipotle, "Chipotle and Jamie Oliver Expose the Horrors of Processed Food This Halloween," October 6, 2010, http://ir.chipotle.com/phoenix.zhtml?c=194775&p =irol-newsArticle_print&ID=1479718&highlight= (accessed October 13, 2011).
4. Ibid.
5. Chipotle, "Chipotle Cultivate Foundation Releases Short Film to Promote Halloween Fundraiser," October 12, 2011, http://ir.chipotle.com/phoenix.zhtml?c= 194775&p=irol-newsArticle&ID=1616398&highlight= (accessed October 13, 2011).
6. Ibid.
7. Information supplied via e-mail by Chipotle spokesman Chris Arnold., October 17, 2011.
8. PetSmart, "Company Information," http://phx.corporate-ir.net/phoenix.zhtml?c= 93506&p=irol-homeprofile (accessed October 21, 2011).
9. Susan Della Maddalena, Telephone Interview by author, September 28, 2011.
10. PetSmart Charities, "Events and News," www.petsmartcharities.org/events-news/ press-releases/sept-2011-national-adoption-weekend.html (accessed October 21, 2011).
11. PetSmart, "PetSmart 2010 Annual Report," 4, http://phx.corporate-ir.net/External .File?item=UGFyZW50SUQ9OTE5MDB8Q2hpbGRJRD0tMXxUeXBlPTM=&t =1 (accessed October 21, 2011).
12. PetSmart, "Company Information."
13. Ibid.
14. Susan Della Maddalena,Telephone Interview by author, September 28, 2011.

15. People Saving Pets Facebook page, www.facebook.com/peoplesavingpets?sk=info (accessed October 2, 2011).

16. Susan Della Maddalena, Telephone Interview by author, September 28, 2011.

17. Stacey Feldman, Telephone Interview by author, October 17, 2011.

18. March of Dimes, "Partners and Sponsors: First Response," www.marchofdimes .com/partnersandsponsors/firstresponse.html (accessed October 11, 2011).

19. March of Dimes, "National Survey Shows Planned Pregnancies May Also Be Healthier Pregnancies," www.marchofdimes.com/aboutus/14458_15615.asp (accessed October 22, 2011).

20. March of Dimes, "March of Dimes Booklet Request," www.milesforbabies.org/ pnhec/first_response.asp (accessed October 11, 2011).

21. FirstResponse, "Preparing for a Healthy Pregnancy," www.firstresponse.com/ devine-healthy-pregnancy.asp (accessed October 22, 2011).

22. Jocelyne Daw, *Cause Marketing for Nonprofits* (Hoboken, NJ: John Wiley & Sons, 2006) 252.

23. Stacey Feldman, Telephone Interview by author, October 17, 2011 in which Feldman, cited Nielsen, FDMx latest 52 52-week data as of October 2011.

24. Stacey Feldman, Telephone Interview by author, October 17, 2011.

25. Ibid.

26. Reading Is Fundamental, "Macy's Be Book Smart Campaign Raises $ 4.9 Million for RIF," Press Release Library, www.rif.org/us/about/press/macys-be-book-smart-campaign-raises-4-9-million-for-rif.htm (accessed October 22, 2011).

27. Ibid.

28. Martine Reardon, presentation at 2010 Cause Marketing Forum conference.

29. Ibid.

30. Ibid.

31. Reading Is Fundamental, 2011 survey of local programs, data provided by Macy's VP of Media Relations and Cause Marketing Holly Thomas.

32. Information provided via e-mail October 18, 2011 by Macy's VP of Media Relations and Cause Marketing Holly Thomas.

33. Martine Reardon, presentation at 2010 Cause Marketing Forum conference.

34. Reading Is Fundamental, "Macy's and Reading Is Fundamental Team Up for "Be Book Smart This Summer," www.rif.org/us/about/press/1968.htm (accessed October 22, 2011).

35. Information provided via e-mail October 18, 2011 by Macy's VP of Media Relations and Cause Marketing Holly Thomas.

36. Information provided via e-mail October 18, 2011 by Reading Is Fundamental.

37. Farmers Insurance Group, "About Farmers," www.farmers.com/farmers_insurance .html (accessed October 22, 2011).

38. Charles Browning, Farmers Insurance vice president of community branding, via Telephone Interview on September 30, 2011 by author.
39. Ibid.
40. Ibid.
41. Ibid.
42. Ibid.
43. Ibid.
44. Roger Daniels, October 2011 interview by author, via telephone.
45. Ibid.
46. Irika Slavin, Interview by author, via telephone October 19, 2011.
47. ibid
48. Katie Ilch, Interview by author, via telephone October 19, 2011.
49. Ibid.
50. Ibid.
51. Ibid.
52. Pearson, "About Us," www.pearson.com/about-us (accessed October 22, 2011).
53. Pearson Foundation, "Readers Nationwide Set New World Record By Reading the Children's Classic *The Snowy Day*," www.pearsonfoundation.org/pr/20101007-readfortherecord.html (accessed October 22, 2011).
54. Information provided by Pearson Foundation President Mark Nieker.
55. Jumpstart 2009 Cause Marketing Halo Award entry form.
56. Information provided by Pearson Foundation President Mark Nieker.
57. Ibid.
58. Marks and Spencer, "About Plan A," http://plana.marksandspencer.com/about (accessed October 22, 2011).
59. Ibid.
60. Marks and Spencer, "Plan A—Partnerships," http://plana.marksandspencer.com/about/partnerships (accessed October 22, 2011).
61. Richard Gillies, Interview by author in Marks & Spencer headquarters in London, September 21, 2011.
62. Ibid.
63. Marks and Spencer, "Plan A Partnerships," http://plana.marksandspencer.com/about/partnerships/macmillan-cancer-support (accessed October 22, 2011).
64. Francesca Insole, Macmillan Cancer Support, Interview by author in London September 20, 2011.
65. Ibid.
66. Marks and Spencer, "Katherine Jenkins and Sir Stuart Rose Brew Up a Storm for Macmillan Cancer Support," http://corporate.marksandspencer.com/media/press_releases/macmillan_cancer_support (accessed October 22, 2011).

67. Richard Gillies, Interview by author in Marks & Spencer headquarters in London, September 21, 2011.

68. Ibid.

69. Ibid.

70. Ibid.

71. Ibid.

72. Marks & Spencer "M&S Calls On to Clear Out Their Wardrobes" (http://corporate.marksandspencer.com/investors/press_releases/one_day_wardrobe_clearout) accessed April 2, 2012.

73. Ibid.

74. Ibid.

75. Ibid.

76. Ibid.

77. Ibid.

78. General Mills Promotion Manager David Fisher presentation at 2004 Cause Marketing Forum conference.

79. Berit Morse Cause Marketing Forum 2009 teleconference presentation.

80. Susan G. Komen for the Cure, "Susan G. Komen for the Cure Named the Non - Profit with Biggest Impact on Cancer," http://ww5.komen.org/KomenNewsArticle.aspx?id=19327353786 (accessed November 2, 2011).

81. Business Wire, "Yoplait Brings the Fight against Breast Cancer to Your Doorstep, with Additions to Save Lids to Save Lives Campaign Emphasizing the True Meaning of Community," www.businesswire.com/news/home/20110913007288/en/Yoplait-Brings-Fight-Breast-Cancer-Doorstep-Additions (accessed October 22, 2011).

82. Berit Morse Cause Marketing Forum 2009 teleconference presentation.

83. Susan G. Komen for the Cure, "A Global Movement," http://apps.komen.org/race forthecure (accessed October 22, 2011).

84. Berit Morse Cause Marketing Forum 2009 teleconference presentation.

85. www.savelidstosavelives.com (accessed October 26, 2011).

86. Facebook, "Yoplait, Save Lids to Save Lives," www.facebook.com/Yoplait?sk=app_248382025172748 (accessed October 22, 2011).

87. Information provided via e-mail on October 11, 2011 by One Sight Executive Director Greg Hare.

88. Petco, "In-Store Adoption Events," www.petco.com/petco_Page_PC_storead options.aspx (accessed October 22, 2011).

89. Michael Siegel and Lynne Doner, *Marketing Public Health: Strategies to Promote Social Change* (Gaithersburg, MD: Aspen, 1998), 321.

Chapter 4 Cause-Related Marketing: Making Contributions to Causes Based on Product Sales and Consumer Actions

1. Calculations performed by Cause Marketing Forum, Inc.
2. Cone Communications, Inc., "Global Consumers Voice Demand for Greater Corporate Responsibility," www.coneinc.com/2011globalcrrelease (accessed October 31, 2011).
3. Information provided by TELUS Vice President of Community Affairs Jill Schnarr.
4. Susan G. Komen for the Cure, "Bank of America," http://ww5.komen.org/Content HeaderOnly.aspx?id=6442450996 (accessed October 31, 2011).
5. eBay, "Sell to Make a Difference," www.ebaygivingworks.com/sell.html (accessed October 31, 2011).
6. Blake Mycoskie, *Start Something That Matters* (New York: Spiegel & Grau,2011), 19.
7. Ibid.
8. Ibid., 30.
9. Ibid., 30–31.
10. Ibid.
11. Ibid., 34–35.
12. Comic Relief, "Record Breaking L102 Million Hit for Red Nose Day," http://cdn2 .comicrelief.com/cdn/md5b5806df54c5c2f2620e1edd07d13851e/sites/default/ files/doc/press_release/Updated%20RND%20total%20release.pdf (accessed October 31, 2011).
13. Jat Sahota, Interview by author in Sainsbury's London Office September 21, 2011.
14. Ibid.
15. Ibid.
16. Ibid.
17. Avon Foundation, "The Avon Breast Cancer Crusade," www.avonfoundation.org/ breast-cancer-crusade (accessed October 17, 2011).
18. Susan Arnot Heaney,Telephone Interview by author, October 17, 2011.
19. Ibid.
20. Avon Foundation, "NAILWEAR PRO Nail Enamel in Power Pink," http://shop .avon.com/shop/product.aspx?src_page=product_list.aspx&level1_id=300& level2_id=380&pdept_id=382&dept_id=0&pf_id=41092 (accessed October 31, 2011).
21. Susan Arnot Heaney, Telephone Interview by author, October 17, 2011.
22. Ibid.
23. Ibid.
24. Ibid.

25. Ibid.

26. Ibid.

27. 2011–2012 APPA National Pet Owners Survey data supplied by Pedigree.

28. 2009 Pedigree Cause Marketing Halo Award Entry Form.

29. Data provided by Melissa Martellotti of Mars Petcare US.

30. 2009 Pedigree Cause Marketing Halo Award Entry Form.

31. Comment supplied by Lisa Campbell of Mars Petcare US.

32. Ibid.

33. This case example draws on information contained in the case study done by Linda Scott, Mary Johnstone-Louis, and Catherine Dolan: "Pampers and UNICEF Part 1: The Marketing Campaign," Said Business School, October 2011. The authors express their appreciation to the case study's authors for permission to reference their work.

34. Ibid., 6–8.

35. Ibid., 9.

36. Ibid.

37. Ibid., 9–10.

38. Ibid.

39. Ibid., 3.

40. Ibid., 11–13.

41. Linda Scott, Mary Johnstone-Louis, and Catherine Dolan, "Teaching Notes: Pampers and UNICEF Part 1: The Marketing Campaign," case study, Said Business School, October 2011, 2.

42. Ibid., 3.

43. Linda Scott, Mary Johnstone-Louis, and Catherine Dolan, "Pampers and UNICEF Part 2: The Marketing Campaign," case study, Said Business School, October 2011, 9.

44. Ibid.

45. Business Wire, "P&G Announces New Social and Environmental Commitments and Recognizes Sustainability Partners at 2011 Clinton Global Initiative," www.businesswire.com/portal/site/home/permalink/?ndmViewId=news_view&newsLang=en&newsId=20110921006975&div=-1633607635 (accessed October 27, 2011).

46. Ibid.

47. Ford, "Ford, General Mills Come Together to Help America's Schools," http://media.ford.com/article_display.cfm?article_id=35372 (accessed October 30, 2011).

48. "Box Tops for Education Tracker—Wave 2," April 2011, provided by Box Tops for Education Director Zack Ruderman.

49. Zack Ruderman, director of Box Tops for Education, Telephone Interview by author on October 12, 2011

50. Ibid.

51. Ibid.

52. Ibid.

53. Ibid.

54. Ibid.

55. Ibid.

56. Ford, "Ford, General Mills Come Together to Help America's Schools, Partner in Box Tops for Education Program," http://media.ford.com/article_display.cfm?article_id=35372 (accessed October 30, 2011).

57. "The Wall Street Journal Market Data Center," *Wall Street Journal*, http://online.wsj.com/mdc/public/page/2_3022-autosales.html (accessed October 10, 2011).

58. Brian Johnson, Subaru Share The Love Event Cause Marketing Forum Teleconference, October 21, 2010.

59. Ibid.

60. Ibid.

61. Ibid.

62. Ibid.

63. Ibid.

64. Ibid.

65. ASPCA, "ASPCA Shelters' Edge Blog May 9, 2011," www.aspcapro.org/blog/2011/05/winners-of-the-2010-subaru-%E2%80%9Cshare-the-love%E2%80%9D-contest (accessed October 31, 2011).

66. Subaru, "Subaru Facebook Fans Vote to Share Their Love with the Make-A-Wish Foundation," www.subaru.com/company/news/index.html (accessed October 10, 2011).

67. Information provided by Brian Johnson of Subaru of America, Inc.

68. Ibid.

69. Association of Fundraising Professionals (AFP), "TELUS Named Most Outstanding Philanthropic Corporation with Global Award," www.afpnet.org/About/AwardsDetail.cfm?ItemNumber=4318 (accessed November 9, 2011).

70. Information provided by TELUS Vice President of Community Affairs Jill Schnarr.

71. Ibid.

72. Ibid.

73. Ibid.

74. Ibid.

75. Ibid.
76. Stephen Chriss, Interview by author, October 13, 2011.
77. Ibid.
78. Ibid.
79. Ibid.
80. Ibid.
81. Ibid.
82. Ibid.
83. Ibid.
84. Ibid.
85. Ibid.

Chapter 5 Corporate Social Marketing: Supporting Behavior Change Campaigns

1. DONATE Powered by Goodwill, "Levi's," http://donate.goodwill.org/levis (accessed October 26, 2011).
2. Goodwill, "A Care Tag for Our Planet: Levi's Care Tags Promote Donating to Goodwill," January 25, 2010, www.goodwill.org/press-releases/a-care-tag-for-our-planet-levis-care-tags-promote-donating-to-goodwill (accessed October 26, 2011).
3. Philip Kotler and G. Zaltman, "Social Marketing: An Approach to Planned Change," *Journal of Marketing* 35 (1971): 3–12.
4. Philip Kotler and Nancy Lee, *Social Marketing: Improving the Quality of Life* (Thousand Oaks, CA: SAGE Publications, 2008).
5. Subway/American Heart Association 2009 Cause Marketing Halo Award Entry Submission.
6. Subway, "Nutritional Leadership," http://http://www.subway.com/subwayroot/about_us/Social_Responsibility/NutritionalLeadership.aspx (accessed October 19, 2011).
7. DONATE Powered by Goodwill, "Levi's."
8. Ibid.
9. Goodwill, "A Care Tag for Our Planet."
10. Ibid.
11. Nancy Lee and Philip Kotler, *Social Marketing: Influencing Behaviors for Good*, 4th Edition (Thousand Oaks, CA: SAGE Publications, 2012), Chapter 17.
12. Best Buy, "e-cycle," www.bestbuy.com/site/Global-Promotions/Recycling-Electronics/pcmcat149900050025.c?id=pcmcat149900050025&DCMP=rdr0001422 (accessed October 24, 2011).

13. Best Buy, "Best Buy Launches Online Sustainability Report: "Our World, Connected," http://pr.bby.com/phoenix.zhtml?c=244152&p=irol-newsArticle&ID= 1585751&highlight= (accessed October 24, 2011).

14. U.S. Fire Administration, "Focus on Fire Safety Smoke Alarms," www.usfa.fema .gov/citizens/focus/smoke_alarms.shtm (accessed October 26, 2011).

15. Ibid.

16. Energizer, "Change Your Clock Change Your Battery," http://phx.corporate-ir.net/ phoenix.zhtml?c=124138&p=irol-newsArticle&ID=1619024&highlight= (accessed October 26, 2011).

17. Allstate, "Helping Teen Drivers Become Safe Drivers," www.allstate.com/auto-insurance/auto-insurance-teen-driver.aspx (accessed October 26, 2011); and Centers for Disease Control and Prevention, Web-based Injury Statistics Query and Reporting System (WISQARS) [Online], National Center for Injury Prevention and Control, Centers for Disease Control and Prevention (producer), www.cdc .gov/ncipc/wisqars.

18. Allstate, "Helping Teen Drivers Become Safe Drivers"; and IIHS teenager fact sheet, www.ihs.org.

19. Allstate, "Helping Teen Drivers Become Safe Drivers"; and NHTSA's General Estimates System (GES) for 2007.

20. Allstate Foundation, "The Allstate Foundation Teen Safe Driving Program," www.allstatefoundation.org/teen-driving (accessed October 26, 2011).

21. Kate Hollcraft, Personal e-mail communication from Allstate, November 8, 2011.

22. "Say 'Boo!' to the Flu" brochure, www.sayboottheflu.com/pdf/sayboo_brochure .pdf (accessed November 3, 2011).

23. "Say 'Boo!' to the Flu" Take the Prevention Pledge, http://saybootheflu.com/ pledge (accessed November 3, 2011).

24. David Kellis, Personal e-mail communication from Clorox, November 3, 2011.

25. RE Journals, "Wisconsin's Miron Construction Earns Environmental Honor," www.rejournals.com/2011/10/20/wisconsins-miron-construction-earns-environ mental-honor/print.

26. Cool Choices, "About," www.coolchoicesnetwork.org/ (accessed October 26, 2011).

27. RE Journals, "Wisconsin's Miron Construction Earns Environmental Honor," www.rejournals.com/2011/10/20/wisconsins-miron-construction-earns-environ mental-honor/print.

28. Cool Choices, "About."

29. RE Journals, "Wisconsin's Miron Construction Earns Environmental Honor," www.rejournals.com/2011/10/20/wisconsins-miron-construction-earns-environ mental-honor/print.

30. V/Line Corporate Social Responsibility, "2011 AMI Award Entry."

31. Ibid.
32. Linda Brennan, Personal e-mail communication, October 28, 2011.
33. Lowe's, "Corporate Citizenship," www.lowes.com/cd_Corporate+Citizenship_674540029_ (accessed October 24, 2011).
34. Lowe's, "Social Responsibility," www.lowescreativeideas.com/social/environment-our-mission.html (accessed October 24, 2011).
35. Sustainable Business Oregon, "EPA Honors Lowe's for Water-Saving Products," www.sustainablebusinessoregon.com/national/2011/10/epa-honors-lowes-for-water-saving.html (accessed October 24, 2011).
36. Ibid.
37. Anglian Water, "About Us," www.anglianwater.co.uk/about-us/ (accessed October 24, 2011).
38. Ibid.
39. Anglian Water, "Anglian Water—The Water and Wastewater Company Serving the Largest Part of England and Wales—Will Launch Its 'Keep It Clear' Campaign Today," Press Release, October 13, 2011.
40. Corporate Culture, "Anglian Water Launch a World Leading Corporate Social Marketing Campaign," October 14, 2011, www.corporateculture.co.uk/blog/anglian-water-launch-world-leading-corporate-social-marketing-campaign (accessed October 24, 2011).
41. Anglian Water, "Anglian Water—The Water and Wastewater Company."
42. Nancy Lee and Philip Kotler, *Social Marketing: Influencing Behaviors for Good*, 4th Edition (Thousand Oaks, CA: SAGE Publications, 2012), Chapter 17.

Chapter 6 Corporate Philanthropy: Making Direct Contributions

1. Committee Encouraging Corporate Philanthropy, "Business CEOs Gather for International Corporate Philanthropy Day," www.corporatephilanthropy.org/pdfs/press/cecppr/ICPD2011PressRelease_Final.pdf (accessed December 5, 2011).
2. Committee Encouraging Corporate Philanthropy, "Giving in Numbers: 2011 Edition," www.corporatephilanthropy.org/pdfs/giving_in_numbers/GivinginNumbers2011.pdf (accessed November 20, 2011).
3. Committee Encouraging Corporate Philanthropy, "Business's Social Contract: Capturing the Corporate Philanthropy Opportunity," 12, www.corporatephilanthropy.org/pdfs/research_reports/SocialContract.pdf (accessed November 20, 2011).
4. Ronald Paul Hill, Debra Stephens, and Iain Smith, "Corporate Social Responsibility: An Examination of Individual Firm Behavior," *Business and Society Review* 108, no. 3 (2003): 339–364.

5. Business for Social Responsibility, "Issue Brief: Philanthropy," www.bsr.org/BSR Resources/IssueBriefsList.cfm?area=all (accessed April 14, 2004).

6. Committee Encouraging Corporate Philanthropy, "Giving in Numbers: 2011 Edition," 4, www.corporatephilanthropy.org/pdfs/giving_in_numbers/Givingin Numbers2011.pdf (accessed November 20, 2011).

7. Forbes, "American Companies that Give Back the Most," www.forbes.com/pictures/ mkl45ejjg/5-bank-of-america (accessed November 20, 2011).

8. Michael Porter and Mark Kramer, "The Competitive Advantage of Corporate Philanthropy," *Harvard Business Review*, December (2002). www.isc.hbs.edu/ HBR_Dec2002_Corporate_Philanthropy.htm

9. PepsiCo, "TED2011 Indra K. Nooyi, March 2, 2011," http://pepsico.com/assets/ speeches/IKN%20TED2011%20Remarks%20-%20Final.pdf (accessed November 24, 2011).

10. Ibid.

11. Ibid.

12. Advertising Age, "Pepsi Refresh Project Faces Cheating Allegations," http:// adage.com/article/news/pepsi-refresh-project-faces-cheating-allegations/148042 (accessed November 24, 2011).

13. PR Newswire, "Role of Citizen Consumer to Tackle Social Issues Rises, as Expectation of Government to Lead Declines," www.prnewswire.com/news-releases/role-of-citizen-consumer-to-tackle-social-issues-rises-as-expectation-of-government-to-lead-declines-106678903.html (accessed November 13, 2011).

14. CMO, "Is There Meaning in PepsiCo's 'Refresh' Campaign Failure," www .cmo.com/social-media/there-meaning-pepsico-s-refresh-campaign-failure (accessed November 24, 2011).

15. "Pepsi Bets on Local Grants, Not the Super Bowl," *The New York Times*, www .nytimes.com/2011/01/31/business/media/31pepsi.html (accessed November 13, 2011).

16. Accion, "The Boston Beer Company Launches a New Philanthropy Program," www.accionusa.org/home/support-u.s.-microfinance/learn-about-u.s.-microfinance/press-releases.aspx?d=1123 (accessed November 24, 2011).

17. Information supplied by The Boston Beer Company via e-mail November 23, 2011.

18. Ibid.

19. Caroline Garro, Telephone Interview by author.

20. PR Newswire, "Samuel Adams Expands Philanthropic Program to Include Craft Brewers Nationwide" www.prnewswire.com/news-releases/samuel-adams-expands-philanthropic-program-to-include-craft-brewers-nationwide-119243499 .html (accessed November 24, 2011).

21. Information supplied by The Boston Beer Company via e-mail November 23.

22. Talya Bosch, Western Union corporate responsibility director, Telephone Interview by author, October 11, 2011.
23. Western Union, "Western Union to Release Third Quarter Results on October 25, 2011," http://ir.westernunion.com/phoenix.zhtml?c=203395&p=irol-news Article&ID=1614415&highlight= (accessed October 13, 2011).
24. Western Union, "Corporate Citizenship," http://corporate.westernunion.com/corporate_responsibility.html (accessed October 11, 2011).
25. Talya Bosch, Western Union corporate responsibility director, Telephone Interview by author, October 11, 2011.
26. Ibid.
27. Ibid.
28. Ibid.
29. Ibid.
30. Ibid.
31. Ibid.
32. Pfizer, "Partnership to End Blinding Trachoma through the International Trachoma Initiative," www.pfizer.com/responsibility/global_health/international_trachoma_initiative.jsp (accessed November 20, 2011).
33. Ibid.
34. Committee Encouraging Corporate Philanthropy, "Corporate Philanthropy Builds Shareholder Value," www.corporatephilanthropy.org/pdfs/corporate_philanthropist/CECP_Fall2001.pdf (accessed November 20, 2011).
35. Council of New Jersey Grantmakers, "A Legal Guide to Corporate Philanthropy," www.cnjg.org/s_cnjg/bin.asp?CID=5174&DID=6298&DOC=FILE.PDF (accessed December 5, 2011).
36. A. Coleman-Jensen, M. Nord, M. Andrews, and S. Carlson, *Household Food Security in the United States in 2010*, United States Department of Agriculture/Economic Research Service.
37. Concepts contained in this case example draw upon L. Wyatt Knowlton and C. Phillips (2012), *The Logic Model Guidebook* (2nd. ed.) (Thousand Oaks, CA: Sage and L. W. Knowlton and C. Phillips [Under Review by The Foundation Review]).
38. "Should Charities Operate Like Businesses?," *Wall Street Journal*, http://online.wsj.com/article/SB10001424052970204554204577024313200627678.html (accessed December 5, 2011).

Chapter 7 Community Volunteering: Employees Donating Their Time and Talents

1. Corporation for National & Community Service, Volunteering in America 2009: State and City Trends and Rankings, www.fs.usda.gov/Internet/FSE_DOCUMENTS/stelprdb5108473.pdf (accessed November 16, 2011).

2. Deloitte, "2010 Executive Summary Deloitte Volunteer IMPACT Survey," www.deloitte.com/view/en_US/us/About/Community-Involvement/50eed830bee48210VgnVCM200000bb42f00aRCRD.htm (accessed November 16, 2011).

3. Bill Shore, *Revolution of the Heart* (New York: Riverhead Books, 1995).

4. Bill Shore, 8.

5. Bill Shore, *xix*.

6. ABC News, "Where's Waldo? Game Brings Smiles to Young Patients," http://abcnews.go.com/Health/wheres-waldo-game-brings-smiles-young-patients-seattle/story?id=14466893 (accessed November 2, 2011).

7. Seattle Children's Hospital, "Children's Community Says Thank You to Ironworkers," http://construction.seattlechildrens.org/2011/10/childrens-says-thank-you-to-ironworkers (accessed November 2, 2011).

8. Q13 FOX News, "Local Iron Workers Are Building Hope, One Beam at a Time," www.q13fox.com/news/kcpq-building-hope-one-beam-at-a-time-20110929,0,6651316.story (accessed November 11, 2011).

9. Seattle Children's Hospital, "Kids on Children's Inpatient Units Say 'Beam Me UP!' to Ironworkers," http://construction.seattlechildrens.org/2011/09/names-on-beams (accessed November 2, 2011).

10. Pfizer, "Who We Are. What We Stand For," www.pfizer.com/about/history/history.jsp(accessed November 8, 2011).

11. Pfizer, "Doing Business Responsibly," www.pfizer.com/responsibility/global_health/meet_our_fellows_zhang.jsp (accessed November 23, 2011).

12. Ibid.

13. Peter Ziaodong Zhang, associate director, public affairs and policy worldwide pharmaceuticals operations, Personal e-mail communication, November 18, 2011.

14. Pfizer, "Who We Are. What We Stand For."

15. Stan Litow, Personal e-mail communication to Nancy Lee, November 9, 2011.

16. IBM, "Top Volunteers Help Change the World," www.ibm.com/ibm100/us/en/service/stories/odc_awards_apr_2011.html (accessed November 1, 2011).

17. Stan Litow, Personal e-mail communication to Nancy Lee, November 9, 2011.

18. Points of Light Institute, "Recognizes Extraordinary Corporate Volunteer Programs," www.pointsoflight.org/press-releases/points-light-institute-recognizes-extraordinary-corporate-volunteer-programs-0.

19. Safe Kids USA, "Preventing Injuries: At Home, at Play, and On the Way," www.safekids.org/our-work/programs/walk-this-way (accessed November 2, 2011).

20. FedEx, "FedEx and Safe Kids—Walk This Way—International Walk to School Day," http://blog.fedex.designcdt.com/safe-kids2011 (accessed November 2, 2011).

21. FedEx, "Child Pedestrian Safety," http://about.van.fedex.com/corporate_responsibility/philanthropy/safety/safe_kids (accessed November 2, 2011).

22. AT&T, "People and Community: Engaging Employees," www.att.com/gen/corporate-citizenship?pid=17885 (accessed November 2, 2011). Note: The financial equivalent is determined by using $21.36 per volunteer hour, which is based on the 2010 industry standard from Independent Sector, a leading nonprofit organization that determines the financial equivalent for a variety of volunteer initiatives.

23. AT&T, "AT&T Contributes $50,000 to American Red Cross Disaster Relief to Support Joplin Storm Relief and Care," www.att.com/gen/press-room?pid=19866&cdvn=news&newsarticleid=31947 (accessed November 2, 2011).

24. Patagonia, "Corporate Social Responsibility," Company Info, www.patagonia.com/us/patagonia.go?assetid=37492&ln=65 (accessed November 8, 2011).

25. Ibid.

26. Mark Shimahara, Personal e-mail communication to Nancy Lee, Patagonia, November 8, 2011.

27. Patagonia, "Environmental Internships," www.patagonia.com/us/patagonia.go?assetid=1963 (accessed November 8, 2011).

Chapter 8 Socially Responsible Business Practices: Changing How You Conduct Business to Achieve Social Outcomes

1. Whole Foods Market, "Whole Foods Market Empowers Shoppers to Make Sustainable Seafood Choices with Color-Coded Rating System," Whole Foods Market Press Room, http://wholefoodsmarket.com/pressroom/blog/2010/09/13/whole-foods-market%c2%ae-partners-with-blue-ocean-institute-and-monterey-bay-aquarium-to-empower-shoppers-to-make-sustainable-seafood-selections (accessed November 15, 2011).

2. Bret Schulte, "Saving Earth, Saving Money: Q&A: Linda Fisher," *U.S. News & World Report*, October 9, 2006, 24.

3. Save Our Food, "Plan for Apple Slices in All Happy Meals Is Good News for Growers," www.saveourfood.org/learn/CurrentNews/tabid/219/articleType/ArticleView/articleId/374/Plan-for-apple-slices-in-all-Happy-Meals-is-good-news-for-growers.aspx (accessed November 30,2011).

4. Business for Social Responsibility Education Fund, *Corporate Social Responsibility: A Guide to Better Business Practices* (San Francisco: Business for Socially Responsible Education Fund, 2000), 179.

5. Ibid., 112.

6. Bret Schulte, "Saving Earth, Saving Money: Q&A: Linda Fisher," *U.S. News & World Report*, October 9, 2006, 24.

7. Ibid.

8. DuPont, "Sustainability: Where We Stand," http://www2.dupont.com/Sustainability/en_US/positions_issues/index.html (accessed November11, 2011).

9. Ibid.

10. DuPont, "Sustainability: 2015 Marketplace Goals," http://www2.dupont.com/Sustainability/en_US/Marketplace_Goals/index.html (accessed November 11, 2011).

11. Nike Biz, "Nike Unveils First-Of-Its-Kind Performance Shoe Designed Specifically for Native Americans," September 25, 2007, www.nikebiz.com/media/pr/2007/09/25_airnativen7.html (accessed November 14, 2011).

12. Ibid.

13. CBC News, "Nike Designs Custom Running Shoes for American Indians," September 2007, www.cbc.ca/news/story/2007/09/26/nike-shoes.html (accessed November 14, 2011).

14. Nike, Inc., "Nike's Native American Business Honored for Special Programs, Product," http://nikeinc.com/news/nikes-native-american-business-honored-for-special-programs-product (accessed December 2, 2011).

15. The Coca-Cola Company, "HIV/AIDS program," http://www.thecoca-colacompany.com/citizenship/foundation_local.html (accessed March 26, 2012).

16. The Coca-Cola Africa Foundation, "HIV/AIDS Report 2006," 12, www.thecoca-colacompany.com/citizenship/pdf/tccaf_2006_hivaids_report.pdf(accessed November 14, 1011).

17. Ibid.

18. The Scottish White Fish Producers Association, "People Want to Buy Sustainable Fish, Concludes Defra Research," April 11, 2011, www.fishnewseu.com/latest-news/uk/5626-people-want-to-buy-sustainable-fish-concludes-defra-research.html (accessed November 15, 2011).

19. Whole Foods Market, "Welcome," www.wholefoodsmarket.com/company (accessed November 15, 2011).

20. Monterey Bay Aquarium, "Seafood Watch," www.montereybayaquarium.org/cr/seafoodwatch.aspx (accessed November 15, 2011).

21. Whole Foods Market, "Whole Foods Market Empowers Shoppers to Make Sustainable Seafood Choices with Color-Coded Rating System," Whole Foods Market Press Room, http://wholefoodsmarket.com/pressroom/blog/2010/09/13/whole-foods-market%c2%ae-partners-with-blue-ocean-institute-and-monterey-bay-aquarium-to-empower-shoppers-to-make-sustainable-seafood-selections (accessed November 15, 2011).

22. Ibid. Photo found at http://wholefoodsmarket.com/pressroom/wp-content/blogs .dir/1/files/seafood-rankings/wfm_wildseafood_poster_mba_0.jpg.

23. Microsoft Corporate Citizenship, "Washington State: Transportation," https:// www.microsoft.com/about/corporatecitizenship/en-us/our-actions/in-the-community/washington-state (accessed November 14, 2011).

24. Ibid.

25. Commuter Challenge, "2010 'Diamond Ring' for Outstanding Leadership," www.commuterchallenge.org/cc/profiles10/microsoft10.html (accessed November 14, 2011).

26. The JobsBlog, "Connector Makes Commuting Smoother, Riders Say," posted November 16, 2009, http://jobsblog.com/blog/commuter-makes-commuting-smoother-riders-say (accessed November 14, 2011).

27. Ibid.

28. Commuter Challenge, "2010 'Diamond Ring' for Outstanding Leadership," www.commuterchallenge.org/cc/profiles10/microsoft10.html (accessed November 14, 2011).

29. Patagonia, "Company Info: Responsibility."

30. Yvon Chouinard, *The Next Hundred Years,* Patagonia, Inc., 1995; also, *Defining Quality: A Brief Description of How We Got Here,* Patagonia, Inc., 1998.

31. Joe Starinchak, Personal e-mail communication to Nancy Lee, November 16, 2011.

Chapter 9 Offense: Choosing a Social Problem to Alleviate

1. Michael E. Porter and Mark R. Kramer, "The Competitive Advantage of Corporate Philanthropy," *Harvard Business Review*, December 2002, 5.

2. Ibid.

Chapter 10 Offense: Selecting an Initiative to Support the Cause

1. Ben & Jerry's Homemade Holdings, Inc., "One Sweet Whirled: One Sweet Campaign to Fight Global Warming," www.onesweetwhirled.org (accessed April 2, 2004).

2. Philip Kotler and Nancy Lee, "Best of Breed: When It Comes to Gaining a Market Edge While Supporting a Social Cause, 'Corporate Social Marketing' Leads the Pack," *Stanford Social Innovation Review* 1, no. 4 (2004): 18.

3. Philip Kotler and Gary Armstrong, *Principles of Marketing,* 9th ed. (Upper Saddle River, NJ: Prentice Hall, 2001), 514–515.

4. Ben & Jerry's, "Global Warming," www.benjerry.com/activism/environmental/global-warming (accessed December 6, 2011).

Chapter 11 Offense: Developing Social Initiative Programs

1. Bill Klyn, Personal e-mail communication to Nancy Lee, December 6, 2011.
2. "What Would You Do If You Knew You Couldn't Fail? Creating S.M.A.R.T. Goals," excerpt from Paul J. Meyer, *Attitude Is Everything*, www.oma.ku.edu/soar/smartgoals.pdf (accessed December 8, 2011). Paul J. Meyer (2003). "What Would You Do If You Knew You Couldn't Fail? Creating S.M.A.R.T. Goals". *Attitude Is Everything: If You Want to Succeed Above and Beyond*. Meyer Resource Group, Incorporated, The. ISBN 9780898113044.
3. Curt Weeden, *Corporate Social Investing* (San Francisco: Berrett-Koehler Publishers, Inc., 1998), 68.

Chapter 12 Offense: Evaluating Efforts

1. Terence Lim, PhD, "Measuring the Value of Corporate Philanthropy," www.corporatephilanthropy.org/pdfs/resources/MVCP_report_singles.pdf (accessed December 8, 2011).
2. The Committee Encouraging Corporate Philanthropy, "The Corporate Giving Standard: A Measurement Model for Corporate Philanthropy," www.givingstandard.com (accessed April 21, 2004).
3. The Committee Encouraging Corporate Philanthropy, "About the CGS: Corporate Giving Standard," www.corporatephilanthropy.org/measurement/cgs.html.

Chapter 13 Summary of Best Practices

1. Kenneth Cole, *Footnotes: What You Stand For Is More Important Than What You Stand In* (New York: Simon & Schuster, 2003), 162–163.

Chapter 14 Defense: No Good Deed Goes Unpunished: Dealing with Cynics and Critics

1. Susan G. Komen for the Cure, "New Balance Athletic Shoe, Inc.," http://ww5.komen.org/Partners/NewBalanceAthleticShoe.aspx (accessed December 9, 2011).
2. "Sick of Pink," *The Boston Globe*, www.boston.com/bostonglobe/magazine/articles/2009/10/04/sick_of_pink/?page=5 (accessed December 9, 2011).
3. The Feed Foundation, "Feed USA for the Gap," http://feedusa.thefeedfoundation.org/feed-usa-for-the-gap (accessed December 9, 2011).
4. Brandchannel, "Gap Apologizes for Made in USA (vs Made in China) Flap," www.brandchannel.com/home/post/2010/12/16/Gap-Response-Made-in-USA.aspx (accessed December 9, 2011).
5. Ibid.

6. "New Charges of Cheating Tarnish Pepsi Fund-Raising Contest for Nonprofits," New York Times http://www.nytimes.com/2011/01/06/business/06charity.html?_r=1&scp=1&sq=cheating%20tarnish%20pepsi&st=cse (accessed December 9, 2011.

7. Anamaria Irazabal, Interview by author at Pepsico headquarters in Purchase, New York, November 30, 2011.

8. "Charity's Share from Shopping Raises Concern" *The New York Times*, www.nytimes.com/2007/12/13/us/13giving.html?pagewanted=all (accessed December 10, 2011).

9. Ibid.

10. Ibid.

11. Greenpeace, "Unilever's 'Monkey Business'—Greenpeace Swings into Action," www.greenpeace.org/international/en/news/features/unilever-monkey-business 210408 (accessed December 9, 2011).

12. Advertising Educational Foundation, "For Unilever, P&G, No Good Deed Is Going Unpunished," www.aef.com/industry/news/data/2008/8017 (accessed December 8, 2011).

13. Ibid.

14. Information provided by Craig Bida of Cone Communications, Inc.

15. Information provided by Carol Cone of Edelman.

16. Ibid.

17. Information provided by Anne Erhard of MSLGROUP Americas.

18. Information provided by Craig Bida of Cone Communications, Inc.

19. Information provided by Anne Erhard of MSLGROUP Americas.

20. Information provided by Craig Bida of Cone Communications, Inc.

21. Information provided by Craig Bida of Cone Communications, Inc.

Chapter 15

1. Bill Shore, *Revolution of the Heart* (New York: Riverhead Books, 1995), 118.

2. Samantha Coker, "Corporate/NGO Alliances: Engaging Corporations in Corporate Social Responsibility Initiatives," Seattle University, Summary Project, 2003.

3. American Cancer Society, "ACS Mission Statement," www.cancer.org/docroot/AA/content/AA_1_1_ACS_Mission_Statements.asp (accessed April 21, 2004).

4. The Nature Conservancy, "How We Work: Conservation Priorities," www.nature.org/ourinitiatives/regions/northamerica/unitedstates/hawaii/howwework/conservation-priorities.xml (accessed December 12, 2011).

5. Microsoft News Center, "Microsoft Gives Kinect to Boys & Girls Clubs Nationwide," www.microsoft.com/presspass/features/2010/nov10/11-03boysgirlsclubs.mspx (accessed December 12, 2011).

6. AT&T Wireless, "Media Relations: About Us," http://www.att.com/gen/investor-relations?pid=5711 (accessed March 26, 2012).

7. Avon Products, Inc., "Mark: Makeup You Can Buy And Sell,"http://pr.meetmark.com/PRSuite/about/pressroom.jsp?ArtID=PRESSRELEASE2&page=1 (accessed April 21, 2004).

8. American Legacy Foundation, "Press Release July 16, 2003: New Research on Young Women and Smoking: Two-Thirds Want to Quit, but Only Three Percent Succeed," www.americanlegacy.org/AmericanLegacy/skins/alf/display.aspx?moduleid=8cde2e88-3052-448c-893d-d0b4b14b31c4&mode=User&action=display_page&ObjectID=8f356b23-f3e2-4cde-925d-63656772acb5 (accessed April 21, 2004).

9. Ibid.

10. March of Dimes, "March of Dimes Sponsors," www.marchofdimes.com/partnersandsponsors/firstresponse.html (accessed December 14, 2011).

Index